MW01062310

THE GANG OF THREE: SOCRATES, PLATO, ARISTOTLE

ANCIENT WISDOM
BOOK 2

NEEL BURTON

ACHERON PRESS

Many things can prolong your life, but only wisdom can save it.

In the Ataraxia series

Begin your journey to peace and power of mind

The Meaning of Madness

Hide and Seek: The Psychology of Self-Deception

Heaven and Hell: The Psychology of the Emotions

For Better For Worse: Essays on Sex, Love, Marriage, and More

Hypersanity: Thinking Beyond Thinking

The Art of Failure: The Anti Self-Help Guide

ANCIENT WISDOM SERIES
INTRODUCTION

To be ignorant of the past is to be forever a child. For what is the time of man, lest it be interwoven with that memory of ancient things of a superior age?

— CICERO

The first three books in the Ancient Wisdom series survey a thousand years of Western intellectual history, from the rise of the Greek city states to the peak height of the Roman Empire. This uniquely fertile period, which encompasses the Golden Age of Athens, began in mystical, mythological thought, and culminated in the hyper-rational, hyper-practical philosophy of the Stoics.

The incipient Christian religion absorbed and adapted, and for a long time occulted, many ancient doctrines, which is why, despite their remoteness, they can seem so strangely familiar. In the late Middle Ages, the rediscovery of Plato fuelled the humanistic Renaissance, which pushed back against the Church of Rome.

The Renaissance was a time of great hope and optimism, which, in many ways, proved premature. Faith provides a compelling reason to live, and a compelling reason to be good, which, for better or worse, many people have lost. For all our progress in science, technology, and education, more than one in five adults are now suffering from some form of depression. It's almost as if we've come full circle, minus the philosophy.

Might it then be time to look afresh at these ancient ideas and find in them a happier way of living? Might it be time, in other words, for a new Renaissance?

CONTENTS

PREFACE

Most people go to Venice with a lover, but I went instead with
Plato's writings on love, the *Lysis*, *Symposium*, and *Phaedrus*,
dispersed across two timeworn, clothbound Loebs that I had
taken down from the top shelf on the top floor of Oxford's best
bookshop. Now that I am acquainted with the ladder of love, as
you will soon be, I can see why those books were kept there, as
near as possible to the sky.

Like many, I had read, and been inspired by, Plato's *Apology*, on
the trial of Socrates, but as a young medical graduate I did not
know much more about the Greek philosophers. All I had was
a vague sense that they, along with Homer, sat at the beginning
of Western thought and civilization, and also at their pinnacle.
The trip would be an opportunity, not only to see Venice, but to
dig a little deeper.

One afternoon, I went for a long, aimless walk, and wound up
in a walled garden, the Parco di Villa Groggia, with a theatre
and follies of ancient ruins. It felt like a garden in Classical
Athens, like, perhaps, Plato's Academy—and the perfect place
to start on the *Phaedrus*. As I read, I experienced one of those

rare ecstatic communions that I discuss in my book on the emotions. Words written more than two thousand years ago, etched with a stylus into wax tablets, had, by some mysterious magic, succeeded in moving me to my very core.

Ecstatic communions, like oracular readings of the kind that set off Socrates, can be life-changing. Within five or six years, I had completed a master's degree in philosophy, and read and outlined the collected works of both Plato and Aristotle. The outlines were published for the time-poor as *Plato's Shadow* (2009) and *Aristotle's Universe* (2011). Little did I know then that those two books would serve as groundwork for this one, the research for which would otherwise have been insurmountable!

My title is inspired by Edward de Bono (d. 2021), who, like me, began as a physician. In a nutshell, de Bono contrasted critical thinking, which is logical, adversarial, and judgmental, with 'parallel' thinking, which is open, cooperative, and, he argued, better suited to real-life problem solving. Critical thinking, with its emphasis on 'the truth', is rooted in the Socratic method pioneered by Socrates and codified by Plato and Aristotle. Renaissance humanists turned to this 'Gang of Three' to deliver them from Christian dogma, but their apparatus has since outlived this purpose, leaving us trapped in a form of thinking that is abstract, limited, and sterile.

The thesis is controversial, but it points to the sorts of issues and stakes involved, and the faintly disparaging title that I took from it, with its connotations of partiality and criminality, serves as a salutary reminder to my reverential self to look for the bad as well as the good.

For better or worse, Socrates, Plato, and Aristotle engineered the Western mind. Above all, they formed part of a movement that stood at the crossroads of mythological and scientific-

rational thought, at the crossroads of *mythos* and *logos*.
Although the path of *logos* had already been beaten by the pre-
Socratics, and would be paved by the Stoics, it is they, the Gang
of Three, that forced the carriage to turn.

This book sets out to do three things: trace the journey
from *mythos* to *logos*; outline the lives and thought of Socrates,
Plato, and Aristotle; and, in the final analysis, consider their
legacy, and what can still be gained from them, especially in the
universal fields of mental health and human flourishing.

Socrates, Plato, and Aristotle were not philosophers in the
narrow sense that we understand today, but in the broader,
historical, etymological sense of being lovers of wisdom. They
knew logic and dialectic, but they also knew how to live, and
how to die—and it is in this, perhaps, that their greater strength
lies.

INTRODUCTION

Greek philosophy, to take off, needed two things: a public square and the written word, which arose in tandem from a centuries-long process of historical change.

In the early twentieth century, digs on Crete, led by Sir Arthur Evans, uncovered the remains of a complex civilization whose people Evans called the Minoans after the mythical King Minos. The Minoans flourished from around 3000 to 1500 BCE, and their society came to revolve around a series of palace complexes, the largest of which was at Knossos in the north of the island.

The Minoans grew rich from trade and gained a hold on some of their neighbours, including perhaps the city of Athens. According to myth, King Minos used to exact a nine-yearly tribute of seven boys and seven girls from Athens, to be fed to the illegitimate son of Minos' queen Pasiphae, the half-man, half-bull Minotaur, imprisoned in the labyrinth beneath the royal palace at Knossos.

Figure 1. The partially reconstructed ruins at Knossos. Photo: Neel Burton.

But when the time came for the third tribute, Theseus, the founder-hero of Athens, took the place of one of the sacrificial boys in a daring bid to end this barbaric practice. Theseus killed the Minotaur with some help from Minos' daughter Ariadne, who had given him a ball of red thread by which to retrace his steps out of the labyrinth. Theseus escaped with Ariadne but later abandoned her on the island of Naxos, to be wedded by the god Dionysus.

Minoan Crete fell into decline from around 1500 BCE, owing, it is said, to a volcanic eruption on the island of Thera (modern-day Santorini) followed by a series of Mycenaean incursions and invasions from the mainland. The Thera eruption might underlie the myth of Atlantis, which is contained in Plato's *Timaeus* and *Critias*—and certainly underlies the island's reputed Assyrtiko wines.

The story of Theseus and the Minotaur served in part to account for the shift in power from Minoan Crete to mainland Greece and, later, to Athens, and it is significant that Theseus also unified Attica under Athens, laying the foundation for the later Athenian Empire.

The Mycenaeans flourished from around 1750 to 1050 BCE in the Peloponnese and mainland Greece, with important centres, each built around a fortified palace, at Mycenae, Pylos, Thebes, and Athens, among others. They were led, or dominated, by a warrior aristocracy, and advanced by conquest rather than by trade as the Minoans had done. Their greatest achievement was the conquest of Troy in around 1250 BCE. The legends surrounding this conquest are the subject of Homer's *Iliad*, which, along with the *Odyssey* and the works of Hesiod, became like a Bible to the Greeks.

Towards the close of the Bronze Age, the Mycenaeans may have come under increasing pressure from the Dorians to the north. The Dorians supposedly descended from the Greek hero Herakles (Hercules), and the Dorian invasion represented the return of the Heraclids to reclaim their ancestral right to rule. Whatever its cause, it took some three hundred years for Greece to recover from the demise of the Mycenaeans. During these Dark Ages, old trade links dissolved, the arts and crafts regressed, and famine set in. Many Greeks took to the seas in search of arable land, beginning a culture of colonization.

Looking to the upside, the disintegration of the rigid hereditary hierarchy of the Mycenaeans prepared the ground for a more open society, leading, in due course, to Athenian democracy. In particular, the loss of the Mycenaean king, or *wanax*, led to a loosening of the bond between myth and ritual so that myth became more detached and disinterested, paving the way for literature and philosophy.

The Mycenaean Linear B script, used for administration and mainly found in palace archives, fell into desuetude during the Dark Ages. Consisting of 87 syllabic and over 100 ideographic signs, Linear B derived from the as yet undeciphered Linear A, used by the non-Greek Minoans to record their mysterious language or languages.

By 770 BCE, close contact with the Phoenicians in the east led to the adoption of a phonetic system of language notation. The Greeks adapted the Phoenician abjad (an alphabet with only consonants), which had been developed for a semitic language, to include vowels, thereby creating the basis of our own modern alphabet.

Significantly, this phonetic script was no longer the preserve of an elite of priests and scribes, used to reaffirm royal power, but a common good, used, more and more, to argue and debate and question the status quo. Life in the emerging city-states [*poleis*] no longer centred on the royal acropolis, now turned over to the gods, but on the public square or *agora*, and the nearby law courts where large citizen juries listened to elaborate speeches and grew familiar with the concept of objective truth.

It can be no coincidence that the hierarchical, anti-democratic Spartans, who privileged military might above all else, prided themselves on the pithiness of their speech. According to Plutarch, when an Attic orator accused the Spartans of being ignorant, Pleistoanax, the Spartan king (r. 458-409 BCE), replied: "What you say is true. Of all the Greeks, we alone have not learnt your evil ways."

TIMELINE AND MAPS

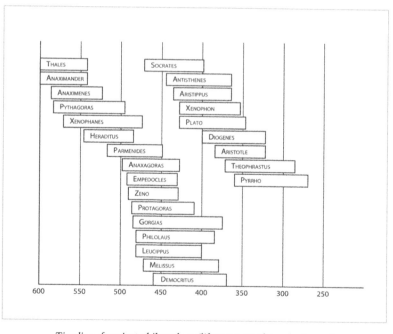

Timeline of ancient philosophers (lifespans are often a best guess)

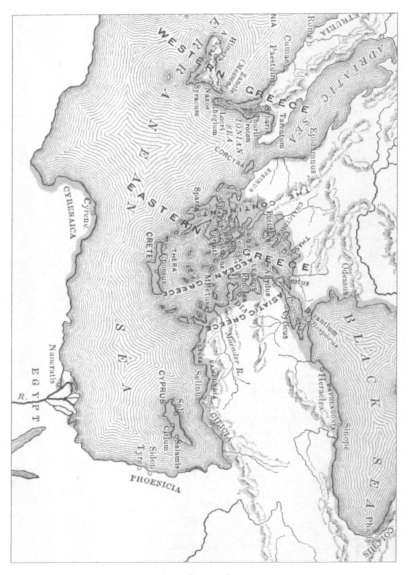

Map 1. Greater Greece

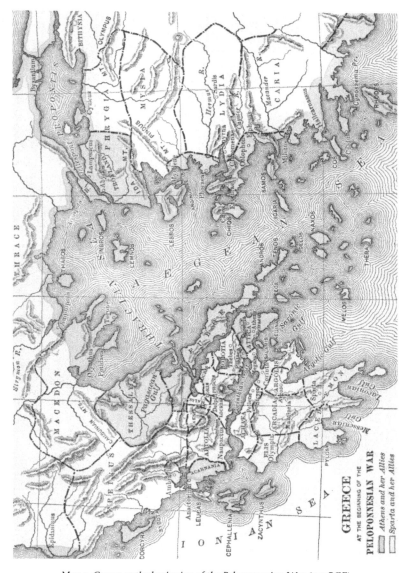

Map 2. Greece at the beginning of the Peloponnesian War (431 BCE)

PART I

THE PRE-SOCRATICS
AND SOPHISTS

Socrates, Plato, and Aristotle did not come out of nowhere, and their life and work can be understood as a response to the pre-Socratics and sophists, who were themselves a product of deep historical change. Socrates died in part because people continued to confuse him with the atheist Anaxagoras, and as many as ten of Plato's dialogues, including the *Protagoras*, *Gorgias*, and *Parmenides*, bear the name of a pre-Socratic or sophist. The first part of this book treats of the major thinkers who led up to Socrates, enabling us to follow the first steps from *mythos* to *logos*.

1

THE PRE-SOCRATIC MOVEMENT

*M*any people have heard of Pythagoras' love for numbers, Zeno's paradoxes, and Heraclitus' obscure aphorisms. But as a group and movement—insofar as they constituted a group and movement—the pre-Socratics remain obscure.

The pre-Socratic movement spanned some two hundred years, from around 600 to after 400 BCE. Its earliest members began to diverge from myth, which, owing to the poet Hesiod (fl. 750 BCE) and others, had by then already acquired an unusual organizing tendency complete with long, intermeshing family trees of gods, heroes, and kings. Its later members were, in fact, contemporaries of Socrates: Democritus was probably ten years younger, and outlived him by some thirty years.

Some pre-Socratics wrote in verse, others in prose. Whether prose or verse, their writings were condensed, and dogmatic, probably because intended to be read before an audience, and to provoke a response from the audience—with the ensuing debate 'filling out' the work.

Heraclitus wrote a single work, later known as *On Nature*, which he deposited in the famed Artemisium [temple to Artemis] of his native Ephesus. According to the biographer of Greek philosophers Diogenes Laertius, the tragedian Euripides gave Socrates a copy of Heraclitus' book. After reading it, Socrates commented, 'What I understand is splendid; and I think what I don't understand is so too—but it would take a Delian diver to get to the bottom of it.'

In Plato's *Apology*, Socrates reveals that the books of Anaxagoras are available 'in the marketplace from time to time for a drachma at most'—a drachma being roughly, at that time, the daily wage of a skilled labourer.

In Plato's *Parmenides*, Parmenides and his student-lover Zeno are visiting Athens at the time of the Great Panathenaia, a major four-yearly civic and religious festival akin to the Olympic Games. In Athens, they are staying at the house of one Pythodorus, where a young Socrates pays them a visit. Socrates is keen to hear the writings of Zeno, which have been brought to Athens for the first time. When Zeno finishes his recitation, he tells Socrates that someone made a copy of his work, so that it began to circulate without his authorization. This, and the entire scene, suggests that thinkers in those days did not make any money from the sale of their books but relied instead on recitations and tutoring.

Some pre-Socratic texts perdured for a thousand years or so. In the sixth century CE, the Neoplatonist philosopher Simplicius of Cilicia was able to consult several, although himself remarks on the rarity of the book by Parmenides. Today, all that remains of the pre-Socratic canon are mere fragments: small sections of original works, or, more often, quotations or paraphrases in later writers, including Simplicius.

These later writers, or doxographers as they are called, tended to rely on a single book by Aristotle's student Theophrastus (d. c. 287 BCE) entitled, *The Opinions of the Natural Scientists*—which has itself largely been lost. Whenever Aristotle reports on the pre-Socratics, it is usually in connection with his own philosophy, and this may also have been true of Theophrastus and others. For instance, in the *Metaphysics*, Aristotle praises Anaxagoras as 'like a sober man compared to his babbling predecessors' simply because, by introducing *Nous* [Mind] as a causal principle, Anaxagoras appears to be heralding his own 'doctrine of the four causes' (Chapter 23).

Doxographers also tended to caricature the pre-Socratics and their ideas, or even to confuse them with one another or merge them.

All this to say that we ought to take whatever information we have about the pre-Socratics with a heavy pinch of salt.

2

THE MILESIAN SCHOOL
THALES, ANAXIMANDER, ANAXIMENES

*T*he first philosophers were from Ionia, on the western coast of Anatolia (modern-day Turkey). More precisely, they were from the Greek city of Miletus, which must then have felt like the centre of the world. With Lydia and Persia to the east, Phoenicia and Egypt to the south, and the Greek city-states to the west, Miletus had prospered from trade and human and cultural interchange. Tales of the early philosophers travelling to the Near East or receiving instruction from Egyptian priests, even if not literally true, attest to the important influence of these rich foreign cultures upon their thought—which, however, amounted to something new and radical.

The Milesian School, consisting of Thales, Anaximenes, and Anaximander, is not to be confused with the Ionian School, of which it is only a subset. The Ionian School of *physiologoi* ['those who discourse on nature'], as Aristotle called them, also includes figures such as Heraclitus of Ephesus and Anaxagoras of Clazomenæ. The Ionians sought, in the main, to establish the origins and nature of the universe, including or especially the basic material out of which all things are made—which sounds quaint and quixotic, until we remember that it is the same quest that our nuclear physicists are embarked upon, this time with the help of giant particle accelerators.

In Plato's *Protagoras*, Socrates numbers Thales of Miletus (c. 624-c. 548 BCE) among the Seven Sages of Greece. According to Aristotle in the *Metaphysics*, Thales held that the Earth floats on water, which is the primary substance from which all else is made. 'Presumably' says Aristotle, 'he derived this assumption from seeing that the nutriment of everything is moist...'

Or perhaps he derived it from similar Egyptian, Babylonian, and Hebrew accounts of creation, echoed already in the first two verses of the Bible:

> In the beginning God created the heaven and the earth.
> And the earth was without form, and void; and darkness
>   was upon the face of the deep. And the Spirit of God
>   moved upon the face of the waters.
>
> — GENESIS 1, 1-2 (KJV).

But in a break with these traditions, Thales sought to explain the origin and nature of the world without resorting to myths and gods, which is why he is often regarded as the first genuine philosopher, as well as the first genuine scientist. When Bertrand Russell declared that 'philosophy begins with Thales', he was, in fact, merely agreeing with Aristotle. Earthquakes, for instance, result not from the trident of Poseidon Seisichton ['Earth-Shaker'], but from disturbances in the water that the Earth floats upon.

At the same time, Thales believed that 'all things are full of gods', arguing that the ability of lodestones (naturally occurring magnets) to induce motion indicates that even 'inanimate' objects are imbued with mind or soul.

According to lore, Thales travelled to Egypt to take instruction from the priests of that land. The story may well be true, not least because Miletus in those days held a trading concession at Naucratis, a Greek colony on the Canopic mouth of the Nile. While in Egypt, Thales measured the heights of the pyramids by measuring their shadows at the time of day when his own shadow was as long as he was tall. He learnt or discovered that triangles with two equal sides are congruent, and applied this insight to 'triangulate' the distances of ships at sea. As well as a geometer, he was an astronomer who determined the dates of the solstices, and even predicted the solar eclipse of 585 BCE which halted the Battle of Halys between the Lydians and the Medes. In Plato's *Theaetetus*, Socrates says that Thales had so little regard for worldly matters that he once fell into a well while gazing at the stars—a story that may be rooted in an ancient belief that looking into a well, or standing at the bottom of one, could assist with stargazing.

Despite all these outstanding achievements, the people of his native Miletus used to mock Thales for his poverty. So one year he predicted a bumper crop of olives, took out a lease on all the olive presses on Miletus, and made himself a fortune, simply to prove to the poor Milesians that a philosopher could easily be rich if only he did not have better things to do with his time.

Thales never married, despite the pleas and entreaties of his mother. As a young man, he would tell her that it was too early to marry; as an older man, that it was too late.

～

Anaximander (c. 610-546 BCE) may or may not have been
taught by Thales. But even if not, he took him as a model and
starting point. Like Thales, Anaximander sought for the
primary substance, or *arkhē*, which he identified with *apeiron*
['the boundless', 'infinite', or 'indefinite'], from which all else is
generated not just in this world but 'in all the worlds'.

Apeiron, which is in constant motion and 'steers' all things,
represents a new level of abstraction in Greek thought—called
for because a more concrete candidate, such as water, which
can only be wet and never dry, could not possibly encompass
all the opposites found in nature.

The following fragment from Anaximander's *On Nature*
preserved by Theophrastus and recopied by Simplicius is the
oldest extant piece of Greek philosophical writing:

> The things that are perish into the things out of which they
> come to be, according to necessity, for they pay the penalty
> and retribution to each other for their injustice in accordance
> with the ordering of time, as [Anaximander] says in rather
> poetical language.

— SIMPLICIUS, PHYSICS 24, 13.

In this fragment, Anaximander, it seems, elaborates upon
Thales by emphasizing the inevitability and cyclicity of change,
and attributing it with a cause or rationale, namely, injustice.

According to Anaximander, the Earth is a cylinder with a
height of one third of its diameter. Thales claimed that the
Earth floats upon water, without specifying (as far as we know)
what the water might rest upon. Anaximander got round this
problem by saying that the cylinder need not be supported:
because it is in the middle of everything, there is no reason for

it to move in one direction rather than another. This is the oldest known argument founded on the principle of sufficient reason, according to which every instance of change must have a reason or cause.

Celestial bodies make full circles and might even pass beneath the unsupported Earth—a truly radical claim for the time. The celestial bodies lie one behind the other: first the stars, then the moon, and the sun furthest behind. They do not fall because they are attached to wheels. Each wheel is filled with fire, which shines through one or several openings in the wheel. The aperture in the lunar wheel changes its shape, accounting for the phases of the moon, while a solar eclipse results from the occlusion of the opening in the solar wheel. Thunder and lightning result from the clashing of clouds rather than the temper of Zeus. Human beings arose from aquatic animals as the Earth began to dry, or developed within certain fish.

Anaximander travelled widely and, according to Ælian, founded the Milesian colony of Apollonia on the Black Sea coast. He introduced the *gnomon* [perpendicular sundial] into Greece, and drew up the first map of the world, with, probably, the Mediterranean Sea at its centre ('Mediterranean', from the Latin *medius* and *terra*, means 'the sea in the middle of the Earth'). Diogenes Laertius claims that he enjoyed singing: 'They say that when he sang, the children laughed; and that he, hearing of this, said, 'We must then sing better for the sake of the children.''

Nietzsche, in his unfinished and posthumous *Philosophy in the Tragic Age of the Greeks*, makes much out of the Anaximander fragment in Simplicius. Underlying the notion of a single *arkhē*, especially an abstract one called the boundless, is a dualism of appearance and essence, and a disregard for the empirical world of appearance which is subject to time and change. More than that, Anaximander seems to imply that all coming-to-be out of *apeiron* is an injustice, or arises out of an injustice, which must be atoned for by a return to *apeiron*. Thus, all coming-to-be is an aberration, 'an illegitimate emancipation from eternal being... for which destruction is the only penance.'

Nietzsche quotes a 'similar reflection' from Schopenhauer, whom he calls 'the only serious moralist of our century':

> The proper measure with which to judge any and all human beings is that they are really creatures who should not exist and who are doing penance for their lives by their manifold sufferings and their death.

The significance in our context is that this early dichotomy between appearance and essence, and the devaluation of appearance, prefigures Plato and his Theory of the Forms. Indeed, in another work, the *Genealogy of Morality*, Nietzsche goes so far as to call Plato 'the sincerest advocate of the beyond, the great slanderer of life'.

Anaximenes (c. 586-c. 526 BCE), an associate or friend of Anaximander, rejected *apeiron* and replaced it with his own *arkhē*, *aēr* [air, but also mist and vapour], which resembles *apeiron* in surrounding the cosmos and bringing about eternal motion. The Earth is flat like a disc and floats on a cushion of *aēr*.

The heavenly bodies, which are also flat, rotate horizontally around the Earth 'like a bonnet about the head', with their rising and setting accounted for by a tilting movement of the Earth.

Anaximenes elaborated upon Thales and Anaximander by positing a mechanism, or two mechanisms, rarefaction and condensation, by which his *arkhē* might pass into and out of everything else. Simplicius tells us that, when *aēr* is rarefied, it becomes fire; when it is condensed, it becomes wind, then cloud, then water, then stones... To support this thesis, Anaximenes appealed to a simple experiment: when one exhales on one's hand, the air is hot, but if one blows through pursed lips, the air becomes cold and dense.

Our breath and soul are akin to *aēr*, suggesting that, more than the air around us, Anaximenes' *arkhē* is a warm, moist, animating stuff. In a rare surviving fragment, he says, 'Just as our soul, being air, holds us together, so do breath and air encompass the whole world.'

Like Anaximander, Anaximenes sought unifying naturalistic explanations for diverse, supposedly divine, manifestations, claiming, for example, that the rainbow, traditionally identified with the goddess Iris, results from the sun's rays falling onto densely compressed air.

With his emphasis on change and its process, Anaximenes might be thought of as a forerunner of Heraclitus (Chapter 3). His influence on Plato is most evident in the *Timaeus*, in which Timaeus, a philosopher of the Pythagorean school who tends to speak for Plato, presents Anaximenes' theory of matter as though it were his own.

Miletus, the greatest Greek city in the East, had prospered through trade. The Milesians had founded more than sixty colonies on the fertile and timber-rich shores of the Black Sea, including Abydos, Cyzicus, and Sinope, and had an important stake in the Greek-Egyptian trading post of Naucratis—whose sister port, Heracleion, was discovered as recently as 2000.

However, in 560 BCE, in the old age of Thales, the middle age of Anaximander, and the youth of Anaximenes, the Greek cities of Ionia were overrun by King Crœsus of Lydia, and remained under Lydian rule until about 540, when Lydia itself was conquered by Cyrus the Great. Thereafter, the Ionian cities were ruled by native tyrants nominated by the Persian satrap in Sardis, the former Lydian capital. These tyrants, backed by the Persian power, had no need to moderate their rule, and began to give tyranny, and Persia, a bad name to the Greeks.

In 499, Aristagoras, the tyrant of Miletus, who inherited the post from his father-in-law, launched an expedition with the Persian satrap Artaphernes to conquer Naxos. When their enterprise floundered, Aristagoras felt threatened and incited all of Ionia to rebel against Darius the Great. The following year, the Ionians, supported by troops from Athens and Eretria, captured and burnt Sardis. But as they repaired to Ionia, Persian troops caught up with them and defeated them in the Battle of Ephesus. Finally, in 494, the Persian army stormed and sacked Miletus, so that the city had to be rebuilt—on a new grid plan designed by Hippodamus of Miletus, the 'father of European urban planning'. According to the historian Herodotus, 'Miletus then was left empty of Milesians.'

In the grander scheme of things, the Ionian Revolt set off the Greco-Persian Wars, and the burning of Sardis with the support of Athens and Eretria led to the first Persian invasion of Greece, starting in 492. According to Herodotus, after hearing about Sardis, and ascertaining who the Athenians were, Darius ordered a slave to say to him three times with every dinner: "Master, remember the Athenians."

THE SECOND PRE-SOCRATIC PHASE
PYTHAGORAS, XENOPHANES, HERACLITUS, PARMENIDES

*P*hilosophy, like art and science, is the flowering of peace and wealth, of leisure and self-assurance. After the downfall of Miletus and its Ionian neighbours, the epicentre of philosophy shifted westwards, towards Athens and the cities of Italy. We know, for example, that Pythagoras left Samos, off the Ionian mainland, for Italy, and that Xenophanes left Colophon, some fifty miles north of Miletus, for a life of itinerancy. At the same time, ideas in this period flowed more freely than ever: Melissus of Samos followed so closely after Parmenides and Zeno, both of Elea in Italy, as to be counted the third member of the Eleatic School.

Compared to the Milesians, the philosophers of this second pre-Socratic phase were even more driven by argument and abstraction, and tended to follow the logic wherever it might lead. Indeed, the works of the Eleatics—Parmenides, Zeno, and Melissus—consisted essentially of long chains of arguments.

Pythagoras of Samos (c. 570-c. 495 BCE) was a contemporary of Anaximander and Anaximenes, and might have met or at least corresponded with Thales, who, it is said, advised him to travel to Memphis to take instruction from Egyptian priests.

At the of age of 40, Pythagoras left Samos, then under the rule of the enlightened but overbearing tyrant Polycrates, for Croton in southern Italy, where he established a philosophically-minded religious community. Pythagoras admitted men and women alike—so that, of the 235 famous Pythagoreans listed by Iamblichus, 17 are women.

The men and women who entered the community's inner circle were governed by a strict set of ascetic and ethical rules, forsaking personal possessions, assuming a mainly vegetarian diet, and—since words are so often careless and misleading— observing the strictest silence. Some of the community's more idiosyncratic rules, such as 'do not break bread' or 'do not poke the fire with a sword', may have stood as riddles or allegories.

Pythagoras' community served as an inspiration and prototype for later philosophical institutions such as Plato's Academy, Aristotle's Lyceum, and Epicurus' Garden, and, subsequently, for the monastic life and associated early universities. Pythagoras' teachings as represented in the *Metamorphoses* of Ovid influenced the modern vegetarian movement to such an extent that, until the word 'vegetarianism' was coined in the 1840s, vegetarians were simply referred to as 'Pythagoreans'.

Music played an important role in Pythagoras' community. Pythagoreans recited poetry, sang hymns to Apollo, and played on the lyre to cure illnesses of body and soul. One day, or so the story goes, Pythagoras passed by some blacksmiths at work, and found that their hammering produced especially pleasing sounds. He then noticed that their anvils were simple ratios of one another, one being half the size of the first, another twice the size, and so on. This insight led to his 'harmony of the spheres', according to which the movements of the heavenly bodies are in a mathematical relationship akin to that between musical notes, and, together, amount to a grand cosmic symphony. The astronomer Johannes Kepler (d. 1630) held that, though inaudible, this 'music of the spheres' might nonetheless be heard by the soul.

As for the famous theorem, concerning the relation between the three sides of a right triangle, that came to bear his name, and make it renowned, Pythagoras might have introduced it to the Greeks, but it had been discovered centuries earlier, and separately, by the Babylonians and Indians.

Pythagoras ['Oracle among the people'] never divorced religion from philosophy and science, which, even in his day, left him open to accusations of mysticism. No doubt under the influence of Orphism, a mystery religion rooted in pre-Hellenic beliefs and the Thracian cult of Zagreus, he came to believe in metempsychosis, that is, in the transmigration of the soul at death into a new body of the same or a different species, until such a time as it became moral. According to lore, he once recognized the cry of his dead friend in the yelping of a puppy. He himself claimed to have lived four lives and to remember them all in great detail: in his first life, he had had the good fortune of being Æthalides, son of Hermes, who had given him the faculty of remembering everything even through death.

In his lost *Protrepticus*, or *Exhortation to Philosophy*, Aristotle relates that when Pythagoras was asked why human beings came into existence, he replied, 'To observe the heavens,' adding that it was for the sake of this that he had passed over into life. Pythagoras coined the word *kosmos*, and held that it is by studying the *kosmos* that we might become *kosmios* ['orderly', 'beautiful', cf. cosmetic, cosmopolitan].

In Croton, Pythagoras laid down a constitution. According to Diogenes Laertius, he and his Pythagoreans governed the state so well that it was 'in effect a true aristocracy (government by the best)'.

After Croton's victory over neighbouring Sybaris in 510, certain prominent citizens pushed for a democratic constitution. When the Pythagoreans rejected it, the supporters of democracy attacked them. In an unlikely story, Pythagoras almost managed to escape, but came over a field of fava beans and refused to step over it. His aversion to fava beans might have owed to a belief that fava beans contain the souls of the deceased, or to favism, an inherited disease that is exacerbated by fava beans.

After Pythagoras' death, the Pythagoreans deified him, and attributed him with a golden thigh and the gift of bilocation [being in two places at once]. He became a paradigm of the sage, so that the Romans tried to assimilate him and claim him as their own. But in his living, Pythagoras had always been a paragon of humility, declining to be called a 'wise man' [*sophos*] and preferring instead to be called 'a lover of wisdom' [*philosophos*]—thereby coining the term 'philosopher'.

In the *Metaphysics*, Aristotle says that Plato's teachings owed much to those of the Pythagoreans; so much, in fact, that Bertrand Russell (d. 1970) upheld not Plato but Pythagoras as the most influential of all Western philosophers. Pythagoras' influence is perhaps most evident in Plato's mystical approach to the soul and in his emphasis on mathematics, and, more generally, reason and abstract thought, as a secure basis for the practice of philosophy.

Xenophanes of Colophon (c. 570-c. 478 BCE) came from Colophon in Ionia, but left in his mid-twenties and 'tossed about the Greek Land' for 67 years—as he himself tells us in one of his 45 surviving fragments. In the *Sophist*, Plato refers to 'our Eleatic tribe, beginning from Xenophanes...' suggesting that he spent some time in Elea. He clearly knew of Pythagoras, whom he discusses in Fragment 7.

Xenophanes famously criticized the likes of Homer and Hesiod for anthropomorphizing the gods (conceiving of them in human form) and portraying them as immoral or amoral:

> But mortals deem that the gods are begotten as they are, and have clothes like theirs, and voice and form ... Yes, and if oxen and horses or lions had hands, and could paint with their hands, and produce works of art as men do, horses would paint the forms of the gods like horses, and oxen like oxen, and make their bodies in the image of their several kinds ... The Ethiopians make their gods black and snub-nosed; the Thracians say theirs have blue eyes and red hair.

But far from being an atheist, Xenophanes instead suggested that there is 'one god, the greatest among gods and men, neither in form like unto mortals nor in thought': 'He sees all over, thinks all over, and hears all over ... But without toil he swayeth all things by the thought of his mind ... And he abideth ever in the selfsame place, moving not at all; nor doth it befit him to go about now hither and thither.' It is perhaps this kind of proto-monotheism that led Plato to assimilate Xenophanes with the Eleatics.

Xenophanes held that the primary substance is earth: 'All things are from earth and in earth all things end.' But he also acknowledged the importance of water to life, and inferred from the existence of inland fossils that the earth had at one time been covered by the sea. He thought that the Earth is bottomless and 'reaches down below without a limit'. Because the sun could not possibly pass beneath the Earth, a new sun must be born with every morning.

Despite pronouncing himself on such weighty matters, he warned that certain knowledge is impossible:

> There never was or will be a man who has certain knowledge about the gods and about all the things I speak of. Even if he should chance to say the complete truth, yet he himself knows not that it is so. But all may have their fancy.

This subtle and original distinction between knowledge and true belief is further developed in Plato, especially in the *Meno* and *Theaetetus* (Chapters 14 and 18).

Another important proto-skeptical point that Xenophanes made is that our perceptions and beliefs are relative and context-dependent: 'If god had not made brown honey, men would think figs far sweeter than they do.'

Two of his 45 surviving fragments mention wine. In one, he says that it is no sin to drink as much as one can take; in the other that one ought to mix wine by pouring the water and then the wine, rather than the other way round.

In Plato's *Republic*, Socrates seems to nod to Xenophanes when he advocates censoring the works of Homer and Hesiod on the grounds that they misrepresent the gods. God, says Socrates, must always be represented as he truly is, that is, as good, and the author of good only.

∾

Heraclitus ('Glory of Hera', c. 535-c. 475 BCE) hailed from Ephesus, not far from Miletus and Colophon. He inherited the honorific office of King of the Ionians, which he abdicated in favour of his brother, explaining that he preferred the company of children to that of politicians. Instead of partaking in pomp and protocol, he played knucklebones with the boys in the precinct of the temple of Artemis, in which he deposited a copy of his single work, later referred to as, *On Nature*.

Theophrastus, who knew the complete work, reports that 'some parts ...are half-finished, while other parts make a strange medley', before putting this down to the author's melancholy disposition. Some 120 fragments survive, although most are no longer than a sentence. In the main, they consist of ambiguous or antithetical aphorisms such as, 'Immortals are mortal, mortals immortal, living their death, dying their life.' For this reason, Heraclitus is sometimes called 'Heraclitus the Riddler' or 'Heraclitus the Obscure' [*ho Skoteinós*].

Owing to his melancholic or misanthropic disposition, he is also called the 'weeping philosopher', and opposed to Democritus, 'the laughing philosopher'. He compared the mass of people to cattle and wished the Ephesians great wealth as a punishment for their worthless lives.

According to lore, Darius the Great once invited him to his resplendent court, but he refused to go, sending the reply:

> All men upon the earth hold aloof from truth and justice, while, by reason of wicked folly, they devote themselves to avarice and thirst for popularity. But I, being forgetful of all wickedness, shunning the general satiety which is closely joined with envy, and because I have a horror of splendour, could not come to Persia, being content with little, when that little is to my mind.

In one fragment, he mentions Pythagoras and Xenophanes, but only to support his claim that 'much learning does not teach understanding'. In Raphael's *School of Athens*, he is one of only two figures to sit alone and apart, the other being Diogenes the Cynic (Figure 2).

Heraclitus' big idea is that everything is in a constant state of flux, as epitomized by his saying that you cannot step twice into the same river. Everything flows, everything moves [*panta rhei, panta chorei*]: the waters are no longer the same, and neither are we.

Figure 2: The School of Athens, by Raphael (c. 1509). Photographic detail from a full-size copy. Photo: Neel Burton.

He picked out fire as his primary substance, perhaps because fire is warm like life, or, more probably, because it symbolizes movement and destruction. 'This world, which is the same for all, no one of gods or men has made; but it was ever, is now, and ever shall be an ever-living Fire, with measures of it kindling, and measures going out.' All change is a product of God's reason or *Logos*, and fire is the expression of *Logos*, and hence of God. Accordingly, a wise man's soul is hot and dry, whereas a drunk 'is led by a beardless lad, tripping, knowing not where he steps, having his soul moist'.

Heraclitus influenced the Stoics, who believed that the cosmos is suffused with *Logos*, and conceived of God as having the nature of fire. It is a testament to the impact of both that the notion of *Logos* entered into the Bible—at John 1:1, no less—with *Logos* (mis)translated into English as 'the Word': 'In the beginning was the Word, and the Word was with God, and the Word was God' [*En arkhêi ên ho lógos, kaì ho lógos ên pròs tòn theón, kaì theòs ên ho lógos*].

The other thing about the river is that 'it rests by changing': it is precisely the flowing of its waters that maintains the river's form and essence. Were it to stop flowing, it would no longer be a river. Heraclitus taught the 'unity of the opposites': that hot and cold are one, as are light and dark and night and day. These opposites appear to be in a constant state of strife, but the resulting tension is, in fact, an expression of essential harmony. All unity is the product of a constant process of change that results in an overall stability—a bit like riding a bicycle.

> It is wise to agree that all things are one ... In differing it agrees with itself, a backward-turning connection, like that of a bow and a lyre ... The path up and down is one and the same.

Heraclitus' unity of the opposites calls to mind that famous phrase from Lampedusa's *Leopard*: 'Things will have to change if they are to remain the same.' Strife is not some aberration, or injustice, as Anaximander thought, but a fundamental feature of the world.

Heraclitus, it seems, did not have any teachers or students, but did in time sprout followers such as Cratylus. According to Aristotle, Cratylus espoused such a radical theory of flux that he berated Heraclitus for saying that one cannot step twice into the same river, 'for he himself held that it cannot be done even once.' Cratylus ended up thinking that one ought not speak, and resorted instead to indiscriminately wagging his finger.

Elsewhere in the *Metaphysics*, Aristotle says that Plato in his youth became acquainted with Cratylus and the Heraclitean doctrine, and continued to believe that the sensible world, being always in a state of flux, is beyond knowing.

In stark contrast to Heraclitus, who held that everything is in a state of flux, Parmenides of Elea (c. 515-c. 440 BCE) argued that nothing ever changes. Parmenides may have been acquainted with Xenophanes, whose work he knew well. In c. 450 BCE, at the age of 65, he travelled to Athens with his student and *eromenos* [younger male lover] Zeno, where, according to Plato, he met with a young Socrates. Their alleged conversation is the subject of Plato's *Parmenides*.

Parmenides wrote a poem, *On Nature*, in hexameter verse, but only 160 lines survive. The work begins with a proem in which the narrator, an unnamed young man (presumably Parmenides himself), ascends to the abode of a goddess, a place 'where day meets night and are the same'.

The goddess reveals to him 'the Way of Truth', what is, and what is not. What is, is, and it is impossible for it not to be. And what is not is not, and it is impossible for it to be. One cannot conceive of what is not, because one cannot think or speak about nothing. Conversely, if one can think or speak about something, then that thing must be, 'for thought and being are the same'. It being possible to think about reality, reality must be—and if it is, it cannot not be. Something cannot come into or pass out of being, because something cannot come into being from nothing, or pass from something into nothing. Thus, if something comes into being, it does so not from nothing but from something—so that it does not really come into being at all.

From this, it follows that there can be no becoming and thus no real change, even though sense experience tells us otherwise. Motion is impossible because it would require moving into a void, that is, moving into nothing, which does not exist. If both motion and change are impossible, the universe must consist of a single, undifferentiated, and indivisible unity, which Parmenides called, 'the One'.

Having disclosed 'the Way of Truth', the goddess goes on to tell the young man about 'the Way of Opinion', which encompasses a cosmological account along the lines of those that came before. Only a small portion of 'the Way of Opinion' survives—perhaps with good reason, since it is unlikely to have been as original and radical as 'the Way of Truth'.

To bolster the philosophy of Parmenides, his *eromenos* Zeno of Elea produced a set of paradoxical arguments, including 'Achilles and the Tortoise', designed to undermine ordinary beliefs about motion, space, time, and plurality. Aristotle outlines 'Achilles and the Tortoise' in the *Physics*: 'in a race the quickest runner can never overtake the slowest, since the pursuer must first reach the point whence the pursued started, so that the slower must always hold a lead.' According to Diogenes Laertius, Aristotle hailed not Socrates but Zeno as the first dialectician, insofar as Zeno also sought to deconstruct the ordinary beliefs of his interlocutors.

What is new about 'the Way of Truth' is that it consists in a long chain of strict *à priori* deductive argumentation from premises that are taken to be necessary truths. The conclusion, startling though it is, seems to follow necessarily from the premises, posing a serious challenge to anyone defending a different and common-sense position. Two thousand years later, Descartes would embark on a similar project in search of truths deemed to be incontrovertible.

Also new and notable about 'the Way of Truth' is that it is the first enquiry into being qua being, so that Parmenides is often regarded as the first ontologist and first metaphysician.

Whereas Xenophanes and Heraclitus had tended to undermine sense experience, and, by extension, science, they did not, like Parmenides, radically, metaphysically discount it.

At the same time, Parmenides was not a skeptic who believed that knowledge is unattainable: truth is within our reach, but only by the use of reason.

Just as Plato leant upon Heraclitus' flux for his conception of the sensible world, so he leant upon Parmenides' unity for his conception of the intelligible world, which he rendered as the ideal, immutable realm of the Forms.

THE THIRD PRE-SOCRATIC PHASE

EMPEDOCLES, ANAXAGORAS, DEMOCRITUS

*T*he third and final pre-Socratic phase can be understood as a reaction to Parmenides and the Eleatics, an attempt to salvage science and sense experience by showing that change need not require that something come out of nothing. Empedocles, Anaxagoras, and Democritus, as we shall see, used similar strategies to get around the so-called Parmenidean problem.

Empedocles (c. 494-c. 434 BCE) hailed from Acragas, now Agrigento, in Italy. He had a reputation as a mystic and miracle-worker, so that people flocked to him for healing. He claimed, among others, that he could cure old age and control the winds. When offered the kingship of Acragas, he turned it down, preferring instead to write poetry in the style of Parmenides and dedicate it to his *eromenos*, the physician Pausanias. Despite his democratic leanings, he dressed flamboyantly, and wrote so ornately that Aristotle credits him with the invention of rhetoric. He is the last Greek philosopher to have expressed his ideas in verse. About 550 lines survive, including 450 lines of his *On Nature*.

Empedocles synthesized the thought of the Ionians by holding that there are four 'roots', or primary substances: air, earth, fire, and water—now referred to as the four classical elements. The four roots are driven together and apart, and combine in various proportions to create the plurality and difference of our sense experience. They are like a painter's primary colours, from which the artist can reproduce all the varied splendours of nature. The four roots of Empedocles inspired or influenced the four-humour theory of medicine, which perdured long enough to be mocked by Molière (d. 1673) in his plays.

In addition to the four roots, Empedocles introduced not one but two causal principles: Love and Strife. Love brings the elements together, and unopposed Love leads to 'the One', a divine and resplendent sphere. But Strife gradually degrades this sphere, returning it to the elements, and this cosmic cycle repeats itself *ad infinitum*. Love and Strife are reminiscent of the justice and injustice of Anaximander, who also put ethics at the heart of his cosmogony.

In sum, contra Parmenides, change can occur, but only in the form of the combination and separation of the four roots, which are themselves unchanging and eternal. Empedocles even developed a crude theory of evolution by survival of the fittest, beginning with the haphazard combination of the elements into random structures and organisms. Over time, only the most successful structures and organisms survived.

Like Pythagoras, Empedocles believed in metempsychosis. To atone for an original sin involving bloodshed, souls must go through a series of mortal incarnations before they are able to re-join the immortal gods. They can however help themselves by adhering to certain ethical rules, such as refraining from

meat, beans, bay leaves, and (heterosexual) intercourse.
Animals and even certain plants are our kin and should not be
killed for food or sacrifice. Empedocles and Pythagoras were
pacifists and vegans long before the hippies came around.
Their mortification of the flesh is, in some sense, the apotheosis
of the pre-Socratic privileging of Apollonian reason over
Dionysian sense experience.

*Figure 3: King Pentheus torn apart by Maenads in a Bacchic frenzy. Roman
wall painting from the House of the Vettii, Pompeii. The Dionysian rite of
sparagmos involved dismembering a living animal or even a human being.
The flesh was then eaten raw, while still warm and dripping with blood.
Pentheus, like Pythagoras and Empedocles, had refused to embrace
Dionysus and the Dionysian.*

Empedocles himself claimed to have already been a bush, a
bird, and 'a mute fish in the sea'. But now, as a doctor, poet, seer,
and leader of men, he had reached the highest rung in the cycle
of incarnations—and could, just about, count himself among
the immortal gods.

In a story that is almost certainly false but too good not to tell,
he killed himself by leaping into the flames of Mount Etna,
either to prove that he was immortal or make people believe
that he was.

The premise of Plato's *Symposium* [Banquet] is that each of the
guests at the banquet is to deliver a speech in praise of love.
Aristophanes, however, chooses to deliver his speech in the
form of a myth about the origins of love. This is the famous
Myth of Aristophanes, which appears to lean upon elements of
the cosmogony of Empedocles.

In the beginning, there were three kinds of people: male,
descended from the sun; female, descended from the earth; and
hermaphrodite, with both male and female parts, descended
from the moon.

These early people were completely round, each with four
arms and four legs, two identical faces on opposite sides of a
head with four ears, and all else to match. They walked both
forward and backward and ran by turning cartwheels on their
eight limbs, moving in circles like their parents the planets.

Because they were wild and unruly and threatening to scale the
heavens, Zeus, the father of the gods, cut each one down the
middle 'like a sorb-apple which is halved for pickling'—and
even threatened to do the same again so that they might hop on
one leg.

Apollo, the god of light and enlightenment, then turned their heads to make them face towards their wound, pulled their skin around to cover up the wound, and tied it together at the navel like a purse. He made sure to leave a few wrinkles on what became known as the abdomen so that they might be reminded of their punishment.

After that, people searched all over for their other half. When they finally found it, they wrapped themselves around it so tightly and unremittingly that they began to die from hunger and neglect. Taking pity on them, Zeus moved their genitals to the front so that those who were previously androgynous could procreate, and those who were previously male could obtain satisfaction and move on to higher things.

This is the origin of our desire for others: those of us who desire members of the opposite sex used to be hermaphrodites, whereas men who desire men used to be male, and women who desire women used to be female.

When we find our other half, we are 'lost in an amazement of love and friendship and intimacy' that cannot be accounted for by mere lust, but by the need to be whole again, to be restored to our original nature. Our greatest wish, if we could only have it, would then be for Hephæstus, the god of fire, to melt us into one another so that our souls could be at one and share in a common fate.

The Myth of Aristophanes, and so Empedocles, came to play an important part in the development of the modern, romantic notion of love as existential and redeeming—about which more in Chapter II.

~

Anaxagoras ('Lord of the Assembly', c. 500-c. 428 BCE), from Persian-held Clazomenæ in Ionia, may have been a pupil of Anaximenes, and may have been acquainted with Parmenides and Empedocles, who were near-contemporaries. In his middle age, he left Clazomenæ for Athens, by then the cultural centre of the Greek Lands, and remained there for some thirty years—making him the first pre-Socratic philosopher to live in the Eye of Greece. The claim that the sun is a blazing mass of metal larger than the Peloponnese led to his prosecution on the grounds of impiety, following which he fled to Lampsacus on the Hellespont. According to Diogenes Laertius, when someone lamented that he would die in a foreign land, he replied, 'The descent to Hades is much the same from wherever we start.'

In fact, the prosecution of Anaxagoras probably owed more to his friendship with Pericles, the principal architect of the Golden Age of Athens. Behind every great man is a great philosopher, and no one, except perhaps for Aspasia, had made a more profound impression on Pericles than Anaxagoras.

According to Plutarch in his *Life of Pericles*:

> ...the man who most consorted with Pericles, and did most to clothe him with a majestic demeanour that had more weight than any demagogue's appeals ... and who lifted on high and exalted the dignity of his character, was Anaxagoras the Clazomenian, whom men of that day used to call 'Nous'...

While in prison in Athens, Anaxagoras attempted to square the circle, that is, to construct, using only compass and straight-edge, a square with the same area as an original circle. The project was finally abandoned in 1882, when *pi* was proven to be a transcendental number. But we still retain the expression, 'to square the circle' for doing something that seems impossible.

Anaxagoras agreed with Parmenides that something cannot come into being nor pass out of being, and with Empedocles that change occurs by the combination and separation of the elements. More originally, he held that everything is infinitely divisible, and that everything contains a bit of everything, albeit in varying combinations—a proposition which may seem outlandish but coheres with modern quantum theory.

Elements such as fire and hair spring out of 'the One' by a process of differentiation mediated by *Nous*, or Mind:

> The other things share a portion of everything, but Mind is infinite and self-ruling and mixed with nothing. But it alone is itself for itself... For it is the lightest of all things and the most pure and it holds all understanding about everything and the greatest power. And all things greater and smaller which have soul, Mind rules them all. And Mind ruled the whole rotation so that the rotation began. And first it began to rotate from a small area and then it rotated more and it will rotate even more. And things combined and separated and distinguished, Mind knew them all...

> — ANAXAGORAS, FRAGMENT B12

This claim that the cosmos was born out of a rotary movement has led some to hail Anaxagoras as the father of the modern Big Bang Theory.

Like Pythagoras, Anaxagoras held that the best life consists in contemplating the cosmos, that is, in turning *Nous* onto itself. So central is *Nous* to his life's work that his contemporaries straight-out nicknamed him 'Nous'.

Anaxagoras made many other claims outside of metaphysics, for example, that wind arises from the rarefaction of air by the sun's rays; that the moon receives its light from the sun and is earthy and inhabited; and that sensation arises out of contrast and, therefore, out of irritation.

Socrates may never have met Anaxagoras, but was taught by one of his students, Archelaus. Upon first hearing about *Nous*, the idea of an intelligent causal principle that orders things for the best greatly appealed to him. In Plato's *Phaedo*, he says that, as a young man, he seized upon the books of Anaxagoras and read them as fast as he could. However, he was left bitterly disappointed by Anaxagoras' failure to develop his account of *Nous*, or even to make use of the concept.

When, in Plato's *Apology*, Meletus accuses Socrates of saying that the sun is stone and the moon earth, Socrates asks whether Meletus might be confusing him with Anaxagoras—suggesting that the prosecution of Anaxagoras loomed large in that of Socrates.

In the *Metaphysics*, Aristotle echoes Socrates in criticizing Anaxagoras for '[availing] himself of Mind as an artificial device for producing order, and [dragging] it in whenever ... at a loss to explain some necessary result...'

Like teacher, like student: Euripides, who had studied under Anaxagoras, used the stage device of *apò mēkhanês theós* ['god from the machine', introducing a god by means of a crane] in the resolution of the greater number of his extant plays.

More than Heraclitus' *Logos*, Anaxagoras' *Nous* introduced a duality of mind and body, or soul and matter, that later thinkers attempted to finesse, and that to this day remains a major trope in philosophy and theology.

Leucippus and Democritus (c. 460-c. 370 BCE) are often spoken of in the same breath as the co-originators of atomism, the culmination of early Greek thought. Leucippus taught Democritus, but little else is known about him, leaving Democritus as the chief exponent of atomism.

Democritus was born in Abdera, on the Thracian coast. He fritted away his considerable inheritance, estimated at over 100 talents (around 2600kg of pure silver), on books and learnt travel, reputedly reaching as far as India where he associated with the gymnosophists, or 'naked wise men'. According to Diogenes Laertius, he went to Athens but, rather than consorting with the likes of Socrates and Euripides, kept himself to himself. Even so, he may have met Anaxagoras and fellow Abderite Protagoras.

Democritus was always ready to laugh at the foolishness of people, whence his epithet, 'the laughing philosopher'. Despite this, the people held him in the highest regard, not least because they believed that he could foresee the future. Like all the early Greek philosophers, he eschewed wealth and power for a prominent place in the history of thought, saying that he would rather uncover a single proof than become king of Persia. He wrote nearly eighty treatises on topics ranging from tangencies and irrationals to farming, painting, and fighting in armour. According to Archimedes, it is he who first determined that the volume of a cone amounts to one-third of the volume of the cylinder with the same height and base area. Although better known for his physics, most of his surviving fragments concern ethics and politics. He seems to have originated the notion of the rise of society from an anarchic 'state of nature', upending the traditional, Hesiodic account of the fall from a golden age.

With regards to his physics, Democritus claimed: 'Nothing exists except atoms and empty space; all else is opinion.' Contra Anaxagoras, matter is not infinitely divisible, but consists of tiny, indivisible bodies called 'atoms' ['uncuttable']. The atom [*den*] and the void [*ouden*] are complementary, so that 'what is not' is no less real than 'what is'. Atoms are infinite in number and variety and do not pass into or out of existence. They are in random motion, like the motes in a sunbeam. Whenever they collide, they can either bounce off one another, or connect into clusters that build up into the objects of sense perception. 'By convention sweet and by convention bitter, by convention hot, by convention cold, by convention colour; but in reality atoms and void.' The universe is a limitless expanse in which atoms, driven by a circular motion, cluster into *kosmoi*, so that our cosmos is but one among many.

Beyond this purely mechanistic account, there is no causal principle or guiding intelligence. Likely for this reason, Plato does not mention Democritus at all—with Diogenes Laertius even claiming that he wanted all his books burnt! Aristotle, for his part, regarded him well enough to write a (now lost) book against his physics. Even the inheritors of atomism, the Epicureans, bore him no love, criticizing him, among others, for leaving no room for human agency.

The pre-Socratics conceived of the universe as an ordered whole—or *kosmos*, as they came to call it. They each attempted to provide a holistic account of its fundamental features without resorting to myths and gods. Instead of accounting for the here and now by the supposed beginning, they accounted for the supposed beginning by the here and now. In so doing, they gave birth to the very idea of philosophy and science.

Other scientific attitudes that they adopted include: conceiving of the world as intelligible; searching for knowledge for its own sake; asking bold questions without fear or favour; seeking to stake claims by force of logic and argument; developing and manipulating abstract concepts; and privileging elegant and economical explanations.

At the same time, the likes of Pythagoras and Empedocles had something of the sorcerer about them, and the pre-Socratics as a whole retained a strong magical or mystical streak. Like the mythologists of old, they were more interested in cosmogony than in uncovering the laws of nature, that is, more interested in grand narratives than in formulating empirically verifiable hypotheses. Although familiar with the work of their forebears and contemporaries—and, it seems, highly driven by it—they did not rigorously critique one another in the way that Aristotle would do in writing a whole book on (or against) Democritus.

The pre-Socratics began the monumental shift from *mythos* to *logos*, even if the two remain entwined in their thought—as perhaps they should when we consider how their divorce has led to the rape of the planet and a dehumanizing loss of vigour and imagination.

Plato himself, for a variety of reasons which I discuss in *The Meaning of Myth*, often resorts to myths, such as the Myth of Aristophanes or Myth of Atlantis, or blends of *mythos* and *logos*, as for instance in the *Gorgias*, when Socrates tells Callicles, "Let me tell you a fine fable. Although you may regard it as a *mythos*, I mean it as a *logos*."

THE SOPHISTS

PROTAGORAS, GORGIAS, PRODICUS, HIPPIAS

*N*ow that the world had been demythologized, the focus of attention shifted from the gods to man, from the shrines and temples to the public square and court of law, and the sophists were far more interested in logic and language ('logic') and ethics and politics ('ethics') than in physics and metaphysics ('physics'). Cicero famously declared that Socrates was the first to 'call philosophy down from the heavens', but the merit may lie rather with the sophists.

The sophistic movement centred upon Athens in its Golden Age and owed to a concatenation of unusual social and political circumstances, not least: a renewed sense of self-confidence and optimism fuelled by the improbable repulsion of two Persian invasions; the great wealth flowing in from the maritime empire that had grown out of an original anti-Persian defensive alliance; and an extreme participatory democracy in which power was wielded by those who were able to carry the crowd. This power was a double-edged sword, since prominent citizens were especially vulnerable to vexatious lawsuits and, rather than hiring a lawyer, had to mount their own defence.

In this climate, the ability to speak became paramount, and the sophists converged upon Athens to deliver public lectures and private classes, typically to young *aristoi* with high political or military ambitions. Other Greek *poleis*, especially in Sicily and Italy, also called upon their services, so that the chief sophists were continually on tour—and could sometimes double up as an ambassador or envoy of their native city. When in Athens, they would often reside at the house of a patron such as the magnate Callias, at whose house Plato's *Protagoras* is set, or the politician Callicles, at whose house Plato's *Gorgias* is set. According to Plato, Callias owned 'the greatest and most glorious house' in Athens (*Protagoras* 337d), and 'spent a world of money on the sophists' (*Apology* 20a). The house is also the setting of Xenophon's *Symposium*.

Callias, once the richest man in town, died penniless, in part because of the astronomical fees of the most prominent sophists. In Plato's *Greater Hippias*, Hippias tells Socrates:

> ...if you were to know how much money I have made, you would be amazed. I won't mention the rest, but once, when I went to Sicily, although Protagoras was staying there and had a great reputation and was the older, I, who was much younger, made in a very short time more than one hundred and fifty minas, and in one very small place, Inycus, more than twenty minas...

In Plato's *Cratylus*, Socrates says, 'If I had not been poor, I might have heard the fifty-drachma course of the great Prodicus, which is a complete education in grammar and language...' Instead, Socrates had only heard the one-drachma course, which Prodicus, presumably, touted as a taster for the more profitable fifty-drachma course.

Sophistês ['expert'] derives from *sophos* ['wise'], and originally designated one who is learnt or skilled in a particular art or craft. But the term began to acquire derogatory connotations even before Plato, who held most sophists in contempt. The comedian Aristophanes had assimilated Socrates with the sophists, leading, ultimately, to the charges of impiety levied against the philosopher. To help rehabilitate the reputation of Socrates, Plato laboured the contrast between Socrates and the sophists, whom he portrayed as venal and amoral and nothing like his poor and pious teacher. As a result, 'sophistry' has come to mean something like, 'the self-interested use of clever but deceptive arguments.' Although he is harshest on the sophists, Plato, in a bid to define, demarcate, and elevate philosophy as a discipline, also sought to undermine poets and orators and all those with a rival but less rigorous or rational claim to the truth. Plato's Socrates often mocks the sophists. For instance, in the *Protagoras*, when Socrates and his friend Hippocrates arrive at the house of Callias, the eunuch at the door mistakes them for sophists and refuses to let them in! Like master, like pupil: Aristotle had such a poor opinion of the sophists that he barely mentions them, so that our principal source on the sophists is... the hardly unbiased Plato.

So, who, in fact, were the sophists? Although they all shared skeptical tendencies, the sophists were not a homogenous group, and Plato treats the likes of Protagoras and Prodicus with much greater respect than second- or third-rate sophists such as Euthydemus and Thrasymachus. Instead of generalizing about the sophistic movement, it might be more profitable simply to discuss a few of its leading exponents: Protagoras, Gorgias, Prodicus, and Hippias.

∾

Protagoras of Abdera (c. 490-c. 420 BCE), an almost exact contemporary of Anaxagoras and Empedocles, hailed from the same city as Democritus. According to lore, his father hosted Xerxes the Great during the second Persian invasion of Greece, so that the boy came to be tutored by magi, or Persian priests.

In the *Protagoras*, Plato intimates that Protagoras invented the role of the professional sophist. He gravitated towards Athens and so impressed Pericles that, in 444, Pericles invited him to draft the constitution of Thurri, his experimental panhellenic colony on the Tarentine Gulf—settled, among others, by the historian Herodotus and the orator Lysias.

Protagoras is especially noted for his maxim that 'man is the measure of all things' [*pantōn chrēmatōn metron estin anthrōpos*], attacked in Plato's *Theaetetus* on the grounds that, if true, nothing could be inherently true or false, or right or wrong—not even the maxim itself (Chapter 18). According to Protagoras, the value of an opinion lies not in its truth but in its usefulness to the person that holds it—a slippery position that could readily be seized upon by scoundrels.

Protagoras is also remembered for the outré opening of his lost work, *About the Gods*: 'About the gods, I cannot be sure whether they exist or not, or what they are like to see; for many things stand in the way of the knowledge of them, both the opacity of the subject and the shortness of human life.'

The agnosticism and relativism of the first and foremost sophist turned him into a controversial figure, and coloured, or tainted, the entire sophistic movement, and even certain proximal *bona fide* philosophers such as Anaxagoras and Socrates. Indeed, the Socrates portrayed by Aristophanes in the *Clouds* is much closer to Protagoras than to the historical Socrates.

In Plato's *Protagoras*, Protagoras claims to teach virtue, even though, as it turns out, he has no grasp of what it is. Plato's attempt to anchor truth in transcendental universals is in part a response to the ethical and epistemological challenge posed by Protagoras and the sophists.

Protagoras charged extortionate fees for his services. According to Aulus Gellius, he once took on a pupil, Euathlus, on the understanding that he would be paid once Euathlus had won his first court case. However, Euathlus never won a case, and in time Protagoras sued him for non-payment.

Protagoras argued that if he won the case he would be paid, and if Euathlus won the case, he would still be paid, because Euathlus would then have won a case.

Euathlus, having assimilated the methods of his master, retorted that if he won the case he would not have to pay, and if Protagoras won the case, he still would not have to pay, because he still would not have won a case!

This so-called Paradox of the Court, and the concomitant Counterdilemma of Euathlus, is also told of Corax ['Crow'] of Syracuse and his student Tisias, the nominal founders of rhetoric. One version ends with the judge throwing them both out of the court with the words, *Kakou korakos kakon ōon* ['A bad egg from a bad crow'].

Gorgias (483-375 BCE) hailed from Leontini in Sicily. He studied rhetoric under Corax and Tisias in nearby Syracuse, and was also acquainted with the teachings of Empedocles. In 427, he led an embassy to Athens to forge a defensive alliance against an overbearing Syracuse.

Gorgias was something of a showman. He specialized in making unconventional, counterintuitive, or absurd arguments appear the stronger, and spoke in a florid, rhyming style that hypnotized his audiences. When in the theatre at Athens, he would say, 'Come, propose me a theme!' He took pride in his ability to take any position, on any subject, and founded the art of extempore oratory. In the *Rhetoric*, Aristotle characterizes his style of oratory as 'ironic', so that his own opinions, if he had any, are hard to decipher. Rather than any positive philosophy, he offered an agnostic art of persuasion which he held to be of the utmost value.

In Plato's *Philebus*, the sophist Protarchus tells Socrates: 'I have often heard Gorgias maintain that the art of persuasion far surpassed every other; this, as he says, is by far the best of them all, for to it all things submit, not by compulsion, but of their own free will.'

Of Gorgias' works, two short display speeches survive, the *Encomium of Helen* and the *Defence of Palamedes*, along with a fragment of a funeral oration and two paraphrases of a lost treatise, *On Non-Being*.

In the *Encomium of Helen*, which aims at praising Helen and exculpating her for leaving Sparta with Paris and sparking the Trojan War, he compares the effect of speech on the soul to the effect of drugs on the body: 'Just as different drugs draw forth different humours from the body—some putting a stop to disease, others to life—so too with words: some cause pain, others joy, some strike fear, some stir the audience to boldness, some benumb and bewitch the soul with evil persuasion.' In sum, he argues that Helen could have been persuaded to leave in one of four ways: by the gods; by physical force; by the power of love; by the power of speech. But whichever way it was, she herself would have been blameless.

In *On Not-Being*, he parodies and refutes Parmenides by arguing that: 1. Nothing exists. 2. Even if something did exist, nothing could be known about it. 3. Even if something could be known about it, this knowledge could not be communicated to others. 4. Even if it could be communicated to others, it could not be understood.

But as ever with Gorgias, it is far from clear whether these stood among his own opinions.

Gorgias spent much of his long life in Thessaly where he enjoyed the patronage of Aristippus of Larissa and Jason of Pheræ. He taught Aristippus' one-time beloved, the Meno who lent his name to Plato's *Meno* (Chapter 14), as well as the orator Isocrates, who came to rank among the ten Attic Orators.

In his autobiographical *Antidosis*, Isocrates tells us that Gorgias:

> ...spent his time in Thessaly when the Thessalians were the most prosperous people in Hellas; he lived a long life and devoted himself to the making of money; he had no fixed domicile in any city and therefore paid out nothing for public weal nor was he subject to any tax; moreover, he did not marry and beget children, but was free from this, the most unremitting and expensive of burdens...

Gorgias died at the grand old age of 108.

Prodicus (c. 465-c. 395 BCE), an almost exact contemporary of Socrates, hailed from the island of Ceos, an early member of the Delian League, and first came to Athens as an ambassador from that place.

Prodicus established himself as a sophist and specialized in the correct use of words and fine discrimination between near synonyms—which led him, in the minds of some, to be linked to Socrates, who more particularly strived to define moral terms such as 'courage', 'temperance', and 'virtue'.

In Plato, he is often mocked for his pedantry and love of gain. Nevertheless, Plato held him in higher regard than the other sophists, having himself argued, in the *Cratylus*, that words can, and should, contain an intrinsic wisdom—the word *alētheia* [truth], for instance, being a compression of the phrase, 'a wandering that is divine.'

In the *Protagoras*, he is presented as less distinguished than Protagoras and even Hippias, but he was sufficiently well known in Athens for Aristophanes to mention him by name in not one but two of his plays (the *Clouds* and the *Birds*).

Prodicus left himself open to charges of atheism by arguing that men had made gods out of the things that they most depended upon, such as the sun, fire, rivers, meadows, crops, and wine.

He is also remembered for Hercules at the Crossroads, a parable preserved in Xenophon and later seized upon by the Stoics. In this parable, an adolescent Hercules arrives at a fork in the road and must choose between the path of virtue and the path of vice. While contemplating this choice, he is visited by the personifications of Vice and Virtue, who each make the case for their way of life. Hercules, of course, chooses the path of virtue, and becomes the greatest of the Greek heroes, to be raised, upon his death, to the rank of an immortal god.

Prodicus taught Isocrates, Euripides, and possibly also the historian Thucydides.

Hippias, a younger contemporary of Socrates and Prodicus, frequently served as an ambassador for his native Elis, in the Peloponnese. He is even harder to reconstruct than Protagoras, Gorgias, and Prodicus.

In two dialogues of disputed authenticity, the *Greater Hippias* and *Lesser Hippias*, Plato presents Hippias as vain and arrogant, and utterly oblivious to the mocking irony of Socrates. He is also depicted, more charitably this time, in the *Protagoras*, as another guest at the house of Callias. In the *Greater Hippias*, he is due to deliver a speech on the *kalon* [the beautiful, excellent, or noble] but proves quite unable to define the term.

Hippias claimed to be an authority on everything and wrote many books. He had, it seems, an elephant's memory: in his *Lives of the Sophists*, Philostratus claims that, upon hearing fifty names, he could repeat them all in the order in which he had heard them. In mathematics, in attempting to solve the angle trisection problem, he discovered a transcendental curve, now called the quadratix (or trisectrix) of Hippias. He held that the purpose of life is *autarkeia* [self-sufficiency], and boasted of presenting himself at Olympia wearing nothing that he had not himself made, down to his sandals, seal-ring, and strigil.

Hippias drew a contrast between natural law, which is universal and eternal, and positive (as in, 'posited') law, which is socially constructed and subject to variation and alteration. In the *Protagoras*, when he rises to speak, he begins by making an argument for cosmopolitanism: 'All of you who are here present I reckon to be kinsmen and friends and fellow-citizens, by nature and not by law; for by nature like is akin to like, whereas law is the tyrant of mankind, and often compels us to do many things which are against nature.' In the *Greater Hippias*, Socrates leans upon this dichotomy between *physis* [nature] and *nomos* [convention] when he jokes that the Spartans must be breaking their laws by not giving Hippias their money. The dichotomy also surfaces in the *Antigone* of Sophocles (c. 441 BCE), when Antigone seeks to justify her attempt to bury her brother Polynices by claiming the superiority of divine over man-made law.

In his bid to distinguish Socrates from the sophists, and, more generally, philosophy from sophistry, Plato painted the sophists in an unflattering and possibly unfair light as being more concerned with themselves than with wisdom or virtue.

From our own discussion, it does seem that many sophists had a strong and potentially self-serving skeptical streak. Although they did raise many questions, they seemed more interested in expediency than in knowledge for its own sake—their primary purpose being to create effective public speakers and enrich themselves in the process, without due regard for the long-term consequences of creating a cohort of venal and amoral leaders.

Their habit of attacking and undermining the traditional gods turned many conservatives and ordinary people against them, and, ultimately, against Socrates, who was condemned by (false) association.

Their successors in Rome, such as Cicero and Quintilian, confined themselves more narrowly to education, rhetoric, oratory, and matters of style.

PART II

SOCRATES

Unlike the more academic and aristocratic Plato and Aristotle, who succeeded, by and large, in removing themselves from the world, Socrates was a philosopher of the street and very much immersed in the tumultuous currents of history. Even though he had the good fortune of living right through the Golden Age of Athens, which, more than anyone, he came to epitomize, he had to submit to several long and brutal military campaigns, suffer the defeat and subjugation of his people, and defend his character and ideals in a court that sentenced him to death.

HISTORY OF ATHENS UP TO THE TIME OF SOCRATES

From the eighth century BCE, the scattered communities remaining on mainland Greece began to organize around a much larger centre under the rule of an aristocratic elite. In Athens, those born into the foremost families—the *Eupatridæ*, or 'sons of good fathers'—could be elected by their peers to join the ruling council of *archons*.

By the seventh century, a prominent middle class had emerged, and its exclusion from the ruling council gave rise to social unrest. In around 632, Kylon, an aristocrat and former Olympic champion, sought to take advantage of this discontent by setting himself up as sole tyrant—before having to flee to his father-in-law, the tyrant of Megara.

To pacify the people, the aristocrat Draco published a written code of law which put justice firmly into the hands of the state, so that aristocrats could no longer act as they saw fit. On the other hand, the laws treated debtors of a lower status than their creditors differently to debtors of a higher status, with the long-term effect of consolidating the aristocracy's land holdings. Draco had his laws inscribed onto three-sided pyramids [*axones*], which could be pivoted by the reader. Draco's laws were 'written not in ink, but in blood', with the death penalty meted out for even minor offences such as stealing potherbs or fruits or even just opting for idleness. When asked why he had made death the penalty for most offences, Draco replied that he considered the lesser offences to deserve it and had no harsher punishment for the greater ones. In time, Draco was chased out of Athens to end his life on Ægina.

In 594, Solon, who was also a poet, was appointed as archon, and acquired such a reputation for justice and wisdom as to be given a free rein in reforming the city. He proceeded to cancel or limit debts, redeem forfeited land, outlaw debt slavery, and restructure the class system to broaden political participation. Solon's reforms may have averted a revolution and subsequent tyranny; even so, the Eupatrids so resented them that, for two years from 589, they returned no archons—a period referred to as the Anarchy ['Without archons'].

Solon had laid the foundations for Athenian democracy, and in Plato's *Protagoras* is numbered among the seven sages of Greece alongside Thales of Miletus, Pittacus of Mytilene, Bias of Priene, Cleobulus of Lindus, Myson of Chen, and Chilon of Sparta. The tradition of the 'seven sages' encapsulates an era of social crisis in Greek history in which wisdom and equity came to prevail.

The tyranny of the Peisistratids

There is an ancient tradition, discredited by Aristotle, that Solon had a younger lover by the name of Peisistratos. In 561, Peisistratos, by now a popular Athenian general, staged an attempt on his own life, and rode on the public outcry to seize power. He ruled as tyrant for some five years before being banished by an aristocratic faction led by Megakles.

In around 556, Megakles recalled Peisistratos, who rode into the city in a golden chariot. As part of their pact, he married the daughter of Megakles, but refused to lie with her 'in the normal way' so as not to compromise the political futures of his sons, Hippias and Hipparkhos. Taking offence, Megakles drove him back into exile.

Ten years later, in 546, Peisistratos returned at the head of a foreign army and reinstated himself as tyrant. It would be third time lucky: up until his death in 527, he ruled as an enlightened despot, patronizing the arts while championing the people. His legacy included the institution of the Great Panathenaia.

When Peisistratos died, his son Hippias took over, but Hippias did not have his father's charisma or ability and came to be resented. According to Aristotle, the tyranny of Peisistratos was often spoken of proverbially as 'the age of gold', 'for when his sons succeeded him the government became much harsher.'

In 514, two lovers, Harmodius and the older Aristogeiton, plotted to assassinate Hippias and Hipparkhos but succeeded only in taking out Hipparkhos. Harmodius was killed in action, and Aristogeiton captured and tortured to death.

Having lost his brother, Hippias became increasingly ruthless. Kleisthenes, a son of Megakles exiled by Hippias, asked or bribed the Delphic oracle to tell the Spartans to liberate Athens. In 510, King Kleomenes of Sparta entered the city, restoring the democracy and forcing Hippias to flee.

Hippias joined the court of Darius and, after the Ionian Revolt, inclined him to invade Greece. He even accompanied the Persian fleet, and it is he who suggested Marathon as a battle site. According to Herodotus, the night before reaching Attica he dreamt of making love to his own mother—which he somehow interpreted as a good omen.

Despite their aristocratic lineage, the lovers Harmodius and Aristogeiton became martyrs for democracy, and the Athenians raised many statues by which to remember them—and, by the same token, forget King Kleomenes and the debt that they owed to Sparta.

The reforms of Kleisthenes

After the deposition of Hippias, Kleisthenes and Isagoras vied for power. Isagoras ruled for a time with the support of Sparta, until Kleisthenes and the democrats ousted him. Kleisthenes is remembered as 'the Father of Athenian Democracy' for his isonomic ['equal before the law'] reforms of 508.

Long-standing rivalries between the four traditional clans had led to the tyranny. To guard against infighting, Kleisthenes divided the people of Attica into ten new geographic tribes [phulai], which he subdivided into 139 demes. Each deme belonged to one of 30 trittyes, with three trittyes per tribe—the significance being that each one of a tribe's trittyes had to issue from a different territorial classification: Coast, Inland, or City.

Kleisthenes also reformed the Solonian Boule, creating a Council of Five Hundred, with every deme proportionally represented and government positions filled by lot. This reformed Boule ran ordinary affairs and set the agenda for the popular assembly [ekklesia] of around six thousand.

To safeguard the democracy, Kleisthenes (it was probably him) introduced the oft abused system of ostracism, whereby the ekklesia could vote, by means of pot shards [ostraca, cf. oyster], to exile any incipient tyrant for ten years.

Still, isonomia only applied to adult male citizens. Women, slaves, and metics (resident aliens) did not benefit from anything like the same rights and privileges.

The First Persian War

In 490, a mighty Persian army, having already sacked and burned Eretria in revenge for its role in the Ionian Revolt, landed at Marathon with the intention of invading Athens and mainland Greece.

One Pheidippides ran the 240km from Athens to Sparta to summon help, only to be rebuffed by the Spartans, who were observing *Carneia*, a sacrosanct period of peace to honour Apollo Karneios. The Spartan ephors informed Pheidippides that the Spartan army could not march until the full moon.

From their camp at Marathon the Persians had dispatched a contingent by sea to Athens, so that the Athenians, assisted only by the Platæans, had not only to defeat the Persians at Marathon, but also to rush back and defend their city—an almost impossible task.

As the Persians advanced onto the battlefield, the Athenian *strategos* [commander on land or at sea] Miltiades ordered his vastly outnumbered troops to converge onto the centre of the Persian infantry line, which miraculously began to crumble.

Instead of pursuing the fleeing Persians, the Athenians marched back to their city, arriving just in time to stave off an attack.

According to lore, the Athenians had sent Pheidippides ahead of them to announce their victory at Marathon. Pheidipiddes ran the 40km from Marathon to Athens, burst into a meeting of the *ekklesia*, and breathed *nenikékamen* ['we are victorious'], before dying on the very spot (Figure 4).

Not only had Athens defeated the Persians, but it had done so without Sparta.

*Figure 4. The Soldier of Marathon (Pheidippides giving word of victory
after the Battle of Marathon), by Luc-Olivier Merson (1869). Pheidippides
supposedly shed his armour and even his clothes to run the better.*

The Second Persian War

The discovery, in 483, of silver in the mines at Laureion brought
immense wealth to Athens. The archon Themistocles
persuaded the Athenians to spend it on building a naval fleet of
almost two hundred triremes (warships with three banks of
oars) to defend Athens and Greece against Xerxes, the son and
successor of Darius. So palpable was the Persian threat that
Sparta, Athens, Corinth, and 28 other Greek *poleis* agreed to the
creation of a joint army under the overall command of Sparta.

But this only represented about a tenth of the Greek *poleis*, so
that when the Persians returned in 480 they far outnumbered
the Greeks. The Greeks took position in the narrow pass at
Thermopylæ ['Hot gates', after its sulphur springs—in myth,

one of the entrances to Hades] and dispatched their fleet to Artemision to prevent the Persian fleet from uniting with the Persian army. However, Xerxes diverted his elite troops of Immortals on a back route that had been revealed to him by a treacherous goatherd. As the assembled Greek army pulled out of Thermopylæ, King Leonidas of Sparta, with 300 Spartans and 700 Thespians, succeeded in holding the pass for three days, fighting to the last man standing.

The poet Simonides composed their epitaph at Thermopylæ:

Go tell the Spartans, passerby
That here, by Spartan law, we lie.

Meanwhile at Artemision, the Persians lost many of their eight hundred battleships to storms and several more to the Greeks. The remainder of the Persian fleet sailed south to find the Persian army. By the time the Persian army entered Athens, the Athenians had fled to the island of Salamis, where they were joined by the Greek fleet under Themistocles. The Persians looted and burnt down Athens, and desecrated and destroyed the Acropolis.

In emulation of Thermopylæ, Themistocles funnelled his three hundred triremes into the narrow strait between Salamis and the mainland, leaving a small number of ships behind, tucked away in the Bay of Ambelaki. When the Persian fleet followed into the strait, the more manoeuvrable Greek ships suddenly turned around to face the enemy. The Persian fleet fled back down the strait, only to be ambushed by the Greek ships at Ambelaki. The performance of Queen Artemisia of Caria, who commanded five ships on the Persian side, prompted Xerxes to remark, "My men have turned out to be women and my women men!"

Cut off from the remnants of its navy, the Persian army retreated north for the winter. Xerxes returned to Asia Minor, leaving his son-in-law Mardonius in command. In the spring of 479, the Persian army once again marched south. Pausanias, acting as regent for the young son of Leonidas, led the Greek army north near Platæa. The Persian army attacked while the Greek army was on manoeuvres, but the Greek troops managed to regroup and the Persians suffered a devastating defeat with even Mardonius killed. The Greek fleet pursued the fleeing Persian fleet, which the Persians beached at Mycale. The Greeks stormed the beach and burnt down every last ship.

Within a few years, in c. 470, Socrates would be born.

The Delian League

Athens received much of the credit for the double defeat of the Persians, although Themistocles would follow Miltiades in falling from grace. In the winter of 478-77, ambassadors from several Greek *poleis* met on the sacred island of Delos to forge a defensive anti-Persian alliance, the so-called Delian League.

Athens soon asserted itself over the Delian League, reducing its nominal allies to the condition of vassals and tributaries, as Kimon, the son of Miltiades, further enlarged the Athenian Empire by recapturing Persian-held territories. The immense wealth flowing into Athens, now under the enlightened rule of Pericles, led to a cultural efflorescence the likes of which had never been seen.

This Golden Age lasted from 478 to 405 (or, more narrowly, 478 to 430, the first year of the Plague of Athens), and in it moved a remarkable concentration of great men and women, including Pericles and his life partner Aspasia; the orators Andocides, Antiphon, Isocrates, and Lysias; the sculptors Phidias, Myron, and Polycletus; the historians Herodotus, Thucydides, and Xenophon; the dramatists Æschylus, Sophocles, Euripides, and Aristophanes; and, of course, the philosophers Parmenides, Anaxagoras, Democritus, Protagoras, Socrates, and Plato.

In his *Alcestis* of 438, Euripides wrote:

> I have found power in the mysteries of thought,
> Exaltation in the changing of the Muses;
> I have been versed in the reasonings of men;
> But Fate is stronger than anything I have known.

The First Peloponnesian War

In 464, Sparta suffered a devastating earthquake after which its disenfranchised peasantry, the helots, took the opportunity to revolt. Sparta appealed to Athens for help, and Kimon—who had such a strength of feeling for Sparta [Lacedæmon] as to have named his son Lacedæmonius—persuaded the assembly to send him at the head of an expeditionary force. 'Let not Greece' he said, 'be lamed, and thus Athens herself be deprived of her yokefellow.' But when the Athenians arrived in Sparta, they started sympathizing with the helots, so that the Spartans felt obliged to dismiss them. Following this diplomatic disaster, relationships between Athens and Sparta soured, and, in 460, war broke out.

The First Peloponnesian War lasted for 15 years during which Athens and Sparta attacked each other's allies without either belligerent gaining a decisive upper hand. Finally, in 446, both sides agreed to a truce of thirty years known as the Peace of Pericles: for thirty years, Hellas would remain a house divided, with Athens maintaining supremacy over the seas but shelving its ambition to establish a land empire to rival that of Sparta.

The Second Peloponnesian War

Within just 15 years, war broke out again. Pericles avoided engaging the Spartan army but used the Athenian fleet to diminish Sparta's allies. Meanwhile, Sparta carried out a series of attacks on the Attic countryside, leading many to seek refuge within the city's newly rebuilt walls—connected, via the Long Walls, to the port of Piræus, Athens' gateway to the seas.

In 430, overcrowding within the city walls led to an outbreak of a plague that in some respects resembled Ebola. The plague spread up from Piræus and killed a third of the population of around 300,000, including Pericles and both his sons— seeming to confirm the conviction of conservatives that the plague had been sent by the gods as a punishment for their neglect by Pericles and his humanist friends and allies.

The *strategos* and historian Thucydides also contracted the disease, but survived to write about it in gory detail, noting that even carrion animals stayed away from the dead, or died from feeding upon them. Thucydides also relates that people began to behave lawlessly when it seemed that death would outrun the courts, an episode that might have inspired the passage in Plato's *Republic* in which Glaucon argues that a man who could get hold of the fabled Ring of Gyges and make himself invisible would behave in whatever way he wanted.

As Athens suffered, parts of its empire revolted, including, in 428, the town of Mytilene on Lesbos. Under the spell of the radical demagogue Kleon, the assembly voted to have all the men of Mytilene executed and all the women and children sold into slavery. Mercifully, the issue was revisited on the following day, and a messenger ship arrived in Mytilene just in time to avert a massacre.

In the summer of that year, Sparta and its allies captured
Platæa, and showed no compunction, despite Platæa's part at
Marathon, in executing all the men, enslaving all the women
and children, and razing the city to the ground.

In 424, some cities in north-east Greece that had formerly been
loyal to Athens decided to revolt. Sparta sent up a large force
under the command of Brasidas, who, by strength or by guile,
won over several of the cities. When Brasidas attacked
Amphipolis, Athens dispatched Thucydides at the head of an
army. But Thucydides arrived too late, for which the Athenians
had him exiled. This enabled him to record the history of the
war more dispassionately, 'not as an essay with which to win
the applause of the moment, but as a possession for all time.'

When, in 422, Kleon attempted to recapture Amphipolis, both
he and Brasidas were killed, clearing the ground for the Peace
of Nicias. Some of Sparta's allies felt hard done by the terms of
the peace and defected to Argos. In 420, a handsome aristocrat
by the name of Alcibiades—a long-time protégé of Socrates—
argued in the assembly that Sparta's former friends were now
her enemies, and therefore the friends of Athens. As a result,
Athens forged an alliance with Argos and its allies Mantinea
and Elis. The allies attempted to seize Tegea near Sparta, but
lost the ensuing Battle of Mantinea, leading to the dissolution
of their alliance and the restoration of Spartan hegemony in the
Peloponnese.

Athens fell back on the time-honoured strategy of attacking
and annexing Sparta's allies. In 416, Athens attacked the island
of Melos, and did to the Melians that which it had threatened
to do to the Mytilenes.

In 416, the city of Egesta in Sicily asked Athens for assistance
against its neighbour Selinous, and Alcibiades persuaded the
ekklesia to let him lead a force to Sicily. But as the Athenian

fleet was about to set sail, all the *hermai* [sculptures with the head and genitals of Hermes] in the city were vandalized. The assembly recalled Alcibiades to face charges of impiety, prompting the scoundrel to defect to Sparta!

Now under the command of Nicias—who features alongside Socrates in Plato's *Laches*—the Athenian force prepared to invade Syracuse in an ambitious attempt to conquer all of rich Sicily. But as Nicias prevaricated and delayed, a Spartan force arrived and joined with the Syracusans to defeat Athens. The assembly responded to Nicias' plea for reinforcements by sending a second fleet under Demosthenes, but the Athenians suffered another defeat. Demosthenes called for a retreat, but Nicias hesitated, and then a lunar eclipse seemed like a bad omen for raising anchor. Forced into a major battle in the harbour of Syracuse, the Athenians suffered a final and crushing defeat, with Nicias and Demosthenes executed and seven thousand prisoners taken.

The failure of the Sicilian Expedition so diminished Athens that its empire began to crumble. Meanwhile, Alcibiades left Sparta to serve as an advisor to the Persian satrap Tissaphernes. He leveraged his newfound position to persuade a number of Athenian *strategoi* to stage a coup, and, in 411, the conspirators succeeded in installing an oligarchy known as the Four Hundred. Grieved at not being recalled, Alcibiades, ever the turncoat, made himself an ally of the exiled democrats. Four months later, he received the command of the Athenian army after the democrats came back in with an intermediate regime known as the Five Thousand. Athens rebuilt its fleet and carried on warring, scoring victories at Cynossema and then, under Alcibiades, at Cyzicus. In the aftermath of the Battle of Cyzicus, the Athenians intercepted a laconic dispatch from the Spartans: 'Ships lost; Mindarus dead; men starving; can't figure out what to do.'

Athens refused Sparta's entreaties for peace. Cyrus, the youngest son of Darius, helped to finance the Spartan fleet, which, under Lysander, went on to win an important victory at Notium—leading to the final downfall and exile of Alcibiades.

Fortunes were reversed the following year at Arginusæ, but a sudden storm prevented the Athenians from picking up their survivors and some three thousand were left to die. Despite the protests of Socrates, whose turn it was to chair the assembly, the *strategoi* at Arginusæ were tried as a body and executed.

Once again, Athens refused Sparta's entreaties for peace. In 405, Lysander mounted a surprise attack on the Athenian fleet, which had been beached at Ægospotami in the Hellespont. In the ensuing Battle of Ægospotami, the Spartans captured the near entirety of the Athenian fleet, bringing the 36-year-long Peloponnesian War to an end. The ship carrying the news of the defeat arrived in Piræus at night. According to Xenophon, 'one man passed it on to another, and a sound of wailing arose and extended first from Piræus, then along the Long Walls until it reached the city. That night no one slept. They mourned for the lost, but more still for their own fate.'

Mercifully, the Spartans resisted calls to turn Athens to pasture, but Athens had to surrender to Sparta's terms and became a Spartan territory under Spartan control. The Spartans decided that Athens should be ruled by thirty individuals, mostly conservative, pro-Spartan aristocrats such as Plato's uncles Critias and Charmides. Because they blamed the democrats for their defeat, the Athenians initially lent their support to the so-called Thirty Tyrants. But soon enough, the brutal oligarchy had alienated all but its most ardent supporters. After the democratic forces in exile defeated the oligarchic army and allied Spartan garrison, Sparta reluctantly restored a diluted democracy to Athens.

It is in this period, in 399, that the seventy-year-old Socrates was condemned to death.

Plato, who attended the trial, would then have been in his early twenties.

Aristotle would not be born for another twenty years.

7

THE SOCRATIC QUESTION

*T*he Socratic question, or Socratic problem, refers to the difficulty in reconstructing the historical Socrates from the sometimes contradictory sources on his life and thought. The three primary, contemporary sources on Socrates are his followers Plato and Xenophon, and the comedian Aristophanes. Except for the odd fragment, the Socratic works of the other followers of Socrates, such as Antisthenes and Æschines, have all been lost. Later biographies of Socrates, including those of Plutarch and Diogenes Laertius, lean heavily on Plato and Xenophon, but may also draw on scraps from Aristotle, his student Aristoxenus, and a few others.

Aristophanes

Aristophanes' depiction of Socrates in the *Clouds* is unusual in at least two respects: it is hostile, and it dates from Socrates' own lifetime.

In the *Clouds*, an old Strepsiades seeks to enrol into the 'Thinkery' to learn how to make weak arguments into winning ones, and, in this way, evade his creditors. At the Thinkery, a student tells him about the head of the school, Socrates, who has recently discovered the source of the buzz of a gnat in its trumpet-like rear and devised a new unit for measuring the distance jumped by a flea. Socrates himself then appears, borne aloft in a basket from which he has been studying the sun. Although he conducts the induction ceremony, he later expels the inept Strepsiades, who persuades his son Pheidippides to enrol in his stead. When Pheidippides graduates, he gives Strepsiades a thrashing, and proceeds to debate a son's right to beat his father. An enraged Strepsiades arms his slaves with torches and leads them in a frenzied attack on the Thinkery.

The Socrates of the Thinkery is a representative of the New Learning, a composite of sophists such as Protagoras, natural philosophers such as Anaxagoras, and the historical Socrates, who stood alone and apart for being an ascetic, and for having no knowledge of his own. Possibly, the historical Socrates did for a time embrace natural philosophy, as suggested in Plato's *Phaedo*. He might even have had something of the sophist about him, an aspect that Plato and Xenophon would have been keen to downplay.

Aristophanes (c. 446-c. 386 BCE) would have been a mere 23 years old in 423, when the *Clouds* was first staged, while Socrates would have been in his mid-forties. According to Ælian, Socrates attended the City Dionysia to watch the play. When some out-of-towners seemed confused about who Socrates was, he rose up from his seat and stood there in silence for the rest of the performance, as if to say, 'I am Socrates.'

In favour of Ælian's account, Socrates does seem to have been in the habit of standing motionless for long periods. In Plato's *Symposium*, he keeps falling behind on his way to Agathon's banquet. When Agathon sends out a slave to search for him, the slave reports that he is standing on a neighbour's porch, apparently lost in thought. 'How strange' says Agathon, 'then you must call him again, and keeping calling him.' Aristodemus objects: 'Let him alone... he has a way of stopping anywhere and losing himself without any reason. I believe that he will soon appear; do not therefore disturb him.' When Socrates finally arrives, Agathon beckons him to recline next to him, so that he might touch him 'and have the benefit of that wise thought which came into your mind in the portico...' Later in the *Symposium*, Alcibiades relates how, at Potidæa, Socrates once stood for an entire day and night absorbed in reflection. That Aristophanes is also present at the banquet—which, if it took place, took place in 416—suggests that he and Socrates were not on bad terms.

When Socrates went to see the *Clouds* (if he did go), it would have been in competition with *Konnos* by Ameipsias and the *Wineflask* by Cratinus. Interestingly, *Konnos* seems to have had the same subject as the *Clouds*, and even to feature a character called Socrates. This suggests two things. First, that Socrates had by then already become something of a stock character. Second, that the New Learning was weighing on people's minds as much as the ongoing war. But not as much as wine, and first prize went to the *Wineflask*, in which the almost centenarian Cratinus defended his own drinking with the line, 'You'll never fashion anything clever by drinking water!'

The *Clouds*, which Aristophanes later called his masterpiece, came last. So poorly was it received that Aristophanes felt obliged to rewrite it, and it is this revised, probably more hostile, version that has come down to us. Although the revised version was never completed and never performed, it circulated in manuscript form and is mentioned in Plato's *Apology* as a contributing factor in the trial of Socrates.

Socrates: These clouds here are the only divinities. Everything else is a crock.

Strepsiades: But what about Olympian Zeus? Come on! Surely he's a god?

Socrates: What Zeus? Don't be an idiot. There's no such thing.

— ARISTOPHANES, *THE CLOUDS*

Xenophon

Xenophon led a more interesting life than Aristophanes. The story goes that Socrates met the young and handsome Xenophon (c. 430-c. 354 BCE) in a narrow alleyway. Socrates barred the passage with his staff, and asked Xenophon where such and such wares might be bought and sold. At last, he asked him where men might be made virtuous. When Xenophon could not reply, Socrates said, "Follow me, then, and learn." Xenophon became a devoted student of Socrates.

Xenophon left Athens two years before the death of Socrates and did not return for some forty years. In his *Anabasis* ['The March Up Country'], he relates his attempt to capture Babylon as part of the Ten Thousand, an army of Greek mercenaries hired by Cyrus the Younger in a veiled and failed attempt to seize the throne of Persia from his brother, Artaxerxes II. When, after much hardship and heroism, Xenophon finally made it back to Greece, he found himself fighting on the side of Sparta, for which the Athenians banished him. Only in 362 did they pardon him, after his eldest son Gryllus died fighting on the side of Athens at the Battle of Mantinea.

Xenophon wrote some forty books on various topics including horsemanship and hunting with dogs. In the *Hellenica*, he picks up the *History of the Peloponnesian War* where Thucydides left off. Already in antiquity, he came to be known as the 'Attic Muse' for his limpid prose. He most likely composed his Socratic works on his estate in Elis in the Peloponnese, where he would have had access to the writings of other Socratics including Plato—so that his Socratic works are not fully or necessarily independent of Plato's.

Like Plato, Xenophon had the highest possible regard for Socrates, and would have been keen to defend his character and preserve his memory.

This is how he concludes his *Memorabilia of Socrates*:

> All who knew what manner of man Socrates was and who seek after virtue continue to this day to miss him beyond all others, as the chief of helpers in the quest of virtue. For myself, I have described him as he was: so religious that he did nothing without counsel from the gods; so just that he did no injury, however small, to any man, but conferred the greatest benefits on all who dealt with him; so self-controlled that he never chose the pleasanter rather than the better course; so wise that he was unerring in his judgement of the better and the worse... To me then he seemed to be all that a truly good and happy man must be. But if there is any doubter, let him set the character of other men beside these things; then let him judge.

Xenophon's Socratic works include an *Apology*, a *Symposium*, and the *Memorabilia*. His *Apology*, or account of the defence offered by Socrates, is much shorter than that of Plato, who, unlike Xenophon, had attended the trial. There are also some differences of substance. For instance, whereas Plato rebuts the charge of impiety by presenting it as a misrepresentation of philosophy, Xenophon does so by emphasizing the traditional piety of Socrates. And whereas Plato depicts Socrates' boastful manner of speaking [*megalēgoria*] as an attempt to set or reveal a higher standard, Xenophon depicts it as a wilful attempt to court death. The *Memorabilia of Socrates* consists of four books of reports, mostly in direct speech, of Socrates' conversations. Compared to the Platonic Socrates, the Xenophontic Socrates is more down to earth, not to say more pedestrian, with irony, dialectic, and abstract philosophy taking second place to piety, morality, and practical advice. Another of Xenophon's Socratic works, the *Œconomicus*, pertains to household management and agriculture rather than elevated Platonic themes such as language or knowledge. It has been argued that the Socrates of Plato is the more accurate representation on the grounds that the Socrates of Xenophon could not have inspired the likes of Plato or, conversely, attracted the censure of the Athenians. In the final analysis, it may be that Xenophon could not fully grasp a mind so much greater than his own—a problem that we must all grapple with when approaching the Gang of Three.

About a hundred years after the death of Socrates, a young merchant from Citium in Cyprus suffered a shipwreck and wound up in Athens with nothing more than the clothes on his back. Having recovered from his ordeal, he asked an oracle what he should do 'to live the best life'. The oracle replied that he ought to 'have conversation with the dead', after which he began frequenting a bookshop in the agora. One day, he picked up a copy of the *Memorabilia* and was struck by Xenophon's portrayal of Socrates. On putting the book back down, he turned to the bookseller and asked, 'Where might such men be found?' At that very moment, the Cynic philosopher Crates of Thebes happened to be passing by. The bookseller pointed to him and said, 'Follow yonder man.'

Zeno of Citium is remembered as the founder of Stoicism.

Plato

Plato's authorship spanned some fifty years, from the death of Socrates in 399 to his own death in c. 348. He is traditionally ascribed with 35 dialogues, although around ten of these are or may be spurious. Today, the dialogues are often classified into three periods, 'early', 'middle', and 'late', based upon their presumed order of composition, with the intention of tracing the likely development of his thought. Since historical anchors and internal references are scant, scholars have for the most part relied on comparisons of format, content, and style to determine their approximate order of composition.

The early dialogues are relatively short and accessible. They are sometimes referred to as the Socratic dialogues because they set forth more of the historical Socrates, typically debating ethical subjects such as temperance (the *Charmides*), courage (the *Laches*), or friendship (the *Lysis*) with youths, friends, or a supposed expert. Although the *mise en scène* may be a fiction, and the conversation an elaboration, the broad-brush portrayal of Socrates is faithful to the historical Socrates. The early dialogues include three more explicitly biographical works, the *Euthyphro*, *Apology*, and *Crito*, around the trial and execution of Socrates. The more sophisticated *Protagoras*, *Gorgias*, and *Meno* are considered early transitional or middle period dialogues.

From these beginnings, Plato gradually developed distinct philosophical ideas, such as his Theory of the Forms, which features in middle dialogues such as the *Phaedo*, *Symposium*, and *Republic*. In these long, literary dialogues, the character Socrates is less of the historical Socrates and more of a mouthpiece for Plato. He is accordingly more didactic, putting forth positive doctrines and no longer content merely to question and refute.

In the *Metaphysics*, Aristotle could not be more clear that Socrates did not originate the Theory of the Forms:

> Two things may properly be ascribed to Socrates, inductive
> reasoning and definition by universals—both belonging to
> the very fundamentals of science. But Socrates did not assign
> to the universal or the definitions an independent existence. It
> was the others who made them separate, and called these
> separate entities the Forms of everything that exists.

Other middle dialogue doctrines that are unlikely to owe to Socrates include the Theory of Recollection, the Theory of Reincarnation, and the Theory of the Tripartite Soul.

Compared to the early and middle dialogues, the late dialogues are more abstract and technical, and more akin to expositions than to lively debates. The character Socrates remains, but in name only, as a convention rather than a *dramatis persona*. In the *Timaeus* and its unfinished sequel the *Critias*, he only appears briefly at the beginning before giving way to the dialogue's namesake. Similarly, in the *Sophist* and *Statesman* he soon fades away, leaving a Parmenidean, the so-called Eleatic stranger, to do most of the talking. The last and longest of Plato's dialogues, the *Laws*, which remained unpublished at the time of his death, is the only one from which Socrates is entirely absent.

The French have a saying that to overcook meat is to kill the animal twice: by turning him into a puppet, Plato killed Socrates a second time.

Some of Plato's dialogues, most obviously those around his trial and execution, feature events in the life of Socrates. In the *Charmides*, Socrates is just back from the army and greeted by a barrage of questions. In the *Symposium*, his long-time protégé

Alcibiades publicly declares his love for him. In the *Parmenides*, he appears, uniquely, as a young man who spars with the great Parmenides in the presence of Zeno, Hippias, Prodicus, and others. Did this meeting and conversation ever take place? Did the symposium ever take place?

Plato would have been around ten years old in 416, the dramatic date of the symposium, so could not possibly have been in the room, or *andron*. He is a not a historian but a philosopher, and more interested in ideas than in events. When it comes to Socrates, his main concerns are to preserve his teaching and method and to rehabilitate his reputation, even at the cost of historical accuracy or completeness. If Plato had intended to write a biography of Socrates, he could easily have done so, rather than writing dialogues and blurring the lines by turning him into his mouthpiece.

There are other reasons to be cautious. Unlike Plato, Xenophon could claim to be a historian, but notions of history were not then what they are now. Plato and Xenophon wrote on wax or papyrus, in upper-case letters without punctuation marks or accents or breathings or even spaces (Figure 5). To preserve and disperse their contents, these originals would have been copied and recopied several times over the centuries, by far removed people with agendas and sensibilities, and a mother tongue, of their own. Over time, the 'missing' bits, the punctuation marks, accents, and spaces, would have been added in, sometimes in the wrong places. The few manuscripts that have come down to us are, in effect, inaccurate copies of inaccurate copies, with plenty of scope for further muddying the waters. Did Socrates' *daimonion* [divine inner voice] positively tell him what to do, as Xenophon claims, or merely prevent him from making grave mistakes, as Plato claims? Nuances such as these may owe as much to the copying as to the original claims of the authors.

*Figure 5. Papyrus Oxyrhynchus 24. Third century
fragment of Plato's Republic.*

But to put things into perspective, we are lucky to have
anything at all, let alone so much. Given that the works of the
later Greek Stoics, including the more than seven hundred
books of Chrysippus, have all been lost, it is a miracle that we
seem to have the entirety of Plato's authentic dialogues and
even a few spurious ones. No doubt his Academy, which far
outlived him, would have helped in their preservation.

Even if Plato's early dialogues contain fictional elements, this
need not mean that they misrepresent Socrates. Indeed, the
young Plato probably stumbled into the unorthodox dialogue
form precisely because it could best capture the essence of
Socrates. Having understood the advantages of the dialogue
form, including, perhaps, its popularity, he made it his own and
stuck with it long after it had outlived its original purpose—
leading to the literary masterpieces that we know.

All extant mediaeval Greek manuscripts of Plato are based on a first century compilation by the Egyptian grammarian and literary commentator Thrasyllus of Mendes, a close confidant of the emperor Tiberius. The oldest surviving complete manuscript for twenty-four of the dialogues is the so-called Clarke Plato, written in 895 by John the Calligrapher for Arethas of Patræ, later Archbishop of Cappadocia. In 1801, the clergyman Edward Clarke purchased it from the monastery of St John the Theologian on Patmos and sold it on to Oxford's Bodleian Library, which has recently put it online.

Modern editions of Plato use a system of referencing called the Stephanus pagination, after a 1578 edition of Plato by Henri Estienne [Henricus Stephanus]. The text is divided into numbers which refer to the page numbers of the 1578 edition, with each number further divided into equal sections a, b, c, d, e. As the 1578 edition runs into multiple volumes, page numbers can recur, and, to refer uniquely, must be used in conjunction with a title. An example is '*Symposium* 197a', which contains the phrase, 'He whom love touches not walks in darkness.'

8

SOCRATES AT FIRST

*S*ocrates ['Safe in strength'] was born in c. 470 BCE, ten years after the Persians had stormed Athens, and ten years before the start of the First Peloponnesian War. Although the Persians had been repulsed from Greece, the scars of war would have been everywhere to see.

Socrates belonged to the deme of Alopeke, just outside the city walls. Alopeke was renowned for its stoneworkers, and Socrates' father Sophroniscus is likely to have been a sculptor or stonemason. Socrates' early education and military service as a hoplite (who would have needed to purchase and maintain a full panoply) suggest that his family was relatively well off. If Sophroniscus was indeed a stonemason, perhaps he owned a masonry that employed other stoneworkers.

In Plato's *Laches*, Lysimachus claims to have been friends with the late Sophroniscus, whom he describes as 'a most excellent man'. Lysimachus was the son of the statesman Aristides the Just, one of the *strategoi* at Marathon, whom Herodotus calls 'the best and most honourable man in Athens'—seeming to confirm that Sophroniscus was no ordinary stonemason.

Perhaps he, too, had been a hoplite, and had impressed himself upon Lysimachus while fighting off the Persians.

In Plato's *Alcibiades*, Socrates reminds the impeccably blue-blooded Alcibiades that he used to watch him as a child, playing dice: even back then Alcibiades seemed to know the nature of justice and injustice, crying out if one of the other boys appeared to be cheating. This suggests that Socrates and his father were familiars of Pericles, who was the guardian of the young Alcibiades. One might imagine Pericles working with Sophroniscus on his ambitious building projects, including the Periclean Acropolis.

In Plato's *Theaetetus*, Socrates names his mother as Phænarete, a brave and burly midwife. When Socrates asks the young Theaetetus to define knowledge, Theaetetus replies that he has long struggled with the problem of knowledge and suffers from his inability to solve it. Socrates tells him: 'These are the pangs of labour, my dear Theaetetus; you have something within you which you are bringing forth.' Socrates goes on to compare himself to a midwife who attends not to the labour of the body but to the labour of the soul, helping others 'discover within themselves a multitude of beautiful things, which they bring forth into the light'. Like the midwife, who is past bearing age, he too is barren—not of children, but of wisdom. All he can do is bring forth the wisdom of others, and the triumph of his art consists in 'thoroughly examining whether the thought which the mind of the young man brings forth is a false idol or a noble and true birth'.

Socrates warns that should Theaetetus give birth to a phantom or false idol, he will tear it away from him:

And if I abstract and expose your first-born, because I discover upon inspection that the conception which you have formed is a vain shadow, do not quarrel with me on that account, as the manner of women is when their first children are taken from them. For I have actually known some who were ready to bite me when I deprived them of a darling folly.

Sometimes, the young man takes all the credit for the birth, leaves him sooner than he should, and begins once again to set more value upon phantoms than upon the truth. When this happens, the young man loses whatever he gave birth to and miscarries whatever remains in him. Then one day he realizes that he is an ignorant fool and falls upon his knees, begging to be taken back.

Given this extended 'midwife of the mind' metaphor, and that 'Phænarete' means 'Revealing virtue', it could be that the midwife mother is no more than a literary invention. In favour of his mother having been a midwife is Socrates' lifelong interest in medicine and his conception of philosophy as a process of healing or rebirth.

Socrates may even have been acquainted with Hippocrates of Kos (c. 460-c. 370), an almost exact contemporary who, in his own field of medicine, was caught up in the same broad humanist movement. Plato certainly knew of 'Hippocrates of Kos, the Asclepiad', who he mentions twice: once in the *Protagoras* and again in the *Phaedrus*.

Later, a legend arose that Hippocrates came to Athens at the call of Pericles and brought the plague to an end by lighting a huge bonfire.

∾

Socrates' remarkable strength and resilience might be accounted for by an early apprenticeship into his father's trade, which may have involved quarrying and transporting, or at least manipulating, large blocks of stone. Pausanias (c. 110-c. 180 CE), the world's first travel writer, reports that, in his time, there stood at the entrance to the Acropolis a Hermes of the Gateway along with draped figures of the Graces, 'which tradition says were sculptured by Socrates, the son of Sophroniscus...' Although Diogenes Laertius also attributes these sculptures to Socrates, he may simply have been parroting Pausanias, who, in this case, probably confused Socrates with his less famous namesake, the sculptor Socrates of Thebes.

Whether or not Socrates trained as a stonemason, we know from Plato's *Crito* that his father provided him with a well-rounded education that included 'music' and 'gymnastic'. In Plato's *Menexenus*, Socrates claims to have learnt rhetoric from Aspasia, the mistress of Pericles, and music from Connus, who was a greater teacher even than Lamprus: 'No wonder' Socrates says of himself, 'that a man who has received such an education should be a finished speaker.' In both Plato and Xenophon, Socrates often and sometimes extensively quotes the likes of Homer, Hesiod, and Simonides. In the *Cratylus*, he offers a long list of subtle etymologies, and in the *Ion* his commentary on Homer outclasses that of the rhapsode Ion, whose job it is to lecture on Homer.

In the *Cratylus*, Socrates points out that Homer ascribes two names to Hector's son: Skamandrios and Astyanax. He quotes Homer in saying, of Hector, that 'he alone defended their city and long walls' and argues on this basis that it seems more appropriate to call Hector's son Astyanax, which means 'Lord of the city'. Moreover, Hector itself means 'Holder', which is similar in meaning to 'Lord of the city'. If it is right to call a lion's whelp a lion, or a horse's foal a horse, then it must also be right to call the son of a king a king. Thus, those born according to nature should be given the same name as their father, even though the names of father and son may, as in the case of Hector and Astyanax, vary in their syllables.

Even if all this astounding knowledge is from Plato, it had at least to sound credible in the mouth of Socrates—who, after all, was educated enough to have impressed the likes of Alcibiades, Euripides, and, of course, Plato.

Although this is nowhere to be found in Plato and Xenophon, the reliable Theophrastus indicates that Socrates was a pupil of Archelaus, who was himself a pupil of Anaxagoras and his successor in Athens after he fled the city. Another of Aristotle's foremost students, Aristoxenus of Tarentum, wrote the earliest formal biography of Socrates. Unfortunately, Aristoxenus' *Life of Socrates* has been lost, but in it he made the astonishing claim, preserved in the *Suda*, that Socrates was the beloved of Archelaus: 'Aristoxenus says that at first Socrates heard Archelaus teach; in fact he was his boy-lover [*paidia*], and was very devoted to sex, but free of wrong-doing, as Porphyry says in his *History of Philosophy*.'

The Neoplatonic philosopher Porphyry's third century *History of Philosophy* has also been lost, but the fragment in question seems to have been preserved by the theologian Theodoretus of Cyrus in his fifth century *Cure for the Maladies of the Greeks*: 'Of Socrates it was said that as a boy he did not live a very good or orderly life… At the age of 17 Archelaus the student of Anaxagoras approached him, calling himself his lover; and Socrates did not reject Archelaus' advances or his company, but spent many years with him, and in this way Archelaus inspired his turn to philosophy.'

Diogenes Laertius relates, on the authority of the tragic poet Ion of Chios (d. c. 420 BCE), who was a contemporary of Socrates, that the young Socrates 'visited Samos in the company of Archelaus'. If Socrates and Archelaus did go to Samos, it might have been on campaign, to fight in the Samian War of 440-439 wrought by Athens on behalf of Miletus. Or it might have been an earlier peacetime voyage to meet Melissus of Samos, who followed so closely after Parmenides and Zeno as to be counted the third member of the Eleatic School. That the pair went to Samos to fight seems the less probable of the two possibilities, but has the merit of not contradicting Plato's claim in the *Crito* that Socrates never left Athens other than on campaign, except once to attend the Isthmian Games.

If the story about Archelaus contains even a grain of truth, Socrates did not become acquainted with the teachings of Anaxagoras by avidly reading his books, as claimed in the *Phaedo*, but through his teacher and likely lover Archelaus. The story also suggests that, rather like Saint Augustine at the same age, Socrates was not always the contained or self-restrained sage of his later years.

In the *Phaedo*, Socrates says that, as a young man, he had a passion for the natural sciences, but soon realized that he had no aptitude for this kind of enquiry—which, in any case, only ended up making him more confused. Some time later, he became enthused by the teachings of Anaxagoras, according to which *Nous* [Mind] is the cause of all things. But upon reading his books, he felt let down by Anaxagoras, who, instead of developing his account of *Nous* and showing how intelligence orders things for the best, resorted to 'introducing winds, waters, and other eccentric notions'. In the end, his system amounted to little more than providing physical, scientifical explanations for things: 'It was as if a person had said that Socrates is sitting here [in prison] because he is made up of bones and muscles, instead of telling the true reason—that he is here because the Athenians have thought good to sentence him to death, and he has thought good to await his sentence.'

Socrates then issues a warning that even or especially modern scientists might heed:

> I thought that as I had failed in the contemplation of true existence, I ought to be careful that I did not lose the eye of my soul; as people may injure their bodily eye by observing and gazing on the sun during an eclipse, unless they take the precaution of only looking at the image reflected in the water...

It could be conjectured that it is out of dissatisfaction with the natural sciences that Socrates travelled to Samos to meet and learn from Melissus, who seemed to offer a deeper, more unified account of things. Probably, he would have been equally disappointed by the abstract and remote theorizing of Melissus and the Eleatics.

Both Plato and Xenophon tell us that, in later life, Socrates shunned metaphysical speculation, arguing that the truth of these matters could never be known to man, and that, in any case, knowing them would make no difference to our lives. In the *Memorabilia*, Xenophon tells us very clearly that 'in contrast to others [Socrates] set his face against all discussion of such high matters as the nature of the universe; how the 'kosmos', as the savants phrase it, came into being; or by what forces the celestial phenomena arise.'

Xenophon continues:

To trouble one's brain about such matters was, he argued, to play the fool. He would ask first: Did these investigators feel their knowledge of things human so complete that they betook themselves to these lofty speculations? Or did they maintain that they were playing their proper parts in thus neglecting the affairs of man to speculate on the concerns of God? He was astonished they did not perceive how far these problems lay beyond mortal ken; since even those who pride themselves most on their discussion of these points differ from each other, as madmen do... One sect has discovered that Being is one and indivisible. Another that it is infinite in number. If one proclaims that all things are in continual flux, another replies that nothing can possibly be moved at any time. The theory of the universe as a process of birth and death is met by the counter theory, that nothing ever could be born or ever will die.

Instead, Socrates concentrated on what seemed to be man's proper ken and concern: knowledge of the self and of the right way to live. In the *Phaedrus*, as they pass the place where Boreas is said to have carried off Orithyia, Phaedrus asks Socrates whether he believes the tale to be true. Socrates replies that, while he is still in ignorance of his own self, he sees no point in being curious about myths or anything else which is not his concern: 'I must first know myself, as the Delphian inscription says; to be curious about that which is not my concern, while I am still in ignorance of my own self, would be ridiculous.'

Instead of looking to nature and its settled beginnings, Socrates turned his gaze to man and his still open ends, for it was not in the remote past but in the present future that freedom and action lay. This is what he had been looking for in Anaxagoras: an optimistic account of the future, and, in it, a place for man and his intelligence.

9

SOCRATES ON A MISSION

*I*n the *Birth of Tragedy*, Nietzsche blames Socrates, the great denier of the Dionysian abyss, for the alleged poverty of the plays of Euripides, and, beyond that, for the death of tragedy. In essence, Nietzsche's argument is that, by adopting the rationalism of one who could cheerfully drink of the hemlock, Euripides killed the very essence of tragedy. If this is true, it is, in fact, one of the great appeals of Socrates, that he did kill tragedy—leaving the Stoics, who followed in his train, to bury it six feet under.

Even the greatest tragedies, says the Stoic philosopher Epictetus (c. 50-c. 135 CE), are nothing but the ordeals of people who have come to value externals [things that are external to the mind], tricked out in tragic verse:

> You take the *Iliad*: it's nothing but people's impressions and how they dealt with them. An impression [essentially a raw sense impression or idea of the mind] made Paris rob Menelaus of his wife, and an impression got Helen to run away with him. Now, if an impression had come to Menelaus

that perhaps he was better off losing such a wife—well, that would have meant the loss to us not just of the *Iliad* but of the *Odyssey* as well.

Beyond the story in Diogenes Laertius of Euripides giving or lending a copy of Heraclitus' book to Socrates, what evidence is there for a relationship between Socrates and the decade older Euripides? According to the Roman rhetorician Ælian (c. 175-c. 235 CE), Socrates seldom went to the theatre, except when Euripides competed with a new play, 'for he took great delight in the man, evidently because of his wisdom and his excellence in metre.' One of the close followers of Socrates, Æschines of Sphettus, who was present at his death, wrote a now lost Socratic dialogue, the *Miltiades*, which featured Socrates in conversation with, among others, Euripides. Even in the works of Plato, who was not fond of theatre, Socrates periodically quotes Euripides, for instance, in the *Gorgias* ('Who knows whether life be death, and death be life?') and in the *Republic* ('Tyrants are wise by living with the wise'). In the *Republic*, he even declares, 'tragedy is a wise thing and Euripides a great tragedian.' Surely, he would have shared cups with such a man, as we know he did with that other playwright, Aristophanes.

There is even a tradition that Euripides consulted Socrates, who had a hand in some of his plays. Diogenes Laertius preserves a couple of verses from 'Mnesimachus', in fact, the comic playwright Telecleides, who was a contemporary of Socrates and Euripides: 'The Phrygians, that's a new play by Euripides; Actually, Socrates puts on the firewood [*phrygana*].' Diogenes Laertius doubles up by quoting from what I presume is an anterior version of the *Clouds* by Aristophanes: 'Tis he composes for Euripides/ Those clever plays, much sound and little sense.'

These comedic barbs may contain a grain of truth. For instance, the *Hippolyta* of Euripides, which won first prize at the City Dionysia of 428, contains a passage that appears to respond to the Socratic precept that virtue is knowledge. After Phædra, daughter of Minos and wife of Theseus, confesses to being in love with her stepson Hippolytus, she reflects on her plight: 'I think it is not owing to the nature of their wits that [mortals] fare worse than they might, since many people have good sense. Rather, one must look at it this way: we know and understand what is noble but do not bring it to completion. Some fail from laziness, others because they give precedence to some other pleasure than being honourable.' Perhaps Nietzsche did have a point: this sort of philosophical excursus does rather detract from the raw core of tragedy. On the other hand, Phædra is no longer a mere plaything of the gods, but a self-reflective person who is beginning to take charge of her own fate or destiny, as Socrates would have us do. It is perhaps no coincidence that, in the *Symposium*, Socrates himself quotes from the *Hippolyta* in absolving himself from an earlier promise made 'of the lips and not of the mind'.

In the same year, 428, that the *Hippolyta* triumphed at the City Dionysia, Mytilene on Lesbos revolted against Athens. Under the spell of the radical demagogue Kleon, the assembly elected to have all the men of Mytilene executed and all the women and children sold into slavery. Mercifully, the next day, one Diodotus delivered a speech, preserved by Thucydides, which persuaded the assembly to revisit its decision. Like the *Hippolyta*, the speech of Diodotus appears to have been directly or indirectly influenced by Socrates, for instance, in the contentions that anger is inimical to sound judgement; that a politician ought to triumph by sound argument rather than intimidation; and that moderation, as well as being just and compassionate, is in our own self-interest.

These Socratic outpourings, if that is what they are, suggest that, by 428, Socrates was no longer a natural philosopher, or only a natural philosopher, but recognizable, and influential, as the moral thinker that we know today.

~

When and how did this shift occur?

Socrates had a characterful long-time friend by the name of Chærephon. In the *Clouds*, Aristophanes portrays him as the associate of Socrates at the Thinkery; in the *Birds*, he nicknames him 'the bat' in reference, perhaps, to his physical appearance or sleeping habits. In the *Memorabilia*, Xenophon includes him in the list of the 'true companions of Socrates'; in Book II, Socrates attempts to heal the relationship between him and his brother Chærecrates. In the *Charmides*, he is described as 'a kind of madman' and runs up to greet Socrates upon his return from the Potidæa campaign—indicating that they were already intimates by 429, the dramatic date of the *Charmides*. In the *Gorgias*, he accompanies Socrates to meet Gorgias, and makes them late by chatting too long in the agora.

By the dramatic date of the *Apology*, Chærephon is dead. Socrates tells the jurors that he was 'early a friend of mine, and also a friend of yours, for he shared in the exile of the people, and returned with you'. This suggests that Chærephon, unlike Socrates, had democratic leanings and left Athens during the tyranny of the Thirty—and thus that he died only recently. Socrates then says, 'Well, Chærephon, as you know, was very impetuous in all his doings, and he went to Delphi and boldly asked the oracle to tell him whether ... there was anyone wiser than I was, and the Pythian prophetess answered that there was no man wiser.'

Figure 6. Speculative illustration of ancient Delphi by architect Albert Tournaire (1894). Ecole des Beaux-Arts, Paris. The temple of Apollo is the large central structure.

Knowing that he knew nothing, Socrates was perplexed. To discover the meaning of the oracle, he questioned several supposedly wise men—first the politicians, then the poets, and then the artisans—and in each case concluded: 'I am likely to be wiser than he to this small extent, that I do not think I know what I do not know.'

Socrates was the wisest of all people not because he knew everything or anything, but because he knew what he did not know—or, more subtly, because he knew the limits of the little that he did know. In contrast to the pre-Socratics and especially to the sophists, Socrates seldom claimed to have any positive knowledge; whenever he did, it was always because he had learnt it from somebody else, like Diotima of Mantinea or Aspasia of Miletus, or because he had been 'divinely inspired'. In the *Phaedrus* (Chapter 16), he compares himself to an empty jar, filled through the ears by the words of others.

The world really came together, perhaps for the first time, in the fifth century BCE, with both Confucius and the Buddha echoing from afar the words of Socrates:

> The only true wisdom is in knowing you know nothing.
>
> — SOCRATES

> Real knowledge is to know the extent of one's own ignorance.
>
> — CONFUCIUS

> A fool who recognizes his own ignorance is thereby in fact a wise man.
>
> — BUDDHA

From then onwards, Socrates dedicated himself to the service of the gods by seeking out anyone who might be wise and, 'if he is not, showing him that he is not'. As a result, he acquired a reputation for wisdom and a following among young men of the richer classes, who began to imitate him. But he also earnt the enmity of those whom he had exposed, and of those who stood beside them.

According to Plato, Socrates devoted himself entirely to discussing philosophy, for which he never accepted payment. It is unclear how he supported himself and, later, his young family, but an inheritance from his father combined with meagre needs and rich friends may have tided him along. According to lore, he used to walk through the market and mutter to himself, 'Look at all these things I don't need!'

Plato paints the oracle's pronouncement as the turning point in Socrates' career. By validating his skeptical stance towards the natural philosophy of Anaxagoras and the abstract metaphysics of Melissus and the Eleatics, it gave him the confidence, and the impetus, to develop his own, distinct manner and method of doing philosophy.

But is the oracle story even true, or is it just another of Plato's myths? The oracle story conveniently serves to frame Socrates, who had been put to death as a heretic and corrupter of youths, as having been on a noble, divinely inspired mission, attached by the gods to Athens as upon a great but listless horse which 'needed to be stirred up by a kind of gadfly'. Plato certainly wants us to believe in its truth: after relating the story, Socrates tells the jurors that, although Chærephon is dead, his brother Chærecrates, who is in court, will testify to its truth. More promisingly, the oracle story is also related by Xenophon, although in his version the oracle replies that there is no one more just (rather than wiser) than Socrates. Is Xenophon simply parroting Plato, or is this independent corroboration for the historicity of the oracle story?

If Chærephon did indeed consult the oracle, it is my contention that he must have done so a few years before Socrates left for Potidæa in 432. Plato's *Alibiades*, in which Socrates punctures the pretensions of a young Alcibiades, is set in 432, just before the pair are dispatched to Potidæa. In 432, Socrates would have been in his late thirties, and Alcibiades not yet twenty. The subject of the *Alcibiades* is neither metaphysics nor natural philosophy, but moral philosophy, and the comportment of Socrates in the dialogue indicates that he has already mastered his method. At one point, he tells Alcibiades: 'My good friend, you are wedded to ignorance of the most disgraceful kind, and of this you are convicted, not by me, but out of your own mouth and own argument; wherefore also you rush into politics before you are educated. Neither is your case to be deemed singular. For I might say the same of almost all our statesmen with the exception, perhaps, of your guardian, Pericles.' This last sentence suggests that, by 432, Socrates had interrogated most, if not all, of the city's most prominent politicians.

Although the authenticity of the *Alcibiades* is disputed, that of the *Charmides* is not. The *Charmides* is set on the day following Socrates' return from Potidæa in 429. As soon as he is back in Athens, Socrates reverts to type, visiting his 'old haunts', enquiring about the youth, and picking up the part of the public, and moral, philosopher. Critias introduces him to the young Charmides, and the dialogue ends with Charmides protesting that he can hardly be expected to know whether he is sufficiently temperate if Socrates and Critias, who are his elders, cannot even define temperance.

Plato might also have intended the oracle story as an origin myth for the Socratic method, or method of elenchus. Although Socrates may have perfected the method of elenchus, it is unlikely that he independently originated a mode of conversation that seems so naturally and fundamentally human. Diogenes Laertius, for his part, claims that it was Protagoras who 'first introduced the method of discussion which is called Socratic'—although this seems just as doubtful. In the *Parmenides*, Parmenides, who was about a generation older than Protagoras, himself uses the method of elenchus on the Platonic Socrates to undermine Plato's own Theory of the Forms. But it remains that while the sophists tried to make a show of their knowledge, Socrates tried to make a show of his and everyone else's ignorance.

The method of elenchus, especially as employed by Socrates, consists in questioning one or more people about a concept such as justice or virtue with the covert aim of exposing a contradiction in their initial (and often cherished) assumptions and provoking a reappraisal of the concept. As the process is iterative, it leads to an increasingly precise or refined definition of the concept, and, in due course, to a shared recognition that it eludes our understanding—and hence that we know far less than we thought we did. With our dogmatism transmuted into a state of puzzlement and suspended judgement [*aporia*, 'lacking passage'], we are ready to become much more open and subtle thinkers—assuming, of course, that we have not first become angry and resentful.

To have our understanding of a moral concept undermined is also to have our values undermined, and, with that, our sense of self. To manage their anger and other feelings, and to keep them talking, Socrates often flattered his interlocutors while himself playing the fool. In the *Orator*, Cicero esteems that, 'for irony and dissimulation, [Socrates] far excelled all other men in the wit and genius which he displayed.' Simon Blackburn in the *Oxford Dictionary of Philosophy* defines Socratic irony with brio as 'Socrates' irritating tendency to praise his hearers while undermining them, or to disparage his own superior abilities while manifesting them.'

Here is an example, from the *Meno*, of Socratic irony, so pushed as to be almost parodic:

> Had I the command of you as well as of myself, Meno, I would not have enquired whether virtue is given by instruction or not, until we had first ascertained what it is. But as you think only of controlling me who am your slave, and never of controlling yourself, —such being your notion of freedom, I must yield to you, for you are irresistible.

The technique resembles the one used by the TV character Lieutenant Columbo to trap villains. One of the few miscreants who can see through Columbo's fumbling and forgetful façade is the husband-killer Leslie Williams:

> LW: You know, Columbo, you're almost likeable in a shabby sort of way. Maybe it's the way you come slouching in here with your shopworn bag of tricks.
>
> LC: Me? Tricks?
>
> LW: The humility, the seeming absent-mindedness, the uh, homey anecdotes about the family: the wife, you know?
>
> LC: Really?
>
> LW: Yeah, Lieutenant Columbo, fumbling and stumbling along. But it's always the jugular that he's after.

Despite its pitfalls, and its potential for underhandedness, the Socratic method remains popular in education, especially at its acme, and has also been severally adapted for psychotherapy. In the 1990s, during an institutional audit at the University of Oxford, a team of external assessors met the philosophers and asked about recent developments to their teaching methods. The question was met with a stunned silence, finally broken by Christopher Peacocke FBA, the then Waynflete Professor of Metaphysical Philosophy, who observed that Socrates had discovered the right way to teach philosophy more than two thousand years ago, and that nobody since had been able to significantly improve upon it.

10

SOCRATES AT WAR

*W*hile on his intellectual journey, Socrates would also have been training as a hoplite, a heavily armed foot soldier that fought in the close phalanx formation. Practising manoeuvres in heavy armour would have further developed his strength and agility. The *pyrrhike* war dance, so ancient as to have been performed by Achilles around the burning pyre of Patroclus, is described by Plato in the *Laws*, and involved imitating movements of attack and defence 'in a direct and manly style'.

In Plato's *Apology*, Socrates proudly tells the jury that, just as he did not desert his post at the battles of Potidæa, Amphipolis, and Delium for fear of dying, so he will not now abandon the life of the philosopher.

The earlier of the three battles that he mentions, the Battle of Potidæa, took place in 432, when he would have been around 38 years old, suggesting that he may also have taken part in other, earlier campaigns.

Unlike Pythagoras and Empedocles, who had a pacifist outlook, Socrates did not particularly question warfare, which he looked upon as his patriotic duty.

But he did refuse to carry out unjust orders, and, like Jesus four centuries later, rejected the ancestral law of retaliation, stating, in the *Crito*, that 'we ought not to retaliate or render evil for evil to anyone, whatever evil we may have suffered from him.'

In the *Laws*, Plato goes one further, arguing that war ought only to be waged for the sake of peace.

Socrates did not particularly question slavery either. Like the Stoics after him, he considered that true slavery is the slavery of the mind, and that this is part of the natural condition of man, while true freedom exists only in virtue and in death.

In the *Alcibiades*, he argues that he who is not wise cannot be happy, and that it is better for such a person to be commanded by a superior in wisdom: since what is better is also more becoming, slavery is more becoming for such a person.

That said, Socrates did, it seems, object to unnatural master-slave relationships. As a boy, the handsome and high-born Phaedo of Elis was captured, sold into slavery, and forced into prostitution, before being ransomed at the behest of Socrates.

After that, Phaedo grew close to Socrates, and was present when he drank of the hemlock. In his namesake dialogue, the *Phaedo*, he says that Socrates 'stroked my head and gathered the hair on my neck into his hand—he had a habit of playing with my hair on occasion—and said, 'Tomorrow [when I am dead], perhaps, Phaedo, you will cut off this beautiful hair.'

~

The siege of Potidæa, a city-state which had rebelled against Athens, lasted until 429, depleting the Athenian treasury at a time of plague and undermining the position of Pericles.

In the *Symposium*, Alcibiades says that Socrates singlehandedly saved his life at Potidæa, and that he took the hardships of the campaign 'much better than anyone in the whole army'. At the same time, no one enjoyed a festival more than he did; if compelled, he could drink everyone under the table, yet no one had ever seen him drunk. During a severe frost, he marched barefoot and, even then, outdid his shod comrades, who 'looked daggers at him because he seemed to despise them'.

One day, in the summer, he stood motionless from dawn to dusk, apparently lost in thought, so that some Ionian soldiers slept out in the open just to see whether he would remain there all night. Only at daybreak did he finally offer a prayer to the sun and depart. This salutation to the sun might have been painted in by Plato to portray Socrates as a religious orthodox, and distance him from Anaxagoras, who thought of the sun as no more than a blazing mass of metal.

Socrates' habit of standing motionless for long periods, as he did also in 423 during a staging of the *Clouds*, and in 416 on his way to the symposium, has led some to suggest that he suffered from catalepsy, a trance-like state accompanied by muscular rigidity and fixity of posture, and linked with neuropsychiatric conditions such as Parkinson's disease and epilepsy.

Although Socrates had saved his life, it is Alcibiades, on account of his birth and rank, who received the prize for valour. When Alcibiades remonstrated with the generals that the prize ought to go to Socrates, Socrates was more eager than anyone that Alcibiades should have it.

∾

In Plato's *Charmides*, which is set on the day after his return from Potidæa, Socrates visits one of his old haunts, the palæstra of Taureas, a wrestling school frequented by boys and men. He is saluted on all sides and, having tired of talking about Potidæa, enquires about life in Athens: about the present state of philosophy, and about the youth. He asks whether any of them are 'remarkable for wisdom or beauty, or both'—an odd concern, perhaps, in the midst of a deadly plague. In any case, this is how he is introduced to the young Charmides. When Charmides (an uncle of Plato) sits down, he catches a glimpse of the inwards of his garment and is 'overcome by a sort of wild-beast appetite': 'But I controlled myself, and when he asked me if I knew the cure of the headache, I answered, but with an effort, that I did know.' This is quite the start for a dialogue on temperance and self-control!

Socrates proceeds to tell Charmides about a charm for headaches that he learnt, presumably at Potidæa, from the mystical physician to the King of Thrace. However, this great sorcerer warned that it best to cure the soul before curing the body, since health and happiness ultimately depend on the state of the soul:

> He said all things, both good and bad, in the body and in the whole man, originated in the soul and spread from there... One ought, then, to treat the soul first and foremost, if the head and the rest of the body were to be well. He said the soul was treated with certain charms, my dear Charmides, and that these charms were beautiful words. As a result of such words self-control came into being in souls. When it came into being and was present in them, it was then easy to secure health both for the head and for the rest of the body.

This is an astonishingly integrated and insightful view of health and disease which recognizes that many physical ills originate in the mind, from accumulated stress, anxiety, anger, and more general lack of control and self-control. Instead of palliating the superficial and external manifestations of the diseased soul, as we still do, it is much better to treat the soul itself, and the root and branch treatment that Socrates advocates is 'beautiful words', that is, something akin to psychotherapy—more than two thousand years before Sigmund Freud.

The Battle of Delium, in Bœtia, took place in 424, about five years after Potidæa, and ended in a costly defeat for Athens. In the *Laches*, the *strategos* Laches says that Socrates was his companion in the retreat from Delium, and that if only others could have been like him, 'the great defeat would never have occurred.' In tribute to his valour at Delium, Laches invites Socrates to teach and contradict him as much as he likes, without regard for his superior age and rank.

During the retreat from Delium, Alcibiades chanced upon Socrates and Laches. In the *Symposium*, he says that, even in retreating, Socrates appeared so calm and confident that no one dared attack him or his companions, preferring instead to pursue those who had turned in headlong flight.

In the *Laches*, also known as *On Courage*, the *strategos* Nicias concludes that courage amounts to knowledge of the fearful and hopeful in war and every other sphere and situation. Socrates says that if Nicias means that courage is knowledge of the grounds of fear and hope, then courage is very rare among men, while animals could never be called 'courageous' but at most 'fearless'—as ordinary language use seems to confirm. Nicias concurs, adding that the same is also true of children:

'Or do you really suppose I call all children courageous, who fear nothing because they have no sense?'

Socrates next proposes to investigate the grounds of fear and hope. Fear, he says, arises from anticipated evil things, but not from evil things that have happened or that are happening; hope, in contrast, arises from anticipated good things or, at least, anticipated non-evil things or less evil things. But, in any field of study, there is not one science of the future, one science of the past, and one science of the present: knowledge of the past, present, and future are all the same type of knowledge. Therefore, courage is not merely knowledge of the fearful and the hopeful, but knowledge of all things, including those that are in the past and in the present. A person who had such knowledge could not be said to be lacking in courage, but neither could he be said to be lacking in any of the other virtues: justice, temperance, and piety.

Socrates points out that, in trying to define courage, he, Laches, and Nicias have succeeded in defining virtue herself. Virtue is knowledge, which is why people with some measure of one virtue usually have a similar measure of the other virtues and of virtue in general—a thesis known as the Unity of the Virtues. Laches and Nicias are suitably impressed, but Socrates insists that he does not as yet fully understand the nature of either courage or virtue. On this note of aporia, the dialogue ends.

In the *Laches*, then, Socrates defines courage as knowledge, or knowledge of the good. But knowledge of the good is not enough. What we also need is the Socratic strength to persevere with our conviction through pleasures, desires, and, above all, fears. Thus, in the *Republic*, the mature Plato redefines courage as 'the conservation of the conviction ... about fearful things'.

~

The Battle of Amphipolis took place in 422, two years after the
Battle of Delium, when Socrates would have been around 48
years old—very old for a shield-carrying hoplite [*hoplon*,
circular shield]. The *Clouds* had been staged the year before,
and it is possible that Socrates' notoriety, especially among
ordinary people, rested as much on his bravery in battle as on
his more intellectual pursuits. At Amphipolis, Athens was once
again routed, but the deaths of Kleon on the Athenian side and
Brasidas on the Spartan side prepared the ground for the Peace
of Nicias and, for Socrates, a return to the philosophy of the
street.

11

SOCRATES IN LOVE

*S*ocrates was remarkably full-blooded for an ascetic philosopher. In Xenophon's *Symposium*, he says, 'For myself I cannot name the time at which I have not been in love with someone.' In Plato's *Symposium*, Alcibiades claims that Socrates is crazy about beautiful boys, and follows them around 'in a perpetual daze'.

But Alcibiades also claims that it could not matter less to him whether a boy is beautiful: 'You can't imagine how little he cares whether a person is beautiful, or rich, or famous… He considers all these possessions beneath contempt, and that's exactly how he considers all of us as well.'

The contradiction does seem hard to square. When, during the Renaissance, the works of Plato began to recirculate in Europe, Socrates became a rare model of same-sex love, and 'Socratic love' [*amor socraticus*] a euphemism for same-sex love, pederasty, and anal intercourse. In French, the verb *socratiser* came to mean, 'to moralize' but also, secondarily, 'to have anal intercourse with'.

By all accounts, Socrates' greatest same-sex love was with the blue-blooded Alcibiades (c. 450-404 BCE), who was by some twenty years his junior. Alcibiades was the son of Cleinias, who claimed descent from the Telamonian Ajax, and Deinomache, the granddaughter of Kleisthenes the Lawgiver and the first cousin and former wife of Pericles. After the death of Cleinias at the Battle of Coroneia in 447, the four-year-old Alcibiades and his younger brother, also Cleinias, passed into the guardianship of Pericles. In the *Protagoras*, Socrates says that Pericles feared that Alcibiades would corrupt Cleinias and had them separated for a time. In the *Alcibiades*, Socrates reminds Alcibiades that he used to watch him as a child, playing dice—suggesting that he, like Anaxagoras, frequented the house of Pericles. He might even have been employed by Pericles to tutor or tame the unruly Alcibiades, who acquired the nickname, 'the Lion'. Once, when his wrestling adversary accused the boy of biting like a woman, Alcibiades retorted, 'Not like a woman, but like a lion!'

The *Protagoras*, which is set in around 434, opens on an unnamed friend gently mocking Socrates for chasing the teenage Alcibiades. The friend remarks that, despite sprouting a beard, Alcibiades remains quite charming—to which Socrates responds: 'What of his beard? Are you not of Homer's opinion, who says, 'Youth is most charming when the beard first appears?'' Even so, he has not been paying much attention to Alcibiades since 'a stranger from Abdera' (meaning the elderly Protagoras) has arrived in Athens. When his friend asks incredulously whether this stranger could really be fairer than Alcibiades, Socrates replies, 'And is not the wiser always the fairer, sweet friend?'

Plato's purpose in writing the *Alcibiades*, if he did write the *Alcibiades*, may have been to exonerate Socrates from the charge of having corrupted the young Alcibiades. Its broad themes are justice, virtue, self-knowledge, and wisdom, which all turn out to be one and the same thing. Socrates warns Alcibiades, who is about to enter public life, that only knowledge can qualify him to advise the Athenians. Being noble, rich, and handsome are simply not good enough. Since politics is about just action, Socrates asks Alcibiades to define justice. When he flounders, Socrates suggests that Alcibiades is perplexed about justice because he is ignorant about justice *and* does not know that he is ignorant about justice. When a person thinks he knows what he does not know, he will make mistakes, which, in politics, will be all the graver.

A humbled Alcibiades promises to take greater pains about himself to get the better of other politicians. Socrates points out that Alcibiades' true rivals are not other Athenian politicians but the Spartan and Persian kings, who, in the long-run, can only be overcome by virtue. So could Alcibiades tell him, what is virtue?

Alcibiades is at great pains to define virtue and variously suggests that it is 'the better order and preservation of the city', 'friendship and agreement', and 'when everyone does his own work'. At last, he despairingly admits defeat: 'But, indeed, Socrates, I do not know what I am saying; and I have long been, unconsciously to myself, in a most disgraceful state.'

Socrates continues: to make ourselves better, we must first know who or what we are. Neither the physician, nor the trainer, nor any craftsman knows his own soul, for which reason their arts are accounted vulgar and not such as a good man would practise. He who cherishes his body cherishes not himself but that which belongs to him, and he who cherishes money cherishes neither himself nor that which belongs to him but that which is at one further remove from him. He who loves the person of Alcibiades does not love Alcibiades but his belongings, whereas the true lover is the one who loves his soul. The lover of the body fades away with the flower of youth, but the lover of the soul remains for as long as the soul follows after virtue:

> ...your beauty, which is not you, is fading away, just as your true self is beginning to bloom. And I will never desert you, if you are not spoiled and deformed by the Athenian people; for the danger which I most fear is that you will become a lover of the people and will be spoiled by them.

There is another similar-themed *Alcibiades*, written by Æschines of Sphettus and preserved in scattered fragments, in which Socrates relates a conversation that he once had with Alcibiades. To emphasize Alcibiades' unpreparedness for public life, Socrates delivers an encomium [a formal expression of high praise] to the great Themistocles, whom Alcibiades arrogantly seeks to emulate and surpass—leading a weeping Alcibiades to place his head in his teacher's lap and beg to be educated. Interestingly, Socrates tells his companion that, if he was at all able to improve Alcibiades, this was not through any knowledge or art that he possessed, but only by the force of the love [*eros*] that the youth had aroused in him.

In the same year, 432, in which Plato's *Alcibiades* is set, Socrates and Alcibiades were dispatched to Potidæa, where the middle-aged plebeian and the young aristocrat became unlikely tent-mates. This, surely, could not have been without the knowledge and approval, or toleration, of Pericles. In his *Life of Alcibiades*, Plutarch relates that 'all were amazed to see [Alcibiades] eating, exercising, and tenting with Socrates, while he was harsh and stubborn with the rest of his lovers.' In Plato's *Symposium*, Alcibiades says that Socrates singlehandedly saved his life at Potidæa and, after that, insisted that he keep the prize for valour... Army life, it seems, offered unparalleled opportunities for romance.

Plato's *Symposium* is set in 416, some sixteen years after his *Alcibiades*, and just before the fateful Sicilian Expedition that led Alcibiades to defect to Sparta. The setting is a drinking party held by the playwright Agathon to celebrate his victory at the Lenaia. Most of the guests have a hangover from the previous night's revels, and all agree to curtail the drinking in favour of conversation. Since Phaedrus has been lamenting that Eros is not sufficiently praised, Eryximachus suggests that each person, from left to right starting with Phaedrus, make a speech in praise of Love.

After Phaedrus, Pausanias, Eryximachus, Aristophanes, and the host Agathon, it is the turn of Socrates to speak. Socrates slips into elenchus mode and gets Agathon to agree that if love is not of nothing, then it must be something, and if it is of something, then it must be of something that is desired, and therefore of something that is lacking.

Socrates then relates a conversation that he once had with a mysterious priestess, Diotima of Mantinea, who, he says, taught him the art of love. This Diotima ['Honoured by the gods'] told him that the something that Love lacks and desires consists of beautiful and good things, and especially of wisdom, which is both extremely good and extremely beautiful. If Love lacks and desires beautiful and good things, and if all the gods are good and beautiful, then Love cannot, as most people think, be a god. In truth, Love is the child of Poverty and Resource, always in need but always inventive. He is not a god but a great spirit [*daimon*] who intermediates between gods and men. As such, he is neither mortal nor immortal, neither wise nor ignorant, but a lover of wisdom [*philosophos*]. No one who is wise wants to become wise, just as no one who is ignorant wants to become wise: 'For herein lies the evil of ignorance, that he who is neither good nor wise is nevertheless satisfied with himself...' The aim of loving beautiful and good things is to possess them, because the possession of good and beautiful things is called happiness [*eudaimonia*], and happiness is an end-in-itself.

Wild animals enter into a state of love because they seek to reproduce and make themselves immortal. Men too seek to make themselves immortal, and are prepared to take great pains, even to die, to attain fame and honour. Some men are pregnant in body and turn to women to beget children who will preserve their memory, while others, a few, are pregnant in soul and turn to each other to beget wisdom and virtue. As their children are more beautiful and more immortal, men who are pregnant in soul have more to share with one another, and a stronger bond of friendship between them.

Everyone would rather have their children than human ones:

> Who when he thinks of Homer and Hesiod and other great poets, would not rather have their children than ordinary human ones? Who would not emulate them in the creation of children such as theirs, which have preserved their memory and given them everlasting glory?

Diotima then told Socrates the proper way to learn to love beauty. A youth should first be taught to love one beautiful body so that he comes to realize that this beautiful body shares beauty with every other beautiful body, and thus that it is foolish to love just one beautiful body. In loving all beautiful bodies, the youth begins to appreciate that the beauty of the soul is superior to the beauty of the body and begins to love those who are beautiful in soul regardless of whether they are also beautiful in body. Having transcended the physical, he gradually finds that beautiful practices and customs and the various kinds of knowledge also share in a common beauty. Finally, on the highest rung of the ladder of love, he is able to experience Beauty itself, rather than its various apparitions. By exchanging the various apparitions of virtue for Virtue herself, he gains immortality and the love of the gods. This is why love is so important, and why it deserves so much praise.

As the company applauds, a drunken Alcibiades stumbles in supported by a flute-girl. When he sees Socrates, he picks off some ribbons from Agathon's garland and, with them, crowns Socrates, 'who in conversation is the conqueror of all mankind.' When Alcibiades entreats everyone to drink and match him in his drunkenness, Eryximachus objects to 'drinking as if we were thirsty' and suggests that Alcibiades instead make a speech in praise of Socrates.

Alcibiades says that Socrates always makes him admit that he is wasting his time on his career while neglecting his several shortcomings. So he tears himself away from him as from the song of a siren and once again lets his love of popularity get the better of him.

Socrates may look like a satyr and pose as ignorant, but, like the busts of Silenus [the tutor of Dionysus], he hides bright and beautiful images of the gods within him.

Attracted by his wisdom, he tried several times to seduce him with his famed good looks, but each time without success. Eventually, he turned the tables round and began to pursue him, inviting him to dinner and on one occasion persuading him to stay the night.

He then lay beside him and put it to him that, of all his lovers, he was the only one worthy of him, and he would be a fool to refuse him any favours if only he could make him into a better man.

Socrates replied in his usual, ironical manner:

> Alcibiades, my friend, you have indeed an elevated aim if what you say is true, and if there really is in me any power by which you may become better; truly you must see in me some rare beauty of a kind infinitely higher than any which I see in you. Therefore, if you mean to share with me and to exchange beauty for beauty, you will have greatly the advantage of me; you will gain true beauty in return for appearance—like Diomedes, gold in exchange for brass.

After this, Alcibiades crept under the older man's threadbare cloak and held him all night in his arms—but in the morning arose 'as from the couch of a father or an elder brother'.

All this, says Alcibiades, took place before Potidæa. But how much of his drunken account is true, and how much invented by Plato to rehabilitate the reputation of Socrates?

Even after his second downfall and exile, Alcibiades, being an able, experienced, and enterprising *strategos*, remained the best hope for an Athenian revival. For this reason, says Plutarch, Lysander had him murdered in his place of exile. In the *History of Animals* (VI, 26), Aristotle mentions in passing his place of death: 'In the mountain called Elaphoïs, in Arginusa, in Asia, where Alcibiades died, all the deer have their ears divided, so that they can be known if they migrate to another place, and even the fœtus in utero has this distinction.'

~

Socrates also had several women in his life, the earliest, perhaps, being Aspasia of Miletus.

Aspasia, who might have been the great-aunt of Alcibiades, immigrated from Miletus to Athens, where she lived as a metic. After his amicable divorce from Deinomache, she became the concubine of Pericles, who, according to Plutarch, kissed her every morning upon leaving and every evening upon returning. She bore him a son by the same name; when his two sons by Deinomache died from the plague, he successfully petitioned to have Pericles the Younger legitimized and naturalized. Owing to Aspasia's influence, real or imagined, on the person and politics of Pericles, the comedians of the day branded her a prostitute, and in the *Acharnians* Aristophanes even blames her for starting the Peloponnesian War. Beyond this, her reputation has been tarnished, and her significance occulted, by centuries of misogyny.

In Plato's *Menexenus*, Socrates says that he learnt the art of rhetoric from Aspasia, 'an excellent mistress ... who has made so many good speakers [including] the best among the Hellenes —Pericles, the son of Xanthippus.' Socrates agrees to recite a funeral oration that Aspasia recently composed and taught to him. He tells Menexenus that he ought to remember the speech since, each time he forgot the words, Aspasia threatened to slap him! The speech that Socrates delivers resembles, and satirizes, the famous funeral oration delivered by Pericles and preserved for posterity by Thucydides. When Socrates is done reciting, Menexenus marvels that such a speech could have been written by a woman.

This is not the only occasion on which Socrates claims to have been schooled by a wise woman, and the scholar Armand d'Angour has argued that Aspasia of Miletus and Diotima of Mantinea are in fact one and the same person.

Socrates, and Plato, seem to have held enlightened views on women. In Plato's *Republic*, Socrates argues that, just as male and female dogs are expected to perform the same duties, so women in the ideal state ought to be given the same tasks as the men—and ought therefore to receive the same training and education, including in music, gymnastic, and even the art of war.

> Are dogs divided into hes and shes, or do they both share equally in hunting and in keeping watch and in the other duties of dogs? Or do we entrust to the males the entire and exclusive care of the flocks, while we leave the females at home, under the idea that the bearing and suckling of their puppies is labour enough for them?

Socrates acknowledges that these proposals are so radical and far removed from current mores and customs that they may, if carried out, 'appear ridiculous.'

Socrates might have met Aspasia through a shared concern for the education of Alcibiades, and their connection supports the idea that he did indeed frequent the house of Pericles. Or he might have met her, and, perhaps, been romantically involved with her, before her association with Pericles—in which case it might have been she who introduced him into his circle.

If Aspasia did indeed teach Socrates the art of love, Plato would have wanted to hide her identity, and what better disguise than that of a chaste priestess?

Besides Plato and Xenophon, at least another nine of Socrates' followers wrote Socratic dialogues. Among these dialogues, we know that there are, or were, at least two *Aspasias*, one by Æschines and another by Antisthenes.

Figure 7: The debate of Socrates and Aspasia, by Nicolas-André Monsiau (1800). Standing by Socrates is Alcibiades.

In the *Aspasia* of Æschines, Socrates advises the millionaire Callias to send his son Hipponicus to Aspasia for instruction. Socrates presses his recommendation upon the recalcitrant Callias by citing Aspasia's credentials in rhetoric and marriage guidance—credentials that are confirmed in Plato (rhetoric) and Xenophon (marriage guidance).

In a fragment of the *Aspasia* of Æschines preserved in Cicero, Aspasia demonstrates to a husband (who happens to be called Xenophon) and his wife that neither will be happy with the other so long as they are desirous of an ideal spouse. Therefore, if they are to be happy together, husband and wife alike must endeavour to be or become the best possible spouse.

'Tell me, O you wife of Xenophon, if your neighbour has better gold than you have, whether you prefer her gold or your own?' 'Hers' says she. 'Suppose she has dresses and other ornaments suited to women, of more value than those which you have, should you prefer your own or hers?' 'Hers, to be sure' answered she. 'Come, then' says Aspasia, 'suppose she has a better husband than you have, should you then prefer your own husband or hers?' On this the woman blushed.

But Aspasia began a discourse with Xenophon himself. 'I ask you, O Xenophon' says she, 'if your neighbour has a better horse than you have, whether you would prefer your own horse or his?' 'His' says he. 'Suppose he has a better farm than you have, which farm, I should like to know, would you prefer to possess?' 'Beyond all doubt' says he, 'that which is the best.' 'Suppose he has a better wife than you have, would you prefer his wife?' And on this Xenophon himself was silent.

Then spake Aspasia: 'Since each of you avoids answering me that question alone which was the only one which I wished to have answered, I will tell you what each of you are thinking of; for both you, O woman, wish to have the best husband, and you, O Xenophon, most exceedingly desire to have the most excellent wife. Wherefore, unless you both so contrive matters that there shall not be on the whole earth a more excellent man or a more admirable woman, then in truth you will at all times desire above all things that which you think to be the best thing in the world, namely, that you, O Xenophon, may be the husband of the best possible wife; and you, O woman, that you may be married to the most excellent husband possible.'

— ÆSCHINES, *ASPASIA*, AS QUOTED IN:
CICERO, *DE INVENTIONE*, I, 31.

What is so striking about this dialogue, preserved by Cicero, somewhat obtusely, to illustrate argument by induction, is that Aspasia uses the very same methods as Socrates, namely, elenchus and argument by analogy, to arrive at the very same conclusion as Diotima, namely, that love's highest purpose is to serve as a vehicle of virtue.

What if Aspasia had taught Socrates his method as well as his theory of love?

Late in life, Socrates married the much younger Xanthippe, with whom he had three sons: Lamprocles, Sophroniscus, and Menexenus. That their eldest son, Lamprocles, was named after Xanthippe's father suggests that he was the more eminent of the child's two grandfathers. In Plato's *Apology*, Socrates tells the jurors that he has three sons, 'one almost a man, and two others who are still young.'

In the *Phaedo*, when his friends come to visit Socrates in the state prison, Xanthippe is sitting beside him and holding one of their younger children in her arms. She is in such a state, 'crying out and beating herself', that Socrates asks Crito to have her sent home. Xanthippe is not otherwise mentioned in Plato.

In Xenophon's *Symposium*, it transpires that Xanthippe had quite the character. In the course of the evening, Antisthenes asks Socrates why he does not tutor his own wife, 'instead of letting her remain, of all the wives that are, indeed that ever will be... the most shrewish?' Socrates compares himself to an expert horseman with a fondness for spirited horses, and claims that it is precisely for her temperament that he married Xanthippe ['Yellow Horse']—for '...if I can tolerate her spirit, I can with ease attach myself to every human being else.'

Xanthippe's shrewishness captured the imagination of later writers, who took to inventing or repeating stories about her, for instance, that she trampled upon a cake sent by Alcibiades, or that she emptied the chamber pot over Socrates' head—prompting Socrates to remark, 'After thunder comes the rain.'

There is much confusion and contradiction in later sources as to whether Socrates married twice, and as to whether Myrto, the daughter of Lysimachus, was his first wife, second wife, concurrent wife, mistress, ward, or lodger. However, the primary sources Plato and Xenophon make no mention of Myrto or of a second wife.

Despite his professed ugliness, Socrates seems to have formed profound romantic attachments, including with the much younger Alcibiades, who would have topped any Golden Age list of most eligible bachelors. In Plato's *Symposium*, Alcibiades himself compares Socrates' appearance to that of a satyr.

Cicero relates that the physiognomer Zopyrus, who claimed to be able to read a man's character from his features, examined Socrates and attributed him a host of vices. But when he accused Socrates of being a womanizer, Alcibiades burst out laughing. Socrates rescued Zopyrus by saying that he did have all those vices at birth but had since been able to overcome them by the use of reason.

In the *Theaetetus* (Chapter 18), the geometer Theodorus describes the young Theaetetus to Socrates as 'very like you, for he has a snub nose, and projecting eyes, although these features are not so marked in him as in you.' In Xenophon's *Symposium*, Socrates himself says that he has protruding eyes, a snub nose, thick lips, and a paunch. He jokes that these features are to his advantage, his eyes, for instance, enabling him to 'squint sideways and command the flanks'.

Since Xenophon's *Symposium* is set in 422, Socrates is describing himself at the age of around 48. However, he is likely to have seemed more attractive, or less unattractive, in his younger days, as a fit, battle-ready hoplite.

Moreover, parallels with the satyr Silenus who hid his inner beauty may have led later writers, starting with Plato and Xenophon, to exaggerate his aberrant features.

If Socrates really did look like a satyr, why did Aristophanes, who caricatured him on the stage, not pick up on this?

The younger Socrates, while perhaps not handsome, may not have been all that ugly.

In the *Meno* (Chapter 14), Socrates observes that the wise are very poor at imparting their wisdom: Themistocles was able to teach his son Cleophantus skills such as standing upright on horseback and shooting javelins, but no one ever credited the poor wretch with anything like his father's wisdom—and the same could also be said of Lysimachus and his son Aristides, Pericles and his sons Paralus and Xanthippus, and Thucydides and his sons Melesias and Stephanus.

Perhaps it was too early in 402, the dramatic date of the *Meno*, for Socrates to have added his own sons to the roll of dolts and dunderheads, but Aristotle, who had the benefit of hindsight, tells us that they too grew up to be 'fools and dullards'.

This tendency for an exceptional person to have unexceptional children is nowadays termed, 'reversion to the mean.'

12

SOCRATES ON TRIAL

*W*hile Socrates seldom claimed any real knowledge, he did claim to have a *daimonion* or 'divine sign', an inner voice or intuition that prevented him from making grave mistakes such as going into politics or fleeing Athens after having been sentenced to death.

On the face of it, it is possible that he occasionally experienced auditory hallucinations. As I discuss in the *Meaning of Madness*, auditory hallucinations are common and represent one end of a continuum of normal human experience. In a 2000 survey of samples representative of the general population in the UK, Germany, and Italy, 38.7 per cent of respondents reported having experienced hallucinations of some kind. In many cases, psychotic phenomena are an expression of severe stress or profound emotion, often underlain by a complex, difficult, or deep-seated life problem. In some cases, they may even be a life-enhancing experience, as in, for example, hearing the comforting voices of ancestors or guardian spirits, as is common in certain traditional societies, or having visions that are a source of insight and inspiration.

However, taken together with Socrates' habit of standing
motionless for long periods, which some have associated with
catalepsy, the *daimonion* also suggests a diagnosis of epilepsy
with a focus in the temporal lobe. When, in Plato's *Symposium*,
Agathon sends out a slave to search for Socrates, the slave
reports that Socrates is transfixed on a neighbour's porch.
When Socrates finally arrives, Agathon beckons him to recline
next to him, so that he might touch him 'and have the benefit of
that wise thought which came into your mind in the portico...'
Catalepsy and psychosis can also be symptoms of catatonic
schizophrenia, although this seems too debilitating a condition
to ascribe to Socrates.

In the *Phaedrus* (Chapter 16), Socrates carries out a speech-
making exercise in which he calls love a kind of madness. As he
makes to leave, his *daimonion* manifests itself to tell him that he
has been guilty of impiety and must atone to *Eros*, who, being a
god, cannot be evil.

In reparation, Socrates delivers a second speech in praise of
love. He begins by criticizing his first speech for overlooking
that madness, as well as being an illness, can also be the source
of man's greatest blessings:

> Madness, provided it comes as the gift of heaven, is the
> channel by which we receive the greatest blessings... the men
> of old who gave things their names saw no disgrace or
> reproach in madness; otherwise they would not have
> connected it with the name of the noblest of arts, the art of
> discerning the future, and called it the manic art... So,
> according to the evidence provided by our ancestors, madness
> is a nobler thing than sober sense... madness comes from
> God, whereas sober sense is merely human.

Socrates explains that there are four forms of divine madness: prophecy, from Apollo Pythios; mysticism, from Dionysus; poetry, from the Muses; and love, the highest form, from Aphrodite and Eros.

Presumably, Socrates identified his own *daimonion* as being from Apollo, the god of the oracle to whom he had dedicated his life. But others interpreted it otherwise, and it contributed in no small part to the charge of impiety and 'inventing new gods' that led to his trial and execution.

In Plato's *Apology*, Socrates says that, had he disregarded his *daimonion* and gone into politics, he would have perished long ago and been of no use to anyone. But by heeding his *daimonion* and remaining a private citizen, he was able to help both himself and others. He proceeds to offer proof, 'not in words but in deeds', of the dangers of politics.

When (in 406) his turn came to chair the assembly meeting, he alone opposed the trial as a body of the eight *strategoi* who, owing to a sudden storm, had failed to pick up the survivors at Arginusæ. At the time, the orators had been ready to impeach and arrest him, although later everyone acknowledged the unlawfulness of such a collective prosecution. (Among the six *strategoi* who had returned to face trial, and who were executed, was Aspasia's son Pericles the Younger, and it is possible that Aspasia had interceded and pleaded with Socrates.)

This had taken place under the democracy. But two years later, when the Thirty Tyrants ordered him and four others to bring the innocent Leon of Salamis to be executed, he alone refused, and quietly went home—even though this could have cost him his life.

Socrates saw that, in Athens, 'the law' soon caught up with
those who rose to prominence in public affairs—as it did even
with Solon, Kleisthenes, Pericles, Themistocles, and Alcibiades
—and that it did not help to be upright and unbending:

> For I am certain, O men of Athens, that if I had engaged in
> politics, I should have perished long ago and done no good
> either to you or to myself. And don't be offended at my telling
> you the truth: for the truth is that no man who goes to war
> with you or any other multitude, honestly struggling against
> the commission of unrighteousness and wrong in the state,
> will save his life; he who will really fight for the right, if he
> would live even for a little while, must have a private station
> and not a public one.

It seems that Socrates abstained, in so far as he could, not only
from taking part in politics but also from talking about politics.
In both Plato and Xenophon, he never specifically comments
on politicians and political affairs, not even on Alcibiades, or
Pericles, or the Peloponnesian War. Or perhaps Plato and
Xenophon chose to omit any such comments from the record
and portray him as apolitical. Although he defied an order from
the Thirty Tyrants, he did choose to remain in Athens during
those terrible months, rather than follow his friend Chærephon
and the rest of the democratic opposition into exile—from
which we might infer that he did not lean, or strongly lean,
towards the democrats. From everything that we know about
him, he, like Plato, favoured government by true aristocracy,
that is, government by the best or most wise and virtuous, even
if he himself, on account of his *daimonion*, did or deigned not
get involved.

Plato's *Euthyphro* is set in 399. The tyranny has fallen, and a limited form of democracy has been restored to Athens. Socrates, now in his seventieth year, crosses the mantic seer Euthyphro in the Porch of the King Archon, the chief religious official who handled preliminary proceedings in cases of impiety and bloodguilt. When Euthyphro asks him what he is doing here, Socrates replies that he is being prosecuted by a young and little-known man called Meletus, with a beak, long straight hair, and an ill-grown beard.

Like Meletus, Euthyphro is something of a religious fanatic. He tells Socrates that he has just pressed murder charges against his own father for the inadvertent death of a labourer who had himself, in a fit of drunken passion, murdered a servant. Whereas Euthyphro believes that he is behaving piously in indicting his father, his relatives believe that he is behaving most impiously.

In the ensuing debate, Socrates raises what has come to be known as the Euthyphro dilemma: is the pious loved by the gods because it is pious, or is it pious because it is loved by the gods? If the pious is loved by the gods because it is pious, it cannot be their love that makes it so; but if it is pious because it is loved by the gods, we are none the wiser about what makes it pious/why they love it.

At the end of the dialogue, Socrates says that Euthyphro is more skilful than Dædalus, in that Dædalus could only make arguments move, whereas Euthyphro can make them go round in a circle. Socrates suggests that they begin their enquiry anew, but Euthyphro claims to be in a hurry and scarpers off.

Meletus, Anytus, and Lycon charged Socrates with refusing to recognize the Olympian gods and introducing different gods, and, relatedly, with corrupting the youth. Seeming to associate or confuse him with Anaxagoras and the sophists, they accused him of 'studying things in the sky and below the earth', 'making the worse into the stronger argument', and 'teaching these same things to others.'

Meletus stood as the principal accuser. But as he had never even met Socrates, it is likely that the older Anytus, the real driving force behind the prosecution, had persuaded him to take on the role.

Anytus makes a cameo appearance in the *Meno* (Chapter 14), when Socrates pulls him into the conversation and asks him why there do not seem to be any teachers of virtue. Anytus asserts that all those who give their money to the sophists are out of their mind, and would do better to seek instruction from any one Athenian gentleman, who would have learnt virtue from the previous generation of Athenian gentlemen. When Socrates points out that not even Pericles and Themistocles were able to teach virtue to their sons, Anytus gets angry at Socrates for defaming such eminent men and warns him, ominously, to be careful.

Anytus issued from a prosperous family of tanners. He had served as a *strategos* and, in 409, lost Pylos to the Spartans. He returned to Athens to face charges of treason but succeeded in bribing off some of the jurors—this debacle being a possible reason for his arrangement with Meletus. Later in life, Anytus played a leading role in ousting the Thirty Tyrants, who had confiscated his property and driven him into exile. What he had lost in gold and silver he made up in popularity, which he remonetized by standing for office. Anytus had supported the Amnesty of Eucleides that prohibited the prosecution of offenses committed during or prior to the tyranny; but because the charges levied against Socrates related to activities carried out after 403, they did not fall under the ambit of the amnesty.

Although Socrates had been charged with the crime of impiety [*asebeia*], the real reason for his indictment may have been his anti-democratic leanings and close association with aristocrats such as Charmides and especially Critias, the leader of the Thirty Tyrants. Both Critias and Charmides died in 403, fighting the democratic forces. Although Socrates had refused to be tainted by the tyranny, he had remained in the city throughout, and, for all his moralizing, had done little to actively oppose the regime or intercede with Critias, Charmides, or their compeers. To many democrats, Socrates no longer seemed like the harmless eccentric of old, but like a dangerous and corrupting influence, a breeder of tyrants and the enemy of the common man. In the febrile atmosphere that had taken hold over the city, any accusation, however false or fanciful, could be seized upon as a pretext to punish him and scapegoat him for the sufferings of the tyranny.

Anytus also had some personal reasons for disliking Socrates. His son Aristodemus had once been close to Socrates, who had persuaded the youth to abandon the 'servile occupation' of his father and forefathers in favour of philosophy. Unfortunately, Aristodemus later found himself at a loss and became neither a philosopher nor a tanner but a drunk and a good-for-nothing.

Socrates may have given Anytus any number of reasons for hating him, but none of those could rival the single reason that he had given himself. As a young man, Anytus had fallen madly in love or lust with Alcibiades. Estimating, as one does, that uninvited affection is the most heartfelt form of impudence, Alcibiades returned his advances with the coldest contempt.

One day, Anytus invited Alcibiades to a banquet at his house. Having accepted the invitation, Alcibiades arrived late and already far-gone in drunkenness. Before the singers had even begun, he made to leave, and ordered his slaves to take half of the gold and silver dishes back to his house. When the other guests chided him, Anytus instead excused him, saying that he loved him so much that he would suffer him to take all of the dishes. Since Alcibiades doted on Socrates, Anytus may have blamed Socrates for his lack of success with Alcibiades, and for the humiliation of that evening.

Whatever the case, it remains that, if Critias had borne the palm for cruelty under the tyranny, Alcibiades had exceeded all licentiousness and insolence under the democracy, and that many people, not least Anytus, had come to associate Socrates with the misdeeds of these, the most infamous of his students.

Little is known about the third man, Lycon, except that he was an orator. Like Anytus and Meletus, he may have seen Socrates as a threat to the restored democracy, which was both partial and precarious. And like Anytus, he may have had a more personal axe to grind. Socrates had introduced his son Autolycus to the much older Callias, who went on to seduce the youth. Indeed, the banquet that is the subject of Xenophon's *Symposium* is given by Callias for Autolycus, whose beauty, says Xenophon, 'drew on him the gaze of all...'

Although Lycon would probably not have been invited, Xenophon is careful to depict Autolycus as sat next to his father, while everyone else is reclining on couches—a custom which, like the symposium itself, and much else that is 'Greek' (gods, temples, alphabet, coins...), originated in Asia.

∼

Plato's *Apology*, which is four times as long as Xenophon's, consists of three speeches delivered by Socrates in the supreme court of Athens [*heliæa*]: the first in reply to the charges, the second concerning the appropriate penalty, and the third in response to the passing of the death penalty.

Each of the three accusers makes a speech for the prosecution, after which Socrates clambers onto the platform to respond to the allegations. He begins by telling the five hundred jurors that he could not recognize himself in the words of his accusers. His accusers cautioned the jurors against his eloquence, but unless by 'eloquence' they meant 'true-speaking', he could not be said to be eloquent. Unlike them, he has not prepared a studied speech, but intends only to improvise as per his custom.

Before replying to his accusers, Socrates proposes to reply to his 'older accusers', the silent enemies who, for many years, had been dripping poison into the ears of the jurors. These older accusers all hid behind cloaks of anonymity—all, except for Aristophanes, who had featured him in one of his comedies, floating in mid-air and talking nonsense about divine matters. But as many of the jurors can attest, he has never pronounced himself on divine matters, nor, like the sophists, pretended to understand virtue or taken money from his students.

What, then, has led to these accusations against him? Over the years, he acquired a certain reputation for wisdom, not the superhuman wisdom of the sophists but the sort of wisdom which is within our ken. When he learnt that the oracle of Delphi had pronounced him the wisest of all men, he did not know what to make of this. So he questioned a politician with a reputation for wisdom and cross-examined his words to reveal their inconsistencies and contradictions. But the result was that the politician hated him. Whereas both he and the politician knew nothing, he at least knew that he knew nothing, and in that much was wiser than the politician. After that, he went from one man to another, first the politicians, then the poets, and then the craftsmen, and found that those among them with the greatest reputation for wisdom were in fact the most foolish of all. By this exercise, he came to understand the oracle's meaning: that the wisdom of men is little or nothing, and those who know this are as wise as any man can be. Inspired by this revelation, he entered the service of the god of the oracle, seeking out anyone who might be wise and putting his wisdom to the test. Over the years, he made many friends, but he also made many enemies, people who got angry at him rather than at themselves and who, not knowing why they were angry, made up all sorts of charges against him.

Having said enough about his older accusers, Socrates addresses Meletus and reproaches him for being too eager to sue other men for matters in which he takes no interest. To prove his point, he asks Meletus to name the improver of the youth. After some hesitation, Meletus replies, 'the law'.

> S: Who in the first place knows the laws?
>
> M: The judges, Socrates, who are present in court.
>
> S: What do you mean to say, Meletus, that they are able to instruct and improve the youth?
>
> M: Certainly they are.
>
> S: What, all of them, or some only and not others?
>
> M: All of them.

Coming under pressure from Socrates but trying to remain consistent with himself, Meletus blurts out that members of the assembly also improve the youth, thereby implying that all enfranchised Athenians improve the youth, except for Socrates.

Having proven his point out of Meletus' own mouth, and, at the same time, made a demonstration of the method that landed him in court, Socrates puts it to Meletus that, when it comes to horses, it is not the case that everyone does them good except for one man who does them harm, but rather that no one does them good except for one man, namely, the horse trainer.

Socrates now sets out to show that, if he did corrupt the youth, he could not have done so intentionally:

> S: Do not the good do their neighbours good, and the bad do them evil?
>
> M: Certainly.
>
> S: And is there anyone who would rather be injured than benefited by those who live with him?
>
> M: Certainly not.
>
> S: And when you accuse me of corrupting and deteriorating the youth, do you allege that I corrupt them intentionally or unintentionally?
>
> M: Intentionally I say.

Hereupon, Socrates argues that he could not have corrupted the youth intentionally because he would have known that doing so would have amounted to injuring himself. Thus, if he did corrupt the youth, he must have done so unintentionally, and ought to be educated rather than punished.

This argument reflects his general outlook that people only do wrong because, in the moment, they think that it is the right thing to do. To put this differently, all people incline towards goodness, but are waylaid by their foolishness or narrowness.

Finally, Socrates asks Meletus what he meant when he accused him of teaching the youth to acknowledge gods other than those acknowledged by the state: did he mean that he believed in some gods but not in the right ones, or that he did not believe in any gods at all? The latter, says Meletus, 'since you believe the sun to be stone and the moon to be earth.' Socrates points out that these are in fact the beliefs of Anaxagoras. But as for himself, he would not have introduced different gods, as charged, if he had not believed in at least some gods.

Having done with Meletus, Socrates turns back to the jurors. Despite its dangers, he had chosen the life of a philosopher because it seemed like the right and best thing to do. Had he chosen safety over philosophy, he would have been pretending to a wisdom which he did not possess, for no one knows whether death is the greatest evil or, in fact, the greatest good. It is not death that Achilles feared, but living in dishonour by failing to avenge the death of Patroclus. 'Let me die at once' he said, '...rather than remain here, a laughingstock by the curved ships, a burden upon the earth.'

Just as he, Socrates, had not abandoned his post in battle, so he would not now abandon the life of philosophy:

> Men of Athens, I am grateful and I am your friend, but I will obey the god rather than you, and as long as I draw breath and am able, I shall not cease to practise philosophy, to exhort you and in my usual way to point out to any one of you whom I happen to meet: Good Sir, you are an Athenian, a citizen of the greatest city with the greatest reputation for both wealth and power; are you not ashamed of your eagerness to possess as much wealth, reputation, and honours as possible, whilst you do not care for nor give thought to wisdom or truth, or the best possible state of your soul?

By exhorting men to excellence, he had brought the greatest good to the state. Wealth does not bring about excellence, but excellence makes wealth and everything else that is good for men. Such is the core of his teaching: if it is held to corrupt the youth, then so be it. By condemning him to death, the jurors would be doing themselves a far greater harm than they would be doing him, since putting an innocent man to death is much worse than dying oneself. Besides, they would struggle to replace him. In homage to the god, he had attached himself to Athens like a gadfly to a noble but listless horse, and his poverty was proof enough that he had never taken payment for his service. He had at one time considered going into politics but his *daimonion* had dissuaded him from doing so on the grounds that a dead man is of no use to anyone. Nevertheless, he had behaved in the private sphere with the same integrity as in the public sphere, and it is a matter of record that he opposed the collective prosecution of the *strategoi* at Arginusæ and disobeyed the Thirty when they sought to implicate him in the execution of Leon of Salamis. Although he had freely conversed with rich and poor alike, he had never taught anyone anything, and could be neither praised nor blamed for their subsequent actions. If he did indeed corrupt the youth, why had their fathers and brothers not come forth to accuse him? And why had Meletus not called upon them as witnesses?

This is all the defence that he has to offer. Some of the jurors may take offence that he did not shed tears, resort to prayers and supplications, or bring forth his young children, but such bathetic scenes would hardly have been worthy of him, or them, or philosophy, or Athens.

～

Once all the disks in the bronze urn have been counted, the herald announces the outcome of the ballot. Socrates has been found guilty, if only by a margin of sixty votes.

Socrates arises to respond to the verdict.

He had been expecting this outcome; if he is at all surprised, it is by the near evenness of the vote.

Having been found guilty, he ought to be given that which he deserves, which is not death, but free meals in the *prytaneion* [town hall]. Why should Olympians eat at the state's expense but not he? Olympians provide only the illusion of happiness: he provides the reality.

He had never wronged anyone and was not going to start now by asking the jury for a penalty that he did not deserve. He could ill afford a fine, and imprisonment would turn him into a slave. Exile could be tolerable, but only if he were willing to hold his tongue:

> For if I tell you this would be a disobedience to a divine command, and therefore that I cannot hold my tongue, you will not believe that I am serious; and if I say again that the greatest good of man is daily to converse about virtue, and all that concerning which you hear me examining myself and others, and that the life which is unexamined is not worth living—that you are still less likely to believe.

In the end, Socrates proposes a fine of one mina, but, upon the insistence of his friends, raises the amount to thirty minæ (half a talent, or around 13kg of pure silver).

∼

In the second ballot, eighty more jurors voted for the death sentence than had voted for the guilty verdict, a split, this time, of 360 to 141.

Socrates delivers his final address.

By condemning an old man to death, the jurors had not gained much time, but enabled the city's detractors to say that the Athenians had killed a wise man. If they had condemned him, it was not for a want of words, but for an unwillingness to say whatever it takes. But he would rather die than compromise the thought-through principles of a lifetime. Yes, they had condemned him in his twilight years, but Truth had condemned them in the prime of life, and their punishment would be much worse than his. After his death, new critics would rise up and ask them to account for their lives. Rather than killing them in turn, they would do better to seek bravely after wisdom and virtue.

Socrates now speaks to those jurors who voted to acquit him. His *daimonion* had stayed silent throughout the proceedings, intimating that death is in fact a good thing. If death is a state of unconsciousness, there is nothing to fear. But if it is a journey to a land inhabited by great men such as Homer and Hesiod, he would take infinite delight in conversing with them.

> For in that world they do not put a man to death for this; certainly not... Wherefore, O judges, be of good cheer about death, and know this of a truth—that no evil can happen to a good man, either in life or after death.

Having concluded that it would be better to die than to live, he was not in the least angry with those who had accused and condemned him. For although they had not meant to do him any good, neither had they done him any harm.

He asks only that his friends take good care of his three sons:

> When my sons are grown up, I would ask you, O my friends,
> to punish them; and I would have you trouble them, as I have
> troubled you, if they seem to care about riches, or anything,
> more than about virtue; or if they pretend to be something
> when they are really nothing... The hour of departure has
> arrived, and we go our ways—I to die, and you to live. Which
> is better God only knows.

On the force of the arguments alone, Socrates had produced a
brilliant defence. But instead of behaving with the customary
humility and contrition, he turned the tables round and made
himself judge and jury, cross-examining all of Athens before his
court of philosophy. For the first and last time, he let drop his
ironic mask, and his unapologetic apology turned many a juror
against him. After being found guilty, his arrogance in
suggesting a punishment of free meals and insolence in
proposing a paltry one-mina fine only hardened hearts.

But this, from such a fine psychologist, may well have been the
intention. Socrates knew that his best years lay behind him,
and that a timely death could be a blessing as much as a curse.
Moreover, by martyrizing him, the Athenians promised to
preserve his memory, and, more importantly, the memory of his
method and philosophy. Had the Athenians acquitted Socrates,
you would not have read this book, and I would not have
written it.

For Socrates, the hemlock was never a deadly poison, but the
very elixir of life.

Socrates did not die until one month after his trial because the state galley was out on its annual pilgrimage to Delos and executions could not be carried out until its return. While biding his time in the state prison, he composed a pæan to Apollo, wrote poetry, and set some of Æsop's fables to verse.

He also received his friends, several of whom entreated him to flee to Thessaly, where Crito had some friends. They argued that to remain and die would be to commit an injustice that would please his enemies and leave his children fatherless.

In the *Crito*, Socrates puts it to Crito that to escape would be to wrong the city by breaking his compact to abide by her laws. It was by the city that his parents had married and begat him, and by the city that be had been educated. By electing to remain in the city even though he had had ample opportunity to leave, he had tacitly agreed to abide by her laws. The city is nothing if not her laws, and to break them would be tantamount to destroying her. Moreover, if he fled, those who condemned him would feel vindicated in having done so, for a man who breaks the city's laws is just as likely to corrupt its youth.

Besides, no lawful territory would welcome a man who had broken the laws of the city in which he had abided for seventy years. Where would he go? And what sort of life would he lead if he were no longer able to speak freely? If he wished to save himself for the sake of his boys, he would have to take them with him and deprive them of their Athenian citizenship—or leave them behind to be cared for by friends who would care for them just the same whether he were alive or dead.

But as things stood, he would die as an innocent, a sufferer rather than a doer of evil, a martyr rather than a petty criminal, and fare handsomely before the judges of the underworld.

～

The *Phaedo* covers Socrates' last hours and execution. However, the Socrates of the *Phaedo* sounds a lot more like Plato than the historical Socrates. Plato never mentions himself in his works, except in the *Apology* to indicate that he was present, and in the *Phaedo* to indicate that he was not. Presumably, he wrote himself as present at the trial of Socrates to vouch for the veracity or verisimilitude of his account. Conversely, he may have written himself as ill and absent from the execution of Socrates to suggest that he employed a large measure of artistic license in recreating his mentor's final conversation. Since this final conversation, which is on the immortality of the soul (the *Phaedo* used to be known as *On the Soul*), is not faithful to the historical Socrates, I shall not relate it here, but later, in Chapter 15.

When the conversation in the *Phaedo* comes to a close, a prolonged silence, punctuated only by sighs and sobs, descends upon the gathering. The young Phaedo comes to press against Socrates, who takes to stroking his hair. Socrates says that it is time for him to take his bath and save the women the trouble of washing his corpse. After his bath, he spends some time with his family before returning among his companions. Even the gaoler, who brings in the hemlock cup, struggles to hold back tears as he extols the noble nature of his prisoner. Crito suggests that there is still time to eat and drink, but Socrates feels that it would be unbecoming to cling on in this way to the dregs of life. He offers a prayer to the gods and calmly drinks of the hemlock. Several of his friends start to sob, but he chides and silences them. He stands up and walks about to assist the poison. Having done so, he lies on his back, covers his head with his cloak, and patiently awaits death. As his body stiffens, he uncovers his head and utters his last words: 'Crito, we owe a cock to Asclepius; pay it and don't forget'—the great healer of the soul, in his final act, honouring the god of healing.

PART III

PLATO

If the best way of reaching Socrates is through his life, the best way of reaching Plato is through his copious writing. Many of Plato's early 'Socratic' dialogues have already been considered in the previous section, freeing us in this section to concentrate on his later, mature works. Some of these are among the greatest works of philosophy ever written, as well as being literary masterpieces. The five that I have chosen to present and discuss—the *Meno*, *Phaedo*, *Phaedrus*, *Republic*, and *Theaetetus*—span the full breadth of his middle period. Taken together, they disclose all his major themes and reveal the progression of his style and thought.

13

LIFE AND WORKS

*A*fter the death of Socrates in 399 BCE, his nearest students ran off each with a different aspect of his teaching. While Plato and the Platonic Academy which he founded embraced his theoretical side, Antisthenes inherited his ethical or practical side, advocating an ascetic life of virtue and laying the foundations for the Cynic school. A third follower, Aristippus, had a very different take on their master's ethics, and established the Cyrenaic school which taught that the only true good is pleasure, especially momentary pleasures and above all physical ones—a position far more radical than that later espoused by Epicurus. Between these two extremes of the Cynics and the Cyrenaics came to lie the Skeptics, the Stoics, and the Epicureans, as well as a number of lesser schools such as the Megarian school, founded by Euclid of Megara, and the Elian school, founded by Phaedo of Elis. Phaedo, Euclid, and Antisthenes had been present at the death of Socrates; Plato was ill (or so he said), and Aristippus, the seeker after pleasure, unaccounted for.

What about these later, 'in-the-middle' schools, the Skeptics, the Stoics, and the Epicureans? The Skeptics had latched onto Socrates' incessant questioning, as well as the suspension of judgement with which he tended to conclude his debates. Stoicism can be thought of as an offshoot of Cynicism, and the Stoics upheld Socrates as a model of the wise man or sage. Of the major schools, only the Epicureans did not claim Socrates as a parent or grandparent—although, in the *Protagoras*, Socrates does say that 'things are good just in case they are pleasant, and bad just in case they are painful'. But even if the debt to Socrates went unacknowledged, all the major Hellenistic schools, Epicureans included, imitated Socrates in the conviction that philosophy is about learning how to live, and that this involves the cultivation of wisdom and virtue. For the interested reader, I discuss the post-Socratic Hellenistic schools at much greater length in *Stoic Stories*, but here, of course, I wish to focus on Plato.

In the *Lysis*, two boys, Lysis and Menexenus, argue about who is the elder. This seems odd, until one realizes that people back then did not have birthdays, but only birth years or birth cohorts.

Plato is likely to have been born in 428/427 BCE. His father Ariston claimed descent from Codrus, the last king of Athens (d. c. 1068 BCE), who himself claimed descent from Poseidon. His mother Perictione descended, more humbly but in a shorter line, from Solon. She had Charmides for a brother and Critias for an uncle. Out of a desire to rehabilitate his mother's family line, or hark back to happier times, he often featured his relatives in his dialogues: not only Critias and Charmides, but also his brothers Glaucon and Adeimantus.

Plato probably bore the name of his father's father, Aristocles, but his wrestling coach Ariston of Argos took to calling him 'Plato' on account of his broad shoulders. Alternatively, the nickname derived from the breadth of his eloquence, or his large forehead. Had it not stuck, he might have been known to us as Aristocles of Collytus. According to some later writers, he was not the son of Ariston but of Apollo himself—earning him a couple more epithets, 'Son of Apollo' and 'Divine teacher'. In another legend, as the infant Plato slept on Mount Hymettus, the bees settled upon his lips to augur the honeyed words that would one day flow from his mouth.

When Plato was still a boy, his father died, and his mother married Pyrilampes, her widowed maternal uncle. Pyrilampes already had a son, Demus, who was famed for his good looks, and went on to have another son, Antiphon, with Perictione— making Antiphon Plato's half-brother. Shortly before marrying Perictione, Pyrilampes suffered a shoulder injury at Delium, and it might have been from him that Plato first heard about Socrates and his bravery on the battlefield. Pyrilampes enjoyed a close friendship with Pericles. After the birth of Antiphon, Pericles dispatched him to Persia to represent Athens. When he returned from the court of Darius with a pride of peacocks, scurrilous tongues accused him of breeding the birds to procure freeborn women for Pericles. Possibly, it is he who first introduced the peacock to Europe.

Plato no doubt took an engaged interest in the education of Antiphon ['Responsive voice', the root of 'anthem']. In the *Parmenides*, one Cephalus encounters Glaucon and Adeimantus in the agora and asks to meet Antiphon, who happens to be acquainted with the famous conversation that passed between Parmenides, Zeno, and the young Socrates. But Antiphon has, by now, given up philosophy for horses: when the party arrives at Antiphon's house, they find him with a smith fitting a bridle.

Plato's eldest brother Glaucon ['Owl-eyed', 'Bright-eyed', or 'Grey-eyed'] enjoyed music and mathematics and naturally fell under the spell of the Pythagoreans. Both he and Adeimantus distinguished themselves in the Battle of Megara of 424, and in the *Republic* (368a) Socrates commends him for his 'godlike virtues in battle'. In his mid-thirties, he suffered a minor injury, and thereafter devoted himself to finery, frivolling away his fame and fortune on a large estate that he filled with hunting dogs and pedigreed cocks.

In the *Republic*, Adeimantus ['Without fear'] claims that most philosophers are 'strange monsters, not to say utter rogues' who are made utterly useless by their study (487d). When, in discussing the ideal state, Socrates proposes that the guardians be without property, he objects that they would be unhappy without luxuries.

Neither Plato nor his three brothers had any children, leaving the joys and burdens of family life to their sister Potone, who had no choice in the matter. Pyrilampes and Critias married her off at an early age to Eurymedon of Myrrhinus, whose greatest achievement was to father Speusippus, the nephew who would follow Plato at the head of the Academy.

The young Plato excelled in his studies, including in gymnastics; according to Aristotle's student Dicæarchus, he was a well-known wrestler and competed at the Isthmian Games. It is said that Plato started out as a poet and tragedian, but burnt his works after meeting Socrates. Probably, it is Critias who introduced him to Socrates, who must have seemed like a breath of fresh air after Cratylus.

Socrates too would have been delighted to meet Plato: it is said that, the night before their first meeting, he dreamt of a cygnet on his knees, which at once sprouted feathers and flew up uttering a loud sweet note.

Plato frequented Socrates for, or over, several years. Had Athens been at peace, he might have spent all his days basking in his sunlight. He must have despaired of army life, which he likely looked upon as a rite of passage for a political career.

With the coming of the Thirty, he may have hoped for a new age of rational government by philosophical men such as Critias and Charmides who embodied the sound values of his aristocratic class. But when, in 404, Critias invited him to join their administration, he held back, repelled by its oppression and, more particularly, its attempt to implicate Socrates in the execution of the innocent Leon of Salamis.

Mercifully, the regime only held out for a matter of months before being routed by the democratic forces in exile, with both Critias and Charmides killed in the heat of battle. If the initial restraint and moderation of the restored democracy did fill Plato with renewed hope, the trial and execution of Socrates would have put paid to any remaining illusions that he might have entertained about Athenian politics.

After the fall of the Thirty Tyrants, Plato's name turned from a major asset into a major liability, and his background, politics, and association with Socrates all sat uncomfortably with the mood of the times. In consequence, he retired with other Socratics to Megara in West Attica, where he resided with Euclid, a Socratic and Eleatic who had been present at the death of Socrates.

Euclid, under the influence of the Eleatics, argued in the manner of Zeno, lending force to his ideas by disproving or discrediting those of his opponents. Socrates thought poorly of such eristics and, in his living, had encouraged him to prefer the more cordial and constructive dialectic method. Despite Euclid's antagonistic debating style, Plato, Euclid, and the other Socratics must have had many fertile conversations in Megara. By marrying the ideas of Parmenides and Socrates, Euclid would go on to establish the Megarian school of philosophy.

According to Diogenes Laertius, after a time in Megara, Plato crossed to Cyrene, the Libyan birthplace of both Aristippus and the geometer Theodorus. As he had a higher opinion of Theodorus than of Aristippus, he probably stayed with the former, who features as a friend and contemporary of Socrates in three of his later dialogues, the *Theaetetus*, *Sophist*, and *Statesman* (Chapter 18).

From Cyrene, Plato may have proceeded to Egypt, before, perhaps, being recalled to Greece to serve in a fresh anti-Spartan alliance.

In the five years that Plato had been travelling, an overbearing Sparta had been encroaching upon Persian-held territories, including in Ionia. As a result, the satrap Pharnabazus took to fomenting unrest among Sparta's nominal allies, turning Athens, Thebes, Corinth, Argos, and other smaller *poleis* against Sparta. At sea, at Knidos, Pharnabazus with the veteran Athenian commander Conon defeated the Spartan fleet. A grateful Pharnabazus left Conon with a section of the allied fleet and sufficient funds to rebuild the long walls, which had been torn asunder in the aftermath of Ægospotami.

On land, the returning Spartan army under Agesilaus II crossed through Thessaly and marched down into Bœtia, where, at Coroneia, it clashed with the allied forces. By lying to them about the outcome at Knidos, Agesilaus was able to boost his men to victory.

Even so, with its walls rebuilt and a sizeable fleet, a resurgent Athens took to recapturing some of the territories that had once formed part of its empire.

At Coroneia, Xenophon had fought on the Spartan side, for which Athens banished him.

If Plato did get embroiled in the so-called Corinthian War, he may have returned to Athens after the Battle of Coroneia in 394. Now in his mid-thirties, he no doubt received several marriage proposals, which he turned down in favour of philosophy. He may have started on his dialogues as early as Megara or Cyrene, but now he doubled down. By the time he left for Italy in around 388, he had already written several works, including the *Apology*, *Laches*, and *Protagoras*.

In Taras [modern-day Taranto] on the heel of Italy Plato visited the foremost Pythagorean philosopher Archytas, with whom he may have discussed the problem of doubling the cube, or so-called Delian problem.

According to Plutarch, the forever feuding Delians had turned in despair to the Delphic oracle, who advised them to double the size of their altar to Apollo. In obeisance to the oracle, they built another altar with sides twice as long—but, if anything, their problems only got worse.

When the Delians wrote to Plato for advice, he replied that the oracle may have meant doubling the volume of the cube, rather than simply doubling the length of its sides—in which case their new altar was four times too large. But since no one knew how to calculate the length of side required to double the volume of a cube, the god may in fact have been telling them to moderate their passions by taking up the study of mathematics and philosophy.

In Taras, Archytas is likely to have introduced Plato to his teacher Eurytus, who had himself been a pupil of Philolaus. Like Philolaus, Eurytus believed that numbers give limit to the limitless and form to matter, and that their odd and even values account for opposites such as rest and motion, light and dark, and one and many. The concept is not dissimilar to modern binary code.

Plato was deeply impressed by Archytas and the Pythagoreans, whose influence is evident in middle works such as the *Meno* and *Phaedo* (Chapters 14 and 15). In Taras, Plato may also have met Timaeus, if there did exist a historical Timaeus. If not, he might have calqued the Timaeus of the *Timaeus* on Archytas and other Pythagoreans.

In the *Timaeus*, Timaeus associates each of the classical elements (earth, air, water, and fire) with a regular solid (cube, octahedron, icosahedron, and tetrahedron, respectively).

In addition to the four classical elements, there is also a fifth, invisible element called quintessence which makes up the heavens. Particles of quintessence take on the most perfect shape of a dodecahedron.

At the invitation of a philosopher called Dion, Plato left Taras for the court of Dionysius I, the tyrant of Syracuse in Sicily.

Dion's father Hipparinus had been instrumental to the rise of Dionysius, first to supreme military commander and then to tyrant. Dionysius had in turn married Hipparinus' daughter Aristomache, making Dion his brother-in-law and, later, his adviser and close confidant.

Although taken by Dion, Plato had grave reservations about the dissolute Dionysius, who had made himself tyrant by staging an attack upon his own life and using the attack as a pretext to set up a 'guard'—really, a private army. But Rome had recently been sacked by the Gauls and Plato may have been running out of places to go.

Dionysius sought to surround himself with lettered men to flatter his artistic pretensions and lend himself the aura of an enlightened despot. But he also had a predilection for turning upon them, so that when the dithyrambic poet Philoxenus declined to praise his verses, he condemned him to hard labour in the quarries.

Plato's criticisms of the sybaritic court of Syracuse angered Dionysius. Plato had argued, among others, that a slave with a just and ordered soul is happier than an unjust tyrant. To test this theory, Dionysius sold Plato into slavery!

According to Diogenes Laertius, the Cyrenaic philosopher Anniceris ransomed Plato from Dionysius for twenty minas.

Upon returning safe and sound to Athens, Plato resolved to remain there once and for all.

～

In 387, the King's Peace, negotiated by all belligerents and underwritten by the Persian king Artaxerxes II, brought the eight-year-long Corinthian War to an end. Hoping that the Peace would last, Plato purchased a large house some six stadia (around half a mile) beyond the north-western Dipylon gate. The house gave onto the precinct of the Akademeia, named after the Attic hero Hekademos.

According to an old legend, Theseus carried off Helen, the twelve-year-old daughter of Zeus, from Sparta and deflowered her. For this outrage, her twin brothers Castor and Pollux (also known as the Dioscuri, and later catasterized as Gemini) besieged Athens, insisting upon the return of their sister. When the Athenians sincerely told the Dioscuri that they did not know her whereabouts, the Spartans took to battering the city walls and laying waste to the countryside. By revealing Helen's hiding place, Hekademos saved Athens from destruction, and after his death the people honoured him with a garden. Even the Spartans, who by Hekademos recovered their Helen, held the garden to be sacred, and, despite its exposed emplacement, never defiled or despoiled it.

The Akademeia contained a sacred grove of olive trees that produced the oil for the victors at the Panathenaic Games. Hippias, the son of Peisistratos, had walled the garden and raised statues and temples. Cimon, the son of Miltiades, had diverted the Cephalus river for irrigation and planted large trees including oriental planes, poplars, and elms. By the time Plato arrived, a gymnasium had been added to one corner. Several athletic and religious events took place or ended within the garden, including the Dionysiac procession from Athens and the torch-lit night race to the altar of Prometheus. To Plato, the garden, strewn with solitary temples, stray columns, and dilapidated hermai, must have seemed to contain the solution to every problem—was the solution to every problem.

Figure 8. Attic Panathenaic amphora, attributed to Kleophrades Painter (c. 480 BCE). J. Paul Getty Museum, Los Angeles. Victors at the four-yearly Panathenaia received amphorœ of olive oil from the sacred grove of Athena in the Akademeia. These amphorae were invariably realized by the black-figure technique, even after it had been superseded by the more fluid and three-dimensional red-figure technique. The back of this amphora depicts the prestigious four-horse chariot race.

Plato applied for the permission to establish a school—on paper, a *thiasos*, or religious confraternity. In a nod to the Pythagoreans, he inscribed on the lintel above the door, 'Let none but geometers enter here.' Scholars and students took up residence in neighbouring houses, and those of meagre means lodged with others or further out. When he arrived, Eudoxus of Cnidus could only afford an apartment in Piræus, and, each day, walked the seven miles in each direction. Later, his friends and colleagues raised the funds to send him to Heliopolis in Egypt to pursue his study of astronomy and mathematics.

Gatherings often took place in the garden or gymnasium. In many European languages, secondary schools that prepare students for higher education are still, for this reason, called gymnasia. Although Plato privileged the dialectic method, he also encouraged senior members to deliver the occasional public lecture. The Academy's public lectures became popular, and, after some years, Plato obtained permission to construct a small amphitheatre in which to accommodate them. Plato himself once delivered a lecture entitled, 'On the Good', and it may have been the desire to speak to a lay audience that led him to invent striking metaphors such as the sun, line, and cave (Chapter 17).

In his forty years as *scholarch* [head] of the Academy, Plato must have seen through hundreds of students, not least Aristotle, Speusippus, Xenocrates of Chalcedon, Heraclides of Pontus, Hestiæus of Perinthus, and Philip of Opus.

Among all the men, he is known to have admitted at least two women, Axiothea of Phlius and Lastheneia of Mantinea—who were nevertheless required to dress like men so as not be mistaken for *hetairai* [courtesans].

In 367, twenty years after the foundation of the Academy, the tyrant of Syracuse Dionysius I competed with a play, *The Ransom of Hector*, which won first prize at the Lenaia festival. Dionysius celebrated by drinking himself to death.

Although Dionysius had married Dion's sister Aristomache, he had also married Doris of Locri, and while Aristomache bore him four children it was Doris who produced his heir apparent, also called Dionysius. As the older Dionysius lay on his deathbed, Dion tried to talk him into anointing an heir born of Aristomache, who, unlike Doris, was Syracusan and popular with the people. Hearing of this, the younger Dionysius had his father poisoned by way of his doctors.

The paranoid Dionysius had kept his son and heir confined and uneducated, and Dion felt that education might transform Dionysius the Younger if not into a philosopher-king, then at least into a half decent ruler. On this pretext, Dionysius and the Pythagoreans persuaded Plato to return to Syracuse.

Plato did not have high hopes for Dionysius but felt bound to Dion and reluctant to pass over even the slimmest chance of putting theory into practice. When Plato's trireme docked into Syracuse, Dionysius sacrificed to the gods. But Plato's arrival, and his grip on Dionysius, did not please the tyrant's jealous advisors, who accused Dion of plotting against their man.

As his advisors dripped poison into his ear, Dionysius grew suspicious of the able, experienced, and popular Dion, who behaved or acted as ruler in all but name. In 366, Dionysius walked Dion down to the beach and bundled him into a boat bound for Italy. To prevent Plato from protesting or leaving, he removed him to the citadel and placed him under a 'guard of honour'. In time, Plato cajoled him into letting him go.

∾

When Plato returned to the Academy, he found a new face in the teenage Aristotle, a man, at last, with real and lasting power. Making the most of exile, Dion soon re-joined them in Athens.

Dionysius did everything in his power to persuade Plato to return to Syracuse, even bargaining with the fates of Dion and his wife. In 361, Plato sailed to Syracuse for a third and last time.

Unsurprisingly, the trip did not go well. When Plato kept on advocating for Dion, Dionysius banished him to the barracks to live amid his hostile guards. Plato would have been reminded of Socrates, of his experience with Alcibiades and Charmides, and of his conviction that virtue cannot be taught.

Fortunately, Dionysius soon returned Plato to the palace. And after a time, Plato once again coaxed the tyrant into letting him leave—promising himself, this time, never to return. Later, Dionysius sent a letter to Athens in which he expressed the fear that Plato would complain about him to the other philosophers at the Academy. Plato curtly replied that he would never be at such a loss of subjects to discuss as to seek one in him.

When Dionysius sold Dion's estate and forced his wife Arete to marry another, Dion led a revolt, ousting the tyrant and confining him to the citadel. Dion ruled chaotically for three years before being assassinated by Calippus, a close friend and student of Plato who had been bribed by Dionysius.

Although Dion had once been popular with the Syracusans, his failure as tyrant to pursue democratic reforms led them to turn against him—demonstrating the difficulties in setting up anything approaching Plato's Republican ideal. The same could be said of the broader Syracusan adventure: Dionysius I had loved the arts, Dionysius II Plato, Dion wisdom... and yet.

∾

When Dion died in 354, Plato was in his seventies. He was still writing, now faster than ever, and had also developed a set of more mystical unwritten teachings [*ágrapha dógmata*].

As alluded to in Chapter 7, Plato is ascribed with 35 dialogues and 13 letters. Around ten of the dialogues are spurious, as are most if not all of the letters. Opinion is divided on the long, autobiographical Seventh Letter. But even if the Seventh Letter is a pastiche, it is early in origin and likely to be based in fact. If authentic, it would have been composed after the death of Dion and before the death, one year later, of Calippus.

Although all called 'dialogues', the dialogues vary in form. Most are naked dramas with no narrator, but a few, such as the *Charmides*, *Lysis*, and *Republic*, are narrated in the first person by Socrates or, in the case of the *Parmenides*, by Cephalus. The *Protagoras*, *Phaedo*, and *Symposium* are hybrids that begin as drama but lapse into narration; they are narrated, respectively, by Socrates, Phaedo, and Apollodorus. The *Theaetetus* is, in effect, a drama within a drama, as one of his slaves reads out Euclid's record of an exchange that one passed between Socrates and Theaetetus. Finally, the *Apology* is the first-person defence speech of Socrates, punctuated by two short dialogues with Meletus.

Twenty-five of the dialogues are named for an individual that takes part or features in the conversation. The *Republic*, *Sophist*, and *Statesman* are titled on a theme, as is the *Symposium*, the theme in this case being the 'mad' Dionysian, in which Plato's Apollonian philosophy is rooted. Plato never participates in the dialogues, and only mentions himself in two, the *Apology* and the *Phaedo*. By never adopting a position—even 'Socrates' makes a point of contradicting himself—he avoids coming across like his dogmatic predecessors. Indeed, he is often self-critical, as in the *Parmenides*, in which he has Parmenides demolish his pet Theory of the Forms. Arresting though it may be, the Theory of the Forms, like much else in Plato, is never definitive, and features less prominently in the late dialogues. Part of the pleasure and privilege, and seduction, of reading Plato is that he is thinking with us, rather than simply telling us what he thinks, or what to think.

Taken together, the dialogues amount to more than the sum of their parts. With their large and diverse cast of characters, including philosophers, sophists, politicians, generals, orators, playwrights, seers, and slaves, they bring to life, with a tinge of nostalgia, the Golden Age of Athens. By setting these characters in motion, Plato is also indirectly exploring the psychology and philosophy of philosophy and broader education, asking, among others, how to teach, why to teach, and who can learn.

Plato's dialogues are traditionally arranged in nine tetralogies according to a scheme devised by Thrasyllus of Mendes, the confidant of the emperor Tiberius. The fourth 'book' of the ninth tetralogy consists of the thirteen Letters, or Epistles.

    I. Euthyphro, Apology, Crito, Phaedo
    II. Cratylus, Theaetetus, Sophist, Statesman
    III. Parmenides, Philebus, Symposium, Phaedrus
    IV. First Alcibiades, Second Alcibiades, Hipparchus,
        Rival Lovers
    V. Theages, Charmides, Laches, Lysis
    VI. Euthydemus, Protagoras, Gorgias, Meno
    VII. Greater Hippias, Lesser Hippias, Ion, Menexenus
    VIII. Clitophon, Republic, Timaeus, Critias
    IX. Minos, Laws, Epinomis, Epistles

The division into tetralogies might be modelled on the theatrical tetralogies (three tragedies and one satyr play) that playwrights submitted to competitions such as the Dionysia. The dialogues in the first tetralogy all treat of the last days of Socrates. Beyond this, it could be that the dialogues are grouped thematically, with the second and third tetralogies treating of knowledge and dialectic, the fourth and fifth of education, the sixth and seventh of sophistic, and the eighth and ninth of political philosophy.

As discussed in Chapter 7, it is now more common to group the dialogues chronologically into three periods, 'early', 'middle', and 'late', according to their assumed order of composition. The early 'Socratic' dialogues, which typically conclude in aporia, are intended to prepare the ground for philosophy by creating a sense of bafflement. The middle dialogues feature positive doctrines which respond to the questions raised in earlier dialogues. Since Socrates made a point of not having any, these positive doctrines can safely be ascribed to Plato.

It is often assumed that Plato wrote the early dialogues in one block and the middle dialogues in another block, but he may, on occasion, have gone back and forth, writing a 'positive' dialogue followed by a 'negative' one. The *Republic* is unusual for combining the two genres: Book 1 is an old school 'negative' dialogue on justice, and the remaining nine books are Plato's bravado attempt to complete the project begun by Socrates.

The late dialogues, as well as being longer, are less literary, with Socrates vanishing into the background. Plato, it seems, was running out of time and racing to put his ideas to paper. Although predisposed to the highest abstraction, he was keen to show the practical significance of all his theorizing, which he did in his last and longest work, the *Laws*, which remained unpublished at the time of his death in 348.

14

MENO

The *Meno* is a direct dramatic dialogue featuring Socrates and Meno, with a cameo by Anytus, one of the three men who went on to accuse Socrates of impiety.

The young and handsome Meno (or Menon) was the scion of one of Thessaly's leading aristocratic families. His family had close ties with Athens: his grandfather, also called Meno, had even been granted Athenian citizenship.

In the *Meno*, Meno is visiting Athens on a diplomatic mission. He has come with a large entourage of slaves and is residing with Anytus. The dialogue is likely to be set in 402, after Anytus' return from exile in 403 (the year in which the tyranny fell) and before Meno's departure to Persia in early 401. In the dialogue, Socrates regrets that Meno is unable to remain in Athens for long enough to partake in the annual spring-time initiations into the Eleusinian Mysteries, the most famous of the secret religious rites of Ancient Greece. He claims that Meno would be able to understand him better if he could 'only stay and be initiated'—suggesting that both he and Plato had been initiated into the Mysteries, and regarded them.

At home in Thessaly, Meno had studied under Gorgias, and
often gave speeches on virtue after the manner of Gorgias.
From 401, when still in his early twenties, he served as a
commander of the mercenary troops hired by Cyrus of Persia.
In the *Meno*, he comes across as impatient and impetuous, but
Xenophon in the *Anabasis* paints him as selfish and scheming
and 'manifestly eager for enormous wealth' (II, 6). After the
demise of Cyrus, all the commanders were summarily
beheaded, except for Meno who was imprisoned and tortured
for a year before meeting his end.

The Meno

Meno encounters Socrates of whom he enquires whether
virtue [*arete*] can be acquired by teaching.

Socrates begins by praising the Thessalians for their fabled
riches and horses, as well as their newly found reputation for
wisdom. If Meno were to put his question to a Thessalian, he
would surely receive his answer in the grand and bold style of
Gorgias. But an Athenian would simply laugh in his face,
saying that one ought to know what virtue is before asking
whether it can be taught.

To Meno's surprise, Socrates says that even he does not know
what virtue is. Moreover, he has never known of anyone who
did. Perhaps Meno could define it for him?

Meno, thinking it an easy task, offers that there are different
virtues for men, women, children, slaves, and so on. Thus,
according to Gorgias, the virtue of a man is to manage public
affairs, help his friends, harm his enemies, and protect himself,
whereas the virtue of a woman is to manage the home and
submit to her husband.

Socrates is delighted to be presented with so many virtues, which he compares to a swarm of bees. If bees are many and varied, this is not insofar as they are bees, but in some other respect such as size or shape. However, what is it that makes every bee a bee? Just as the nature of health or strength is the same in a man as in a woman, so the nature of virtue is the same in all its instances.

Meno tries again, and this time defines virtue as the ability to rule over people. If virtue is the ability to rule, says Socrates, how could a child or a slave ever be said to possess virtue? But granting that it is the ability to rule, surely, it is the ability to rule *justly* and not unjustly.

In that case, says Meno, 'justice is virtue'. Socrates asks whether Meno means that justice is virtue or that justice is *a* virtue. Meno replies that justice is *a* virtue, since there are other virtues such as courage and temperance.

Socrates points out that they are once again facing the same problem: what is it that all these virtues—justice, courage, and the rest—have in common? By analogy, a round figure is 'a figure' and not 'figure', just as white is 'a colour' and not 'colour'. Meno turns the tables to become the questioner and asks Socrates to define 'figure' and 'colour'. Socrates defines 'figure' as 'that which limits a solid', and 'colour' after Gorgias as 'an effluence of form, commensurate with sight, and palpable to sense'.

Meno attempts once more to define virtue, this time by quoting from a poet: 'Virtue is the desire of honourable things and the power of attaining them.' Socrates counters that one who desires honourable things desires good things, which is the case of everyone, since evil things are harmful, and no one wishes to be harmed. No one desires evil things, unless they are under some impression that they might be good things, 'for what is misery but the desire and possession of evil?'

In that case, says Meno, perhaps virtue is simply the power of attaining good things. Socrates says that, if by 'good things' Meno means things such as wealth, health, and honour, then virtue would only consist in the power of attaining them justly and piously, and not in the power of attaining them unjustly and impiously, which would amount to vice and wickedness. However, justice and piety are parts of virtue, which cannot simply be defined in terms of its parts.

Meno is stumped, and unflatteringly compares Socrates to the flat torpedo fish, which torpifies all who come near it.

Meno asks Socrates how they are supposed to look for virtue if they do not even know what it is:

> And how will you enquire, Socrates, into that which you do not know? What will you put forth as the subject of enquiry? And if you find what you want, how will you ever know that this is the thing which you did not know?

Socrates grasps Meno's meaning: one cannot enquire about what one knows nor about what one does not know; for if one knows, one has no need to enquire; and if one does not know, one will not know after what to enquire.

However, he once heard certain wise men and women 'who spoke of things divine' say that the soul is immortal, has been born often, and has seen all things on earth and below. Since the soul already knows everything, 'learning' simply means recollecting that which is already known.

Meno asks Socrates whether he can prove this theory. Socrates draws a square in the dirt and asks one of Meno's slave boys to tell him the area of the square, assuming that each side is two feet long. The boy correctly replies, four feet.

Socrates then asks him to work out the length of side required for a square that is twice as large (eight square feet). The boy (this time incorrectly) replies, four feet.

By extending the sides of the square and asking questions, Socrates leads the boy to recognize that the area of a square with a side of four would not be eight but sixteen. Given that the area of a square with a side of two is four, and that the area of a square with a side of four is sixteen, what is the length of side of a square with an area of eight? The boy hesitantly replies, three feet, but Socrates lets him understand that sides of three would amount to an area of nine instead of eight. In an aside to Meno, Socrates points out that, despite being numbed, the boy is already better off than when he began the exercise, as he now knows what he does not know and will wish to remedy his ignorance.

Socrates carries on with the boy, reminding Meno that he is not teaching so much as prompting him. He divides the square of sixteen into four squares of four and draws four diagonal lines that connect the centres of each side of the original square of sixteen (Figure 9). Seeing that the square contained within the four diagonal lines is exactly eight feet, the boy realizes that the required length is the length of the diagonal, and that double the area of a square is the square of its diagonal.

Socrates triumphantly claims to have proven that the boy found this knowledge by recollection. The knowledge was already in him, waiting to be stirred up as in a dream. Thus, we should confidently seek for the things that we do not 'know', rather than believe, with Meno, that this is impossible.

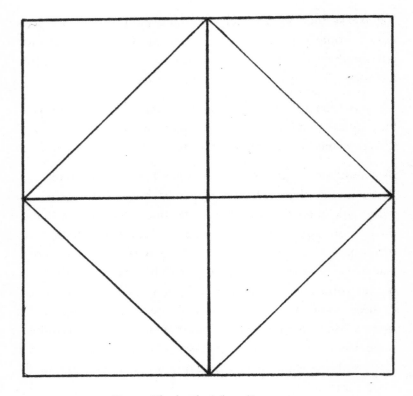

Figure 9: The slave boy's 'lesson' in geometry.

Socrates suggests that they return to defining virtue, but Meno says that he would rather return to his original question of whether virtue can be taught.

Socrates replies with a heavy helping of irony:

> Had I the command of you as well as of myself, Meno, I would not have enquired whether virtue is given by instruction or not, until we had first ascertained what it is. But as you think only of controlling me who am your slave, and never of controlling yourself, —such being your notion of freedom, I must yield to you, for you are irresistible.

Socrates hypothesizes that, if virtue were a kind of knowledge, it could be taught just like any other kind of knowledge. Since virtue is a good, and since knowledge embraces all good, it must also embrace virtue. What is good is beneficial, but such things as wealth, strength, and beauty can be harmful as well as beneficial, depending on how they are used. The same goes for qualities of the soul such as courage, which can be harmful if it amounts to recklessness. Thus, qualities of the soul are only good and beneficial if accompanied by knowledge and wisdom. Since virtue is always good and beneficial, it must be partly or wholly wisdom—and therefore teachable.

However, Socrates is suspicious of this line of reasoning: if virtue is knowledge, and if virtue can be taught, then why are there no teachers of virtue?

Socrates invites Anytus into the conversation. Socrates says that, if one wishes to become a physician, one ought to seek instruction from a physician. Similarly, if one wishes to become wise and virtuous, one ought to seek instruction from a sophist. Although offered in irony, Anytus is horrified by the suggestion: all those who give their money to the sophists are out of their mind! Socrates feigns disbelief: how could a reputed sophist like Protagoras spend forty years plying his trade, and yet remain undetected as a fraud?

Anytus affirms that Meno, to become wise and virtuous, ought to seek instruction from any one Athenian gentleman. Socrates asks how Athenian gentlemen might be able to teach that which they have never learnt. Anytus replies that they did learn virtue, from the previous generation of Athenian gentlemen.

Socrates points out that people of wisdom and virtue, even Athenian ones, seem very poor at imparting these qualities. For instance, Themistocles was able to teach his son Cleophantus skills such as standing upright on horseback and shooting javelins, but no one ever credited the poor wretch with anything like his father's wisdom—and the same could also be said of Lysimachus and his son Aristides, Pericles and his sons Paralus and Xanthippus, and Thucydides and his sons Melesias and Stephanus.

Anytus rages at Socrates for defaming such eminent Athenians and warns him to be careful. Socrates tells Meno that Anytus does not understand the meaning of defamation but will some day.

Meno reports that the Thessalians do not agree whether virtue can be taught. When Gorgias hears other sophists promising to teach virtue, he merely laughs at them. Socrates says that even Theognis [a sixth century lyric poet] doubted the teachability of virtue, in some verses implying that it can be taught and in others that it cannot. If even the supposed teachers of virtue are in two minds about whether virtue can be taught, we can only assume that there are no such teachers, and thus that virtue cannot be taught. And if virtue cannot be taught, it is not, after all, a kind of knowledge.

If virtue cannot be taught, how, asks Meno, did good people come about? Socrates replies that they have so far overlooked that right action is possible under guidance other than that of knowledge. A man who has knowledge of the way to Larisa [a city in Thessaly] might make a good guide, but a man who has only correct opinion of the way, but has never been and does not know, might make an equally good guide. If the man who thinks the truth is just as good a guide as the man who knows the truth, then correct opinion is just as good a guide to right action as knowledge.

In that case, how, asks Meno, is knowledge different from correct opinion, and why should anyone prefer the one to the other? Socrates replies that correct opinions are like the statues of Dædalus, which needed to be tied down if they were not to run away. Correct opinions can be tied down with 'an account of the reason why', whereupon they petrify into knowledge.

Since virtue is not knowledge, all that remains is for it to be correct opinion. This much explains why such virtuous men as Aristides, Lysimachus, Pericles, Themistocles, and Thucydides were unable to impart their virtue. Virtuous men are no different from soothsayers, prophets, and poets, who say many true things when they are inspired but have no real knowledge of what they are saying.

If ever there was a virtuous man who could impart his virtue to another, he would be said to be among the living as Homer says Tiresias [the blind seer of myth] was among the dead: 'He alone has understanding; but the rest are flitting shades.'

Commentary

The influence of Archytas and the Pythagoreans is evident in the *Meno*, which makes prominent use not only of mathematics and geometry, but of Pythagoras' theorem.

The *Meno* is a transitional dialogue that sits between Plato's early and middle periods. It begins in the early negative style, with Socrates in full-blown elenchus mode. Meno responds to Socrates with several definitions of virtue and both end up in a state of aporia, with Meno comparing Socrates to the flat torpedo fish (electric ray) and even going so far as to suggest that new knowledge is impossible.

Socrates' reformulation of this contention is known as Meno's Paradox, or the Learner's Paradox:

> One cannot enquire about what one knows nor about what
> one does not know; for if one knows, one has no need to
> enquire; and if one does not know, one will not know after
> what to enquire.

So far, the *Meno* resembles other early dialogues that try and
fail to define a particular ethical term, such as the *Charmides*
(temperance), *Euthyphro* (piety), *Greater Hippias* (the *kalon*—
fine, beautiful, or good), *Laches* (courage), and *Lysis* (friendship).

It is apparent, especially in the original, unabridged dialogue,
that Meno struggles to understand what Socrates is asking of
him, and the same might also be said of other so-called experts
that engage with Socrates, including Laches in the *Laches* and
Euthyphro in the *Euthyphro*. The confusion of these experts,
some of whom, like Meno, are philosophically trained or at
least philosophically aware, suggests that Socrates' search for
rigorous definitions is something original and radical.

For Socrates, it is not sufficient simply to define an ethical
concept in terms of itself or related concepts, or by a list of its
instances, or according to convention or popular opinion ('piety
is what the gods all love'). Instead, a rigorous definition is one
which, by picking out the nature or essence of the ethical
concept, applies to all its instances and no more. For example,
Meno's definition of virtue as 'the ability to rule over people' is
both too narrow for excluding children and slaves, and too
broad for including those who rule unjustly. When Meno turns
questioner and asks Socrates to define 'figure' and 'colour',
Socrates takes the opportunity to mock the sophists by defining
'figure' in his concise manner ('that which limits a solid') and
'colour' in the florid, frivolous manner of Gorgias ('an effluence
of form, commensurate with sight, and palpable to sense').

For Socrates, one cannot answer questions about virtue or any other ethical concept without first knowing what it is, which is why he keeps on returning the recalcitrant Meno to the subject of defining virtue. More than that, virtue is knowledge, and one cannot possibly be virtuous if one does not even know what virtue is. Had Meno truly understood the nature of virtue, he would have been virtuous, and would not have met his early, grisly end in Persia.

After the voicing of the Meno Paradox, the *Meno* pivots from a negative into a positive dialogue, with Plato's philosophy coming to the fore.

For 'Socrates' [Plato], the Meno Paradox is a false dichotomy between complete knowledge and utter ignorance.

According to the doctrine of recollection [*anamnesis*], the soul, which has been born often, already knows everything, and knowledge is simply a matter of recollecting that which is already known.

Knowledge can be recollected through a dialectical process such as that engaged in by the slave boy, a process that can only begin from a position of perplexity. In an aside to Meno, Socrates points out that the bewildered boy is better off than when he began the exercise, for now he knows what he does not know and will wish to remedy his ignorance. The same may also be said of Meno, and of us, the readers of the dialogue.

The slave boy's 'lesson' in geometry is a reflection, or *mise-en-abîme*, of the dialogue itself, like *Hamlet*'s 'play within a play'—except that the slave boy is earnest in his desire for learning whereas Meno is not.

Learning is, ultimately, a matter of self-motivation, or what I call spiritual energy, for which no amount of teaching, even by the likes of Socrates, can palliate. It's an elitist vision, because spiritual energy is a 'gift of the gods', even if the slave boy outranks his aristocratic master.

The slave boy's 'lesson' in geometry refutes Meno's Paradox and supports (although does not prove) the doctrine of recollection, a theory of innate ideas which has modern correlates in, among others, Carl Jung's collective unconscious and Noam Chomsky's language acquisition device. It is, in part, owing to these innate ideas, even if they remain largely unrealized, that all human beings are inherently worthy of dignity and moral treatment.

Another method of overcoming the Meno Paradox is simply by stating a hypothesis, as Socrates proceeds to demonstrate by hypothesizing that virtue is knowledge, and thus teachable, and then noticing that there are no teachers of virtue. Socrates says that even Theognis doubted the teachability of virtue, in some verses implying that it can be taught and in others that it cannot. In this respect, Socrates is no different from Theognis, arguing in the *Meno* that virtue cannot be taught but in the *Protagoras* that it can.

If virtue cannot be taught, how, asks Meno, did good people come about? Socrates replies that true belief ('correct opinion') is just as good a guide to virtue as knowledge.

In that case, asks Meno, why is knowledge more valued than true belief? This is known as the Meno Problem, or Value Problem of Knowledge (not to be confused with the Meno Paradox above). Socrates' response to the Meno Problem is that knowledge, being *justified* true belief, is more stable and reliable than simple true belief. Socrates returns to the subject of knowledge in the *Theaetetus* (Chapter 18).

The *Meno*, brilliant though it is, raises many more questions than it answers, not least by pushing the problem of learning to one remove—for, if the soul knows all things, there must have been a time when it learnt them.

Even so, we, like the slave boy, although perhaps not Meno, are much the better for the exercise.

15

PHAEDO

*T*he *Phaedo* is named for the young Phaedo of Elis, whom Socrates had rescued from slavery. If you recall, Phaedo had been present at the death of Socrates, who stroked his hair before drinking of the hemlock.

The *Phaedo* covers the last hours and execution of Socrates, although here I am more concerned with the dialogue's Platonic philosophy than its Socratic biography—insofar as it is Socratic biography, given that the Socrates of the *Phaedo* sounds a lot more like Plato than the Socrates of the *Apology*.

In the *Phaedo*, which used to be called *On the Soul*, Socrates offers four arguments for the immortality of the soul, among which the doctrine of recollection and connected Theory of the Forms. The supposed immortality of the soul enables Socrates to remain sanguine in the face of death and offers the ultimate justification for the philosophical life. The dialogue ends with a myth of the afterlife and, of course, the dramatic drinking of the hemlock.

The setting of the *Phaedo* is not in fact Athens but Phlius in the Peloponnese, where the Pythagorean philosopher Echecrates presses the travelling Phaedo to recount the last hours of Socrates. Phaedo devotes almost all of his almost uninterrupted account to the conversation that took place between Socrates and the visiting Pythagorean philosophers Cebes and Simmias, in the presence of Crito, Apollodorus, and several other Socratics—but not, apparently, Plato.

What follows is an outline of this conversation.

The Phaedo

After his wailing wife has been removed, Socrates tells the gathering that a philosopher should welcome death, but not to the point of taking his own life. Man belongs to the gods, and to take his own life would be to incur their wrath.

In that case, asks Cebes, why should a philosopher prefer death over living and, in so doing, giving service to the gods? Socrates replies that death will bring the philosopher to better gods and men.

The philosopher aims at truth, but his body is constantly distracting and deceiving him: 'The body keeps us busy in a thousand ways because of its need for nurture... It fills us with needs, desires, fears, all sorts of illusions and much nonsense...' Although no thought or truth has ever come out of the body, it is for its comfort and preservation that men must go to work and to war.

Absolute justice, absolute beauty, or absolute good cannot be apprehended by the senses, but only by pure thought, that is, by the mind or soul. Thus, the philosopher seeks in as far as possible to separate soul from body. As death is the complete separation of soul and body, the philosopher aims at death, and can be said to be almost dead. Only a true philosopher who does not fear death possesses courage and the other virtues. Those who remain in fear of death can only have, at best, the appearance of virtue; but behind the facade they are frantically measuring their fears and trading the greater for the lesser.

Cebes agrees with all this, but questions whether the soul continues to cohere after it has left the body, or whether it disperses like breath or smoke. There is, says Socrates, an ancient doctrine according to which the living are born of the dead. If so, the soul must continue to cohere after it has left the body. All things come from their opposites: something larger comes from something smaller, something weaker comes from something stronger, and so on. As the opposite of life is death, life must come from death, and *vice versa*.

Simmias asks Cebes to remind him of the proofs for the doctrine of recollection, which implies that the soul existed before this life. One excellent proof, says Cebes, is that 'if a question is put to a person the right way, he will give a true answer of himself' (cf. the *Meno*). Another proof, says Socrates, is when we see one thing and are reminded of another. For instance, when we see equal sticks or stones, we are reminded of the Form of Equality, even though the 'equal' sticks or stones necessarily fall short of perfect equality. This being so, we could not have learnt about Equality through our senses, but must have been born already with the latent knowledge of it. To know something is to be able to explain that thing: if most people are unable to explain what they mean by Justice, Beauty, or Goodness, this is because they are still in the process of recollecting this knowledge.

Cebes and Simmias have been persuaded that the soul exists before birth, but not that it continues to exist after death. Socrates maintains that this has already been proven: if the soul existed before birth as per the doctrine of recollection, and if life comes out of death as per the argument from opposites, it follows that the soul must continue to cohere after death.

That which is compounded is dissoluble, but that which is uncompounded is indissoluble and therefore unchanging. The Forms (for instance, Beauty), which are unchanging, are uncompounded, but their particulars (for instance, a beautiful horse), which are in a constant state of change, are compounded. Particulars are apprehended by the senses, but the Forms can only be apprehended by the mind. Since the soul cannot be apprehended by the senses, it must belong to the class of things that are uncompounded and unchanging.

The embodied soul employs the body as an instrument of perception, but what the body perceives is in a perpetual state of flux, so that the soul is in a state of confusion. But when the soul is once again detached from the body, or when it turns inward to contemplate itself, it passes into the realm of the unchanging and approaches wisdom. The soul rules over the body as the gods rule over men—and, like the gods, it is unchanging and undying.

Upon death, not all souls suffer the same fate. The soul of the philosopher, being the most detached from the body, is able to reach the realm of the unchanging, where it 'lives in bliss and is released from the error and folly of men, their fears and wild passions and all other human ills...'

But unphilosophical souls, which have been weighed down by worldly cares and bodily desires, remain earthbound and pass into another body.

Souls that were unjust as well as unphilosophical might pass into a wolf or a hawk, while gentler souls might pass into a social animal such as an ant or bee or human being.

Figure 10: The Death of Socrates, by Jacques-Louis David (1787). Metropolitan Museum of Art, New York.

A prolonged silence falls upon the gathering. Socrates can tell that Cebes and Simmias are reluctant to share their doubts, lest they disturb him in the moment of his death. He smiles quietly, remarking that if he cannot persuade even his friends that he welcomes death, he is unlikely to persuade anyone else.

With that said, Simmias and Cebes are emboldened to speak their minds. Simmias objects that one might make a similar argument about harmony and the lyre, the lyre being physical and harmony being invisible, beautiful, and divine. But one cannot break the lyre or cut its strings and argue that the harmony still somehow exists.

Cebes, for his part, objects that the soul, though it may outlive the body, or even several bodies, may yet be mortal: a tailor may remake his cloak several times over the course of his life, yet still grows old and dies.

Socrates replies in turn to Simmias and Cebes. If knowledge is recollection, as granted by Simmias and Cebes, the soul must have existed before birth. This is unlike a harmony, which could not have existed prior to the lyre. Secondly, whereas a lyre may be more or less harmonious than another lyre, a soul cannot be more or less soul than another soul: if the soul were akin to a harmony, there could be no such thing as a virtuous or vicious soul. Lastly, whereas the soul rules the body, and may be at variance with it, a harmony does not rule a lyre, and cannot be out of tune with it.

Socrates' complex response to Cebes' tailor argument is the crux of the conversation. He relates that, as a young man, he abandoned the natural sciences in search of the deep causes of things. Anaxagoras' theory that *Nous* is the intelligent and thus benevolent cause of everything seemed appealing, except that Anaxagoras never made anything of it, merely falling back, when needed, on facile physicalist explanations. He thought that having failed in the contemplation of true existence, he ought to be careful not to lose the eye of his soul, as people lose their bodily eye by gazing upon the sun during an eclipse— unless they take the precaution of looking at the image reflected in water. He took a similar precaution in formulating a secondary account of causation which involves not an account of things in themselves, but the formulation of theories about them. Then, whatever accords with the most plausible theory is true, and whatever disagrees with it is false.

Now, the most plausible theory is the Theory of the Forms, according to which there are such things as the Form of Justice, the Form of Beauty, and so on. On this account, something is beautiful because it participates in the Form of Beauty, two is two because it participates in the Form of Duality, and so on. A thing that participates in a Form also participates in other closely connected Forms. For instance, three bundled pencils participate in the Form of Threeness but also in the Form of Oddness. However, opposite forms such as Tall and Short, or Even and Odd, cannot admit of each other. Whenever a soul is embodied, there is invariably life, indicating that the soul is intimately connected with life, and thus that it cannot admit of its opposite, death.

When the body dies, the soul travels to a place of judgement. The Earth is spherical and upheld in the middle of the heavens by its own equipoise. Our world is only one of several pockets of air and water on the surface of the Earth and we are like 'frogs about a marsh'. Above these hollows lies the true surface of the Earth, which contains not air and water but pure ether. Those who live there have sharper senses and keener intellects, and are able to perceive the heavenly bodies as they truly are. We, in contrast, are like the creatures who live at the bottom of the sea, thinking that the sea is the sky and knowing nothing of the purer world beyond.

The Earth's hollows are connected by great subterranean rivers of water, mud, and fire which flow into and out of the deepest hollow, Tartarus. Of these four rivers, Oceanus, Acheron, Pyriphlegethon, and Cocytus, Oceanus is the greatest, and encircles the Earth. The souls of the virtuous ascend to the surface of the Earth, and those that have been purified by philosophy ascend to still higher places.

The souls of the neither-good-nor-bad travel to the shores of the Acherusian Lake where they pay and receive their dues before being returned to an earthly frame. But the souls of the evil go straight down to Tartarus, from where they never return.

As the Pythagoreans have no more objections to raise, the conversation comes to a close. Socrates takes a bath and prepares to drink the hemlock, as related in Chapter 12.

Commentary

The *Phaedo* is a literary masterpiece, with Plato leaning on a
noble and dying martyr to lend gravitas to his philosophy. The
calmness and cheerfulness of Socrates contrasts with the
distress of his wife and dolefulness of his friends. Unusually,
Socrates' interlocutors are philosophers rather than lay people,
enabling the Socratic irony to be dialled down in favour of
elevated themes and elaborate arguments.

Socrates offers four more or less problematic arguments for the
immortality of the soul: the argument from opposites, the
doctrine of recollection, the argument from affinity, and the
Theory of the Forms—with the argument from opposites,
which slips from comparatives (larger and smaller) to absolutes
(life and death), being especially problematic.

Plato seems to assume reader familiarity with the *Meno* and the
doctrine of recollection, which the *Phaedo* leans and builds
upon. For the first time, he explicitly appeals to the Forms,
although does not do much to explain them.

The influence of the pre-Socratic philosophers, especially
Pythagoras (reincarnation and the transmigration of souls),
Heraclitus (the argument from opposites), and Parmenides (the
Theory of the Forms) is perhaps more evident in the *Phaedo*
than in any of Plato's other dialogues.

Simmias and Cebes are themselves Pythagoreans, making
them liable to accept any argument conforming or compatible
with Pythagoreanism. Socrates encourages the pair to resist his
arguments, enabling the reader to engage with Plato's ideas,
since it is, after all, by a thorough process of dialectic that latent
knowledge might be recollected.

For Plato, true knowledge is not of contingent, empirical facts, but of the changeless, eternal Forms.

At the same time, no resistance is offered to the central Theory of the Forms, which is presented as 'the most plausible theory' without any backing or questioning.

Great literature though it may be, the *Phaedo* can be dubious philosophy, with, nonetheless, the occasional flash of brilliance such as Socrates' 'secondary account of causation' which, in acknowledging that we can only work within a paradigm of the truth, anticipates modern scientific theory. As well as being iffy, many of the arguments are question begging. For instance, if knowledge is recollection, when and how did we acquire this knowledge? When, how, and why did the reincarnation cycle begin, and, if it did begin, why can it not end?

Plato does address some of these questions, including about the Forms, in later dialogues, and it is worth noting that the myth of the afterlife in the *Phaedo* prefigures the chariot allegory in the *Phaedrus* (Chapter 16) and the allegory of the cave and Myth of Er in the *Republic* (Chapter 17).

In any case, our main interest in the *Phaedo* is not in its logic but in its impact and influence, which cannot be understated. The *Phaedo* established or entrenched most if not all of the deep divisions or dualities that mark the Western mind, including soul and body, mind and matter, reason and sense experience, reason and emotion, reality and appearance, good and evil, heaven and hell.

In the Western tradition, since the *Phaedo*, the body is the source of all evil. But in the Eastern tradition, for instance, in yoga, we can take control of the mind through the body. More than that, by opening new channels in the body, we can open new channels in the mind.

To me as a psychiatrist, the dichotomies of the *Phaedo* and more generally of the West call to mind the ego defence of splitting, which can be defined as the division or polarization of beliefs, actions, objects, or persons into good and bad by focussing selectively on their positive or negative attributes. Examples of splitting include the religious zealot who divides everyone into blessed and damned, and the child of divorcees who idolizes one parent while shunning the other. Splitting diffuses the anxiety that arises from our inability to grasp a complex state of affairs by simplifying and schematizing it and making it easier to process. On the other hand, such a compartmentalization of opposites leaves us with a distinctly distorted picture of reality and a restricted range of thoughts and emotions.

Although the *Phaedo* is at the root of Western psychology, philosophy, and theology, it is also deeply Eastern in advocating supreme detachment and ego suppression or disintegration as the route to salvation. Also, death is an illusion ... we will be reincarnated ... according to our karma. These, however, are not the aspects that the West has retained.

Although we should not commit literal suicide, we should aim to commit metaphorical suicide. Only once we have 'killed' ourselves can we be truly virtuous, and to be virtuous is to be free—the freedom from fear being the highest, most heroic form of freedom.

16

PHAEDRUS

*T*he *Phaedrus* is a direct dialogue featuring Socrates, Phaedrus, and a written speech by the orator Lysias.

Phaedrus ['Bright', 'Radiant', 'Revealer'] is an attractive youth, the first cousin of Plato's stepbrother Demus.

Lysias, later numbered among the ten Attic orators, is the son of the shield manufacturer Cephalus, who converses with Socrates in the *Republic*, and the brother of Polemarchus, at whose house the *Republic* is set.

The dramatic date is unclear but has to be anterior to 415, in which year Phaedrus fled Athens after being caught up in the affair of the profanation of the Eleusinian Mysteries.

Phaedrus is also present in the *Protagoras*, which is set in around 434, and is somehow still young in the *Symposium*, which is set in 416. It is he who inspires the theme of the banquet by lamenting that Eros is not sufficiently praised. And it is he who delivers the first, relatively unsophisticated, speech, in which he argues, as per the *Phaedrus*, that pederastic love is the most important giver of virtue in life.

The Phaedrus

On a hot day in high summer, Socrates runs into Phaedrus and joins him for a walk beyond the city wall.

Phaedrus has just been listening to Lysias, who gave a speech in which he argued that a youth who is being courted by a lover and a non-lover ought to give his favour to the latter. Socrates suspects that Phaedrus is hiding the speech under his cloak and persuades him to pull it out and read it to him.

The pair amble along the banks of the Ilissus, and then wade in its cool waters, searching for an auspicious place to settle down with the speech. Phaedrus asks whether they are not passing the exact spot where Boreas is said to have carried off Orithyia. Socrates replies that, while he is still in ignorance of his own self, he sees little point in being curious about myths or anything else which is not his concern.

They lie down on the soft grass under a plane and a chaste tree. Phaedrus remarks that Socrates seems like a stranger in the countryside. Socrates explains that he rarely ventures beyond the city gates, since he is a lover of wisdom and the men within the walls are his teachers. But on this occasion, Phaedrus has found 'a drug'—the speech—by which to lead him out.

Phaedrus reads the speech, which begins:

> Listen. You know how matters stand with me; and how, as I conceive, this affair may be arranged for the advantage of both of us. And I maintain that I ought not to fail in my suit, because I am not your lover...

Lysias proceeds to catalogue the many and various reasons for which a youth ought to favour the non-lover over the lover. In sum, the youth ought to give his favour to he who can best return it, rather than he who needs it most because he is 'afflicted with a malady and is not in his right mind'.

Socrates says that Phaedrus' ecstasy in reading the speech drove him into a phrenzy of his own, but Phaedrus calls him out for speaking in irony. Socrates claims that he could cobble up a better speech from various bits and pieces that he has heard. For although he has no ideas of his own, he has been filled, like an empty jar, by the words of others flowing in through his ears. Phaedrus forces the speech out of him by threatening violence.

Socrates covers his head, calls upon the Muses, and begins. Everyone, he claims, is ruled by two principles, a desire for pleasure and an 'acquired opinion which aspires after the best'. These two principles can be in accord, but when they are not one dominates the other. When desire dominates, this is called 'excess'; when it is judgement, this is called 'temperance'. Excess has several forms, such as gluttony, which is the desire to take pleasure in food, and love, which is the desire to take pleasure in the beauty of the beloved.

The lover seeks not to improve his beloved, but merely to make him as personally agreeable as possible. To this end, he may deprive him of family, friends, and other freedoms, and even debar him from philosophy, which is the source of the greatest happiness. Sooner or later, the lover's madness abates, and he disavows all the oaths and promises that he once made.

> Consider this, fair youth, and know that in the friendship of the lover there is no real kindness; he has an appetite and wants to feed upon you: as wolves love lambs so lovers love their loves.

Phaedrus begs Socrates to deliver a similar speech in praise of the non-lover, but Socrates claims to have been overtaken by the riverine nymphs. As he makes to leave, his *daimonion* tells him that he has committed an impiety and must atone to Eros, who is a god and therefore cannot, as he implied, be evil.

To placate the god, Socrates delivers a second speech, this time in praise of the lover. He begins by criticizing his first speech for overlooking that madness, as well as being an illness, can also be the source of man's greatest blessings.

> Madness, provided it comes as the gift of heaven, is the channel by which we receive the greatest blessings... the men of old who gave things their names saw no disgrace or reproach in madness; otherwise they would not have connected it with the name of the noblest of arts, the art of discerning the future, and called it the manic art... So, according to the evidence provided by our ancestors, madness is a nobler thing than sober sense... madness comes from God, whereas sober sense is merely human.

There are, he says, four forms of divine madness: prophecy from Apollo, holy prayers and mystic rites from Dionysus, poetry from the Muses, and love from Aphrodite and Eros.

Socrates then sets out to prove the divine origin of love, starting with an argument for the immortality of the soul. The soul is not only self-moving but 'the beginning of motion' for all else that moves. As the beginning is begotten out of nothing, the beginning is unbegotten—and, therefore, undying, 'else the whole heavens and all creation would collapse and stand still, and never again have motion or birth.'

Figure 11: Apollo's Chariot, by Odilon Redon (c. 1910).
Stedelijk Museum, Amsterdam.

Having established its immortality, he compares the soul to a chariot with a charioteer and two winged horses. Whereas the chariot of a god has two tame horses, that of a mortal has one tame horse and one unruly one which is the cause of much hardship for the charioteer. The soul, he says,

> ...has the care of inanimate being everywhere, and traverses the whole heaven in divers forms appearing—when perfect and fully winged she soars upward, and orders the whole world; whereas the imperfect soul, losing her wings and drooping in her flight at last settles on the solid ground— there, finding a home, she receives an earthly frame which seems to be self-moved, but is really moved by her power; and this composition of soul and body is called a living creature.

The chariot of a god with its two tame horses has no difficulty in soaring to the high edge of heaven, enabling the god to step without and contemplate the essence of reality. The god is taken around in a full circle as he feasts his mind upon Justice and Temperance and Wisdom, not in the form of generation and relation, which men call existence, but in their undimmed, universal Forms.

Despite their unruly horse, the chariots of the imperfect souls that are most alike to the gods can, albeit with great difficulty, ascend high enough for their charioteer to lift his head above the rim of heaven and glimpse, if only fleetingly, at aspects of the Universals.

Sooner or later, all imperfect souls fall down to Earth, but only those that have seen something of the Universals can take on a human form. The imperfect souls that gazed longest upon the Universals are incarnated as philosophers, musicians, and true lovers. As their memories of the Universals are more vivid, they are completely absorbed in ideas about them and forget all about earthly interests. Common people think that they are mad, but the truth is that they are divinely inspired and in love with goodness and beauty.

The madness of love arises from seeing the beauty of the earth and being reminded of true, universal Beauty. Unfortunately, most earthly souls are so corrupted by the body, 'that living tomb which we carry about', that they lose all memory of the Universals. When their eyes fall upon the beauty of the earth, they are merely given over to pleasure, and like brutish beasts rush on to enjoy and beget. But the earthly soul that is still able to remember true Beauty, and so to feel true love, reverences the face of his beloved as an expression of the divine—of Justice, Temperance, and Wisdom absolute. As his eyes catch those of his beloved, a shudder passes into an unusual heat and perspiration. The parts of the soul out of which the wings once grew, and which had hitherto been sealed, begin to melt open, and tiny wings begin to swell and grow from the root upwards.

> Like a child whose teeth are just starting to grow in, and its gums are all aching and itching—that is exactly how the soul feels when it begins to grow wings. It swells up and aches and tingles as it grows them.

The lover feels the utmost joy when he is with his beloved. When they are apart, the parts out of which the wings are growing begin to dry out and close, and the pain is such that they prize each other above all else.

The lover whose soul once followed in the procession of Zeus seeks out a beloved who shares in his god's imperious and philosophical nature, and then does all he can to confirm this nature in him. Thus, the desire of the divinely inspired lover can only be fair and blissful to the beloved.

In time, the beloved, who is no garden fool, comes to realize that his divinely inspired lover is worth more to him than all his other friends and kinsmen put together, and that neither human discipline nor divine inspiration could have brought him any greater blessing.

> Thus great are the heavenly blessings which the friendship of a lover will confer upon you ... Whereas the attachment of the non-lover, which is alloyed with a worldly prudence and has worldly and niggardly ways of doling out benefits, will breed in your soul those vulgar qualities which the populace applaud, send you bowling round the earth during a period of nine thousand years, and leave you a fool in the world below.

~

Socrates claims to have paid his due and redeemed himself to Eros with this 'tolerably credible and possibly true though partly erring myth'. Phaedrus doubts that Lysias could ever write a finer speech, and the conversation turns to the subject of writing.

Socrates suggests that there is no disgrace in writing, but only in bad writing. Rather than nap, Socrates and Phaedrus decide to discuss the differences between good and bad writing, lest the cicadas mock them for avoiding conversation at midday and mistake them for a pair of slaves who have come to their resting place as cattle to a watering hole. On the other hand, if the cicadas see that they are not lulled by their chirruping, they may, out of respect, offer them their god-given gifts. For once upon a time, before the birth of the Muses, the cicadas used to be human beings. But when the Muses were born, song was created, and they were so overwhelmed with the pleasure of singing that they forgot to eat and drink and died without even realizing it. As a gift from the Muses, they were reincarnated as cicadas, singing from the moment they are born to the moment they die without ever feeling hunger or thirst. After dying, the cicadas report back to the Muses in heaven about who is honouring them on earth, and win the love of Terpsichore for the dancers, of Erato for the lovers, and of Calliope, the eldest Muse, for the philosophers.

Phaedrus suggests that a good orator is more concerned with opinion than with the truth. Socrates responds that there can be no genuine art of persuasion without knowledge of the truth; at the same time, truth is more persuasive when allied with rhetoric. Rhetoric and dialectic ought to go hand in hand, since 'he who would deceive others, and not be deceived, must exactly know the real likenesses and differences of things...'

Rhetoric, says Socrates, has the most power with abstract notions such as 'love' and 'justice' which mean different things to different people and even to the same person from moment to moment. By failing to define 'love' in his speech, Lysias treated it as though it were something clear and concrete like 'iron' or 'silver'. He, on the other hand, began by distinguishing between human and divine madness, and the four forms of divine madness. This involved collecting all the various sorts of madness and then dividing them up again 'according to the natural formation'.

Because Lysias did not begin at the beginning, or indeed at all, his speech lacked order and structure, and resembled the trite, interchangeable lines on Midas' grave:

> *I am a maiden of bronze and lie on the tomb of Midas;*
> *So long as water flows and tall trees grow,*
> *So long here on this spot by his sad tomb abiding,*
> *I shall declare to passers-by that Midas sleeps below.*

Every speech must be put together like a living creature, with a body of its own: 'it must be neither without head nor without legs; and it must have a middle and extremities that are fitting both to one another and to the whole work.' The art of composing a speech, and the science of collecting and dividing, properly pertain to dialectic.

Having run the gamut of rhetorical devices, from pithy sayings to pathetic appeals, Socrates and Phaedrus conclude that an orator is like 'a madman or pedant who fancies he is a doctor because he has read something in a book, or has stumbled on a prescription or two, although he has no real understanding of the art of medicine.'

Rhetoric is a kind of leading of the soul: just as a doctor ought to understand the body, how it works and what is best for it, so an orator ought to understand the soul if he is to be persuasive and not end up doing more harm than good.

In the courts of law, men care more for conviction than for truth, so that one might be tempted to exchange an improbable truth for a probable untruth. If a weak but courageous man has attacked a strong but cowardly one, the weak man might say that he could never have attacked such a strong man, and the strong man that he was attacked by several men. A true orator, however, would resist the temptation to lie, because he is not an orator but a philosopher who mastered the art of rhetoric in his pursuit of a much higher goal.

The conversation shifts from writing to the written word itself, prompting Socrates to make up a story about the origins of the written word:

> At the Egyptian city of Naucratis, there was a famous old god, whose name was Theuth; the bird which is called the Ibis is sacred to him, and he was the inventor of many arts, such as arithmetic and calculation and geometry and astronomy and draughts and dice, but his great discovery was the use of letters. Now in those days the god Thamus was the king of the whole country of Egypt; and he dwelt in that great city of Upper Egypt which the Hellenes call Egyptian Thebes, and the god himself is called by them Ammon. To him came Theuth and showed his inventions, desiring that the other Egyptians might be allowed to have the benefit of them; he enumerated them, and Thamus enquired about their several uses, and praised some of them and censured others, as he

approved or disapproved of them. It would take a long time to repeat all that Thamus said to Theuth in praise or blame of the various arts. But when they came to letters, This, said Theuth, will make the Egyptians wiser and give them better memories; it is a specific both for the memory and for the wit. Thamus replied: O most ingenious Theuth, the parent or inventor of an art is not always the best judge of the utility or inutility of his own inventions to the users of them. And in this instance, you who are the father of letters, from a paternal love of your own children have been led to attribute to them a quality which they cannot have; for this discovery of yours will create forgetfulness in the learners' souls, because they will not use their memories; they will trust to the external written characters and not remember of themselves. The specific which you have discovered is an aid not to memory, but to reminiscence, and you give your disciples not truth, but only the semblance of truth; they will be hearers of many things and will have learnt nothing; they will appear to be omniscient and will know nothing; they will be tiresome company, having the show of wisdom without the reality.

When Phaedrus dismisses this made-up tale of Egypt, Socrates reminds him that the first prophecies were uttered by an oak. Back then, men were not as wise as the young of today, but content in their simplicity to listen to an oak or even a stone, so long as it spoke the truth. Phaedrus grants that there is insight in Socrates' tale of Egypt.

Socrates compares a piece of writing to a painting, which, although having the likeness of life, cannot respond to any questions that are put to it. The written word is passed around to the wise and foolish alike. Unlike dialectic, it does not know when to speak and when to keep silent. And if it comes to be abused or misunderstood, it cannot rise up to defend itself.

... it is much nobler to be serious about these matters, and [prefer] the art of dialectic. The dialectician chooses a proper soul and plants and sows within it discourse accompanied by knowledge—discourse capable to helping itself as well as the man who planted it, which is not barren but produces a seed from which more discourse grows in the character of others. Such discourse makes the seed forever immortal and renders the man who has it as happy as any human being can be.

Socrates tells Phaedrus to go to Lysias and tell him what the nymphs have just been telling them: that a person who composes speeches based on truth and knowledge, and defends them ably, deserves the name not of orator but of philosopher.

Phaedrus asks what message he might take to Socrates' young friend, the orator Isocrates. Socrates replies that he will go to Isocrates himself, and tell him that his genius, because it contains an element of philosophy, will come to soar over that of Lysias and every other orator.

Before they leave, Socrates offers a prayer to the local deities:

S: Beloved Pan, and all ye other gods who haunt this place, give me beauty in the inward soul; and may the outward and inward man be at one. May I reckon the wise to be the wealthy, and may I have such a quantity of gold as a temperate man and he only can bear and carry. —Anything more? The prayer, I think, is enough for me.

P: Ask the same for me, for friends should have all things in common.

Commentary

This is the only Platonic dialogue that features Socrates outside of Athens and the Piræus. The spot beneath the plane and the chaste tree is a liminal space between the natural and the supernatural. The supernatural supervenes on the natural in various forms: nymphs, cicadas, and Socrates' *daimonion*, which are all tied to the divine madness [*theia mania*] of which Socrates speaks. Adding to the sense of the numinous is the frequent mention of mythological figures and people from the past ('the men of old...'). Today, the idyllic banks of the Ilissus are no more, although there is a plan to unearth the river.

The ostensible theme of the dialogue is love and pederasty, and the dialogue is full of flirtatious banter and sexual innuendo. Socrates persuades Phaedrus to pull out the speech that he is hiding under his cloak... The grass on which they lie down to read the speech is 'like a pillow gently sloping to the head'... After Phaedrus has read the speech, Socrates says, 'the effect on me was ravishing. And this I owe to you Phaedrus, for I observed you while reading to be in an ecstasy... and, like you, my divine darling, I became inspired with a phrenzy.'

But although the *Phaedrus* seems to be about love, it is more exactly about the education of the soul, which might be led to wisdom through love or dialectic, although not, perhaps, oratory or the written word. Just as the *Phaedo* used to be called, *On the Soul*, so the *Phaedrus* might have been called, *On the Education of the Soul*. In his second speech, in praise of the lover, Socrates supplies an argument for the immortality of the soul which is not among the four in the *Phaedo*: since the soul is the beginning of motion, it precedes motion, and, therefore, cannot die. As in the *Phaedo*, the body, 'that living tomb which we carry about', is a source of corruption that prevents the soul, this time quite literally, from soaring.

Plato tricks the reader into accepting Socrates' first speech, in praise of the non-lover. Fortunately, Socrates is arrested by the nymphs, and then his *daimonion* forces a recantation. In fact, Socrates had reservations about the speech from the beginning, which is why he covered his head before delivering it—a precaution that he did not take for his second, masterful speech. In keeping with the historical Socrates, he also compared himself to an empty jar, filled through the ears by the ideas of others. But for all that, the first speech is not entirely gratuitous: in affirming that everyone is ruled by two principles, essentially, desire and reason, Socrates is setting us up for the two horses of his next speech. The concluding phrase, 'As wolves love lambs so lovers love their loves' is an alliteration that we owe to the great translator of Plato, Benjamin Jowett, who was Master of Balliol College, Oxford, from 1870 to his death in 1893.

In 1880, some undergraduates published a 'Balliol rhyme' lampooning the venerable man:

> *Here come I, my name is Jowett.*
> *All there is to know I know it.*
> *I am the Master of this College,*
> *What I don't know isn't knowledge!*

Socrates' second speech begins with a demonstration of the dialectic method of collection and division, as applied to madness of which love is a kind.

Modern science appears to be catching up with Plato's mystical claim that madness, as well as an illness, can be the source of life's greatest blessings—a thesis that inspired my book, *The Meaning of Madness*.

Figure 12. Caricature of Benjamin Jowett by Leslie Ward,
published in Vanity Fair, *26 February 1876.*

Later, Socrates tells Phaedrus that, unlike Lysias, he began at
the beginning by carefully laying out his terms. There is a
parallel here with the *Meno*, in which Socrates refuses to
discuss whether virtue can be taught until he and Meno have
been able to define it. In a similar vein, Socrates refuses to
discuss the myth of Boreas and Orithyia or anything else which
is not his concern while he is still in ignorance of his own self.
Socrates is the originator of the concept of the self and self-
knowledge, which he intended to be about our nature rather
than our 'issues'. Plato elaborates on the method of collection
and division in the *Statesman*.

Despite his emphasis on Apollonian dialectic and reason, Plato
recognizes that the original impulse for philosophy arises out
of something as irrational and Dionysian as love. However, this
love, though fertile, is not of the reproductive kind, and, like the
unruly horse, needs to be reined in. Although Socrates and
Phaedrus openly flirt with each other, it is no coincidence that
they sit under a chaste tree. According to Pliny the Elder, the
matrons of Athens, at the time of the Thesmophoria [the
festival of Demeter and Persephone], used to place the stems
and leaves of the chaste in their bedding to temper their lust.
When, at the end of the dialogue, Socrates prays to the gods of
the place, he calls himself 'a temperate man'; and when he asks
Phaedrus to complete the prayer, Phaedrus responds, 'Ask the
same for me, for friends have all things in common.' Thus, it is
not as lovers but as friends and equals that they leave. The
genius of Plato is that the relationship between Socrates and
Phaedrus is the very embodiment of the pure, elevating,
ameliorating love of which they speak.

The discussion of madness leads up to the chariot allegory.
Since only the souls that have at some time seen something of
the Universals can take on a human form, all human beings are

acquainted with the Universals, and so capable of recollection. Although Plato does not say so, the capacity for recollection comes close to a definition of a human being and, as I have said, could be used to argue that all human beings, no matter how debased, are inherently worthy of dignity.

Christian angels only acquired their wings in the fourth century, owing in large part to the influence of Plato and the chariot allegory, which, however, has many more parallels with Hinduism. In an echo of the caste system, Socrates goes so far as to rank people according to how much of the Forms their souls are supposed to have seen, with philosophers, musicians [artists], and true lovers in the first class, followed by kings and generals in the second class, politicians and traders, athletes and physicians, prophets and hierophants, poets and imitative artists, artisans and farmers, sophists and demagogues, and tyrants in the ninth and final class. If prophets and poets seem rather low in the pecking low, this is presumably because they are divinely inspired and not acting in their own capacity.

The charming cicada myth serves as an interlude between the discussion on love and the discussion on writing and the written word, which are tied together by the speech of Lysias. The chirruping cicadas are another element of the supervening supernatural, of the nearness of the divine. The cicadas used to be human beings who took such pleasure in singing that they forgot all about their bodies and, like Socrates, died without even realizing it. As a reward for the song that they sang out of love, the Muses returned them as cicadas, winged creatures which, after a time in the earth, shed their shells to become almost pure soul. The proximity and encroachment of nature in the *Phaedrus* also plays on the parallel, first drawn by Democritus, between nature and teaching: 'Nature and teaching are similar, because teaching changes a man's shape, and nature acts by changing shape.'

Early on, Socrates tells Phaedrus that he has found just the 'drug' to lead him out of the city. The drug of oratory can be a cure or a poison, a cure if informed by dialectic, but a poison if not. Socrates compares the dialectician to the husbandman, who is careful to sow the right seed in the right soil in the right season. Teaching is like gardening; it is the gardening of the soul. But even in a fertile plot, a seed, once sown, can take months or years to germinate, if it germinates at all.

Unlike the dialectician, the written word is indiscriminate and indifferent, like a demented doctor who prescribes the same drug to everyone. The written word cannot bring us to recollect the universals but serves only to remind us of what we do not really know, while inviting the most dangerous of delusions: that we know what we do not know. Socrates, the quintessential dialectician, wrote nothing at all, and although Plato wrote copiously, he did not write everything.

The irony is that the *Phaedrus* is itself a piece of writing. Still, it might be of help to those of us who have already intuited it, or parts of it, but not yet made all the connexions.

17

REPUBLIC

The *Republic* is often regarded as Plato's *magnum opus*. It has been voted the greatest work of philosophy ever written, and is the most studied book in the top 10 colleges in the United States. Its title in English derives from Cicero's translation of the Greek *politeia* into the Latin *res publica*. Scipio, the main character of Cicero's *De re publica*, explicitly sets out to imitate Plato and Socrates. Also heavily indebted to Plato's *Republic* are Aristotle's *Politics* (Chapter 20), Zeno of Citium's controversial but lost *Republic*, and Augustine's *City of God*.

The first book of the *Republic* may have been written earlier than the following nine books, and is essentially a negative, aporetic dialogue on the theme of justice. In classic early style, it even features a sophist—the last sophist to feature in Plato. The subsequent nine books are a creative attempt to define justice, while also treating on a great number of interconnected themes, including politics, philosophy, and education.

The Republic

Socrates and Glaucon are returning to Athens from a religious festival in Piræus when they are waylaid by Adeimantus (the brother of Glaucon and Plato), Polemarchus, Niceratus, and others. Arriving at the house of Polemarchus, they encounter his father Cephalus, his brothers Lysias and Euthydemus, Thrasymachus the Chalcedonian, and others.

Cephalus, who seems much aged, chides Socrates for not visiting more often. Socrates reassures Cephalus that he likes nothing better than to converse with the elderly. Can Cephalus tell him what it is like to be old? Old men, says Cephalus, often complain that all the pleasures of life are gone, but, as far as he is concerned, this release from the passions has brought a great sense of calm and freedom. Socrates discloses what many people think: that old age only befits Cephalus because he is rich. In response, Cephalus quotes Themistocles' reply to the Seriphian who attributed his fame to his Athenian citizenship: 'Had you been a native of my country and I of yours, neither of us would have been famous.' Age may not be a light burden upon the good poor man, but neither can the bad rich man ever be at peace.

Socrates remarks that people like Cephalus who have inherited their wealth tend to be indifferent to money, whereas people who have acquired their wealth seem unable to talk about anything else, and, for this reason, make for poor company. The greatest benefit of wealth, says Cephalus, is a clear conscience, since the wealthy rarely feel the need to deceive or defraud anyone. Is there, asks Socrates, nothing more to justice than this: to speak the truth and pay one's debts? Surely, it would be unjust to return his knife to a madman, but just to lie to him about its whereabouts.

Cephalus leaves to overlook some sacrifices and Polemarchus assumes his father's place in the debate. Polemarchus quotes the poet Simonides in saying that justice is the repayment of a debt, that is, the giving to each man that which is due and proper to him. In sum, justice is to do good to one's friends and evil to one's enemies. Socrates points out some problems with this definition of justice, not least that it seems counterintuitive for justice to involve doing evil, and that, owing to our poor judgement, we may not be friends with the best or most virtuous people.

The sophist Thrasymachus barges into the conversation 'like a wild animal': justice, he claims, is nothing other than the interest of the stronger, and it is for subjects to do the bidding of their rulers. Socrates responds that the goal of every art or rule is the interest of the subjects rather than that of the ruler. For instance, the physician, qua physician, aims not at his own interest but at that of his patient. Not so, says Thrasymachus: because the unjust ruler is stronger, his subjects do whatever is in his interest. Compared to the unjust, the just always lose out, both in the private and the public sphere. The highest form of injustice is tyranny, wherein the tyrant is happiest, and those who refuse to do injustice are most miserable. If people censure injustice, it is not because they shrink from committing it but only because they fear for themselves.

Socrates reiterates that the goal of every art or rule is the interest of the subjects, which is why no one is willing to rule without remuneration. This remuneration can take one of three forms: money, honour, or a penalty for refusing to rule. As good men care nothing for avarice or ambition, they are only willing to rule if there is a penalty for refusing, and the worst part of this penalty is that they should be ruled by bad men.

For there is reason to think that if a city were composed
entirely of good men, then to avoid office would be as much
an object of contention as to obtain office is at present; then
we should have plain proof that the true ruler is not meant by
nature to regard his own interest, but that of his subjects; and
all who knew this would choose rather to receive a benefit
from another than to have the trouble of conferring one. So
far am I from agreeing with Thrasymachus that justice is in
the interest of the stronger. This latter question need not be
further discussed at present; but when Thrasymachus says
that the life of the unjust is more advantageous than that of
the just, his new statement appears to me to be of a far more
serious character.

Thrasymachus confirms that he deems the life of the unjust to
be the more advantageous, assimilating injustice with wisdom
and virtue, and justice with their opposites. Socrates says that
the good and wise do not desire to gain more than their like,
but only more than their unlike and opposite. In contrast, the
bad and ignorant desire to gain more than their like and their
unlike. The same could be said of the just and the unjust: the
just desire to gain more than the unjust but no more than the
just, whereas the unjust desire to gain more than the unjust and
the just. Thus, the just are akin to the good and wise, and the
unjust to the bad and ignorant. Justice creates harmony and
friendship, whereas injustice creates discord and enmity.
Compared to the unjust, the just are in a better position to take
concerted action, and so are stronger. In fact, if the bad can at
all organize, this is only because they still have a remnant of
justice.

Justice is desirable because it is the excellence of the soul,
without which a person cannot live well, and without which he
cannot be happy.

Socrates concludes that he is no better off for having risen to Thrasymachus: his original aim had been to define justice, not to show why it is desirable.

Book 2: The healthy vs the luxurious state

Glaucon claims not to have been persuaded that being just is always better than being unjust.

All goods can be divided into one of three classes: goods such as harmless pleasures which are desirable in themselves; goods such as gymnastics, the care of the sick, or the various ways of making money which are desirable for what they bring; and goods such as knowledge, sight, or health which are desirable both in themselves and for what they bring. To which of these classes does justice belong?

To the third, says Socrates.

Most people, says Glaucon, think that it belongs to the second. They think that to do injustice is good, and that to suffer it is bad. Because the bad is greater than the good, they agree among themselves not to do injustice. But if a man could get hold of the fabled Ring of Gyges and make himself invisible, he would behave without restraint—proving that the 'just' man is only so because he is weak and fears retribution. The truly just man who cares only for justice rather than its appearance will be thought unjust and suffer all manner of evil until he learns that he should only *seem* just. Meanwhile, the unjust man who is resourceful enough to seem just will always get the better of everyone and everything.

Adeimantus broadly echoes Glaucon. He challenges Socrates to take the other side of the argument and demonstrate that justice is inherently desirable.

Socrates maintains that there are two kinds of justice, that of the individual and that of the state, and proposes to begin his inquiry into the nature of justice with the justice of the state, which is larger and therefore easier to locate. 'And if we imagine the state in process of creation, we shall see the justice and injustice of the state in process of creation also.'

A state arises out of our necessities for food, shelter, clothing, and the like, and its purpose is to meet these necessities. Different people are naturally suited to different roles, and specialization results in greater quantity and better quality. Thus, each person should exclusively perform the role to which he is naturally suited.

Socrates paints an idyllic picture of this 'healthy' state in which every bare necessity is met. Glaucon objects that people desire more than bare necessities: they desire to lie on sofas, to dine off tables, and to have sauces and sweets. Socrates says that such luxuries call upon greater resources than the state can naturally provide, and lead to warring.

To fight wars, the state requires a specialized class of warriors. If these 'guardians' are to be worthy of the name, they need to have certain physical and spiritual qualities. Since nature cannot be relied upon to provide them, or all of them, with these qualities, nature must be supplemented by education.

The education of the guardians should have two divisions: gymnastic for the body, and music [the arts of the Muses] for the soul. Music includes literature, which may be true or false. From an early age, children are exposed to stories, which are bound to exert a profound influence on their character. For this reason, children's stories should be censored, as should works, including those of Homer and Hesiod, that misrepresent gods and heroes. God must always be presented as he truly is, that is, as good, and the author of good only.

Book 3: The education of the guardians

As future guardians must not fear death, stories should not present heroes as fearful, nor Hades as a horrible place. Heroes should only be portrayed as virtuous: honest, courageous, temperate, pious, and the like. Socrates considers other artforms such as painting, sculpture, and architecture, in each case censuring that which may hinder the education of future guardians. He remarks that, owing to this programme of censorship, the luxurious state is beginning to look like the healthy state.

Socrates also discusses love, which he subsumes under music, 'for what should be the end of music if not the love of beauty?' Whereas true love, which is the love of beauty and harmony, is temperate, the love of the body, which is lust, is intemperate. For this reason, man and boy should not display any form of affection that goes beyond that which may exist between a father and son.

Gymnastic should begin at an early age and consist in military exercises. It is often supposed that music is intended for the soul and gymnastic for the body; in fact, gymnastic too is chiefly intended for the soul. Exclusive devotion to music leads to softness; exclusive devotion to gymnastic leads to ferocity. Instead, music and gymnastic must be practised in such proportions that future guardians be courageous without being hard, and gentle without being soft. Physicians should only be trained to treat those with a single, curable ailment, while those with a chronic illness should be left to die naturally.

Rulers should be chosen from among the guardians after close observation and rigorous testing of their loyalty to the state. Guardians who are chosen as rulers should receive further education; guardians who are not chosen should no longer be known as 'guardians' but as 'auxiliaries'.

All citizens should be told a useful lie to promote loyalty to the state and enforce its three-tiered social order. According to this 'myth of the metals', every citizen is born out of the earth of the state, and every other citizen is his brother or sister. But God has mixed different metals into their souls: gold for rulers, silver for auxiliaries, and iron for producers. Children are usually made of the same stuff as their parents; if not, the child should either ascend or descend in the social order. Should the wrong metal ever come to power, the state will be ruined.

Guardians should not have any private property, but should live communally in housing provided by the state and receive no more than their daily sustenance.

Book 4: Justice as specialization

Adeimantus protests that people would be miserable if they could not own property and enjoy luxuries. To this, Socrates adds that they would not be able to take a journey of pleasure or keep a mistress, 'which is thought to be happiness.' The ideal state [*kallipolis*, 'beautiful city'] aims not at the disproportionate happiness of a few, but at the greatest happiness of all, since it is in this type of state that justice is most likely to be found. Still, it remains possible that the guardians would be the happiest of people in spite, or because, of their deprivations.

The arts and crafts are just as liable to degenerate in wealth as in poverty: 'the one is the parent of luxury and indolence, and the other of meanness and viciousness, and both of discontent.' In the ideal state, there would be no money, and neither wealth nor poverty. Adeimantus asks how a state with no money could go to war, especially against a rich and powerful enemy.

Socrates replies that an army of however many rich men could be no match for an army of however few trained warriors; in any case, allies and neighbours would be happy to assist if promised the spoils of war. Owing to the might of its guardian class, the ideal state need not be particularly large, and certainly not so large as to be ungovernable.

Guardians, since they are friends, will have everything in common, including wives and children. There will be no need for laws since guardians will have a deep understanding of the principles of the ideal state and be able to apply them to each and every individual case. Educated people make informed, rational decisions, which, over time, make life better and the state stronger. So important is education that the original curriculum should never be altered or 'improved'.

Having outlined the ideal state, Socrates is ready to pick out the classical virtues of wisdom, courage, temperance, and justice. Wisdom is in the guardians, courage is in the auxiliaries, and temperance and justice are in every citizen. Justice can be defined as 'doing one's own business', that is, doing what one is best suited to do, and, thus, what is best for the state. If wisdom, courage, and temperance are abstracted from the state, the only remaining virtue is the principle of specialization, which is their cause and condition.

Socrates proposes to verify his definition of justice by locating justice in the individual. The just person is 'he in whom the several qualities of his nature do their work'. Just as society is divided into three classes, so the soul is divided into three parts. In the just person, the rational part rules over the passionate part, which is its ally, and both rule over the appetitive part. The rational part desires truth, the passionate part desires honour, and the appetitive part desires food, drink, sex, and money. The rational part corresponds to the guardians, the passionate part to the auxiliaries, and the appetitive part to the producers, in whom it is most prominent. The just person 'sets in order his own inner life, and is his own master and his own law, and at peace with himself…'

Justice and injustice are to the soul as health and disease are to the body.

> I said: The argument seems to have reached a height from which, as from some tower of speculation, a man may look down and see that virtue is one, but that the forms of vice are innumerable; there being four special ones which are deserving of note.
>
> What do you mean? [Glaucon] said.
>
> I mean, I replied, that there appear to be as many forms of the soul as there are distinct forms of the State.
>
> How many?
>
> There are five of the State, and five of the soul, I said.

The first, virtuous form of the state is monarchy or aristocracy, in which rule is exercised by one or several distinguished persons.

Book 5: Women and children

Socrates begins to enumerate the four vicious forms of the state, but Polemarchus and Adeimantus ask him to return to what he said about wives and children. In response, Socrates elaborates on the place of women and children in the ideal state.

Women ought to have the same duties as men:

Are dogs divided into hes and shes, or do they both share equally in hunting and in keeping watch and in the other duties of dogs? Or do we entrust to the males the entire and exclusive care of the flocks, while we leave the females at home, under the idea that the bearing and suckling of their puppies is labour enough for them?

If women are to have the same duties as men, they must receive the same education, including military training. Woman's nature, though different from man's, divides into the same three faculties, so that both genders ought to have the same pursuits.

The wives of guardians should be held in common, as should their children; no parent should know his child, nor the child his parents. Because all would be considered family, loyalty, rather than being divided between state and family, would be entirely to the state.

The best of both genders should be united as often, and the worst as seldom, as possible. Copulation should only take place during certain festivals; children born from copulation at other times should be put to death. Mates are to be married but only for the duration of the festival, to sanction copulation. To guard against incest, guardians should consider every child born between seven and ten months after they have copulated to be their own.

Despite the community of property and family, guardians would be happier than Olympic champions for having been freed from all the 'little meannesses' of life such as

> ...the flattery of the rich by the poor, and all the pains and pangs which men experience in bringing up a family, and in finding money to buy necessaries for their household, borrowing and then repudiating, getting how they can, and

giving the money into the hands of women and slaves to keep
—the many evils of so many kinds which people suffer in this
way are mean enough and obvious enough, and not worth
speaking of.

...and if any guardian shall try to be happy in such a manner
that he will cease to be a guardian, and is not content with
this harmonious life, which in our judgement, is of all lives
the best, but infatuated by some childish conceit of happiness
which gets up into his head shall seek to appropriate the
whole state to himself, then he will have to learn how wisely
Hesiod spoke, when he said, 'half is more than the whole'.

Socrates also discusses the behaviour of the guardians at war. A
cowardly guardian should be demoted to the productive class.
Children in training to become guardians should attend the
battlefield to learn from and be inspired by their elders; they
should attend on horseback so that they can escape in case of
defeat. Defeated enemies should be treated cordially. If they are
Greek, they should not be enslaved, and their lands should not
be destroyed. But if they be barbarian, anything goes.

Socrates considers whether such an ideal state is realistic or
possible. Words express more than fact: all one can hope for is a
state which resembles rather than coincides with the ideal
state. But even this could not exist 'until all philosophers are
kings, or the kings and princes of this world have the spirit and
power of philosophy, and political greatness and wisdom meet
in one'.

True philosophers are lovers of truth, not mere 'lovers of
sounds and sights' with a sense of beautiful things but no sense
of Beauty, and a sense of just things but no sense of Justice. The
universe is divided into that which is completely, that which is
in no way, and that which both is and is not. That which is

completely is the object of knowledge, that which is in no way is the object of ignorance, and that which both is and is not is the object of opinion. Only the Forms are completely, and only philosophers can apprehend them. Thus, only philosophers can have knowledge.

Book 6: Philosopher-kings

The state should be entrusted to true philosophers, who are the spectators of all time and existence. As such, they are not cowardly or mean, but just and gentle and otherwise virtuous. Adeimantus objects that most philosophers are 'strange monsters, not to say utter rogues'; even the best among them are made useless by their study. Socrates agrees, but explains that, if philosophers are strange monsters, this is because people with a philosophical nature are pressured into other, more 'ambitious', careers. The void that this creates is filled by charlatans with maimed and disfigured souls. Only a small number of the people with a philosophical nature persist with philosophy, perhaps because they are in exile or in poor health, or because they are aristocratic enough to hold society in contempt. If even they are useless to the world, this is the fault of those who will not be guided by them. False philosophers are like little tinkers who have come into a vast fortune; those who ignore philosophy are like mutinous sailors who all want to be captain, while dismissing the true navigators as stargazers.

The philosopher-king, selected from the class of guardians, must have attained the highest knowledge of all, namely, the knowledge of the Form of the Good [*hē toû agathoû idea*] by which all other things are made useful. As the Form of the Good is impossible to describe, Socrates conveys its essence through three connected metaphors: the sun, line, and cave.

The metaphor of the sun

Just as it is by the light of the sun that the visible is made apparent to the eye, so it is by the light of truth and being that the nature of reality is made apparent to the soul. Just as light and sight may be said to be like the sun, and yet not to be the sun, so science and truth may be said to be the Good, and yet not to be the Good. Just as the sun is the author of nourishment and generation, so the Good is the author of being and essence. The Good is beyond being, and the cause of all existence.

The metaphor of the line

A line is cut into two unequal sections, and each section is divided again in the same proportion. The two main divisions correspond to the visible world, below, and the intelligible world, above. The lower segment in the visible division consists of images, that is, shadows and reflections, and is accessed by imagination. The higher segment in the visible division consists of sensible particulars and is accessed by belief. The lower segment in the intelligible division consists of Forms and is accessed by thought, but via sensible particulars and hypotheses, as when geometers trace a triangle to reason about triangularity, or appeal to axioms to prove theorems. The higher segment in the intelligible division also consists of Forms but is accessed by understanding, a purely abstract faculty which requires neither sensible particulars nor hypotheses, but only a first principle, namely, the Form of the Good.

The purpose of education is to progress the philosopher through the various sections of the line until he arrives at the Form of the Good.

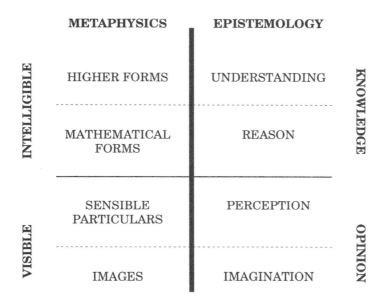

Figure 13: Plato's line.

Book 7: The metaphor or allegory of the cave

Human beings spend all their lives in an underground cave with its mouth open towards the light. They have their legs and necks shackled so that they can only see in front of them, towards the back of the cave. Behind the prisoners, a fire is blazing, and between them and the fire there is a low wall behind which men carry diverse statues above their heads, such that the fire casts the shadows of the statues onto the back of the cave. Because these shadows are all the prisoners ever see, they suppose that the shadows are the objects themselves.

If a prisoner is unshackled and turned towards the light, his eyes suffer sharp pains, but in time they grow accustomed to the light and he begins to discern the statues. He is then dragged right out of the cave, where the light is so bright that he is only able to look, first at the shadows, and then at the reflections, of the actual objects. At last, he is able to gaze upon the objects themselves, of which the statues were but pale imitations. In time, he looks up at the sun, and understands that the sun is the cause of everything that he sees around him, of light, and sight, and the objects of sight.

The true purpose of education is to drag the prisoner as far out of the cave as possible; not merely to instil knowledge into his soul, but to turn his whole soul towards the sun, which is the Form of the Good. Once freed, the prisoner is reluctant to go back down into the cave and muddy himself in the menial matters of men. When he eventually does, his vision is no longer accustomed to the dark, and he seems ridiculous to other men. Nonetheless, he must be made to return into the cave and partake of human labours and honours, because the State aims at the happiness not of a single escapee but of all its citizens. Moreover, he has a duty to give service to the state, since it was by the state that he was educated to see the light of the sun.

> The state in which the rulers are most reluctant to govern is always the best and most quietly governed, and the state in which they are most eager, the worst... You must contrive for your future rulers another and a better life than that of a ruler, and then you may have a well-ordered state; for only in the state which offers this, will they rule who are truly rich, not in silver and gold, but in virtue and wisdom, which are the true blessings of life... And the only life which looks down upon the life of political ambition is that of true philosophy. Do you know of any other?
>
> Indeed, I do not, [Glaucon] said.

Socrates returns to the education of the philosopher-kings. In addition to the normal curriculum, prospective philosopher-kings should be educated in mathematics and, especially, in dialectic, as it is by abstract reasoning that the soul can be drawn from becoming to being. However, dialectic should not be taught to anyone under the age of thirty, and it is only at the age of fifty that the most distinguished students should raise the eye of the soul to the universal light and behold the Form of the Good.

Socrates suggests that the ideal state might be instituted by taking over an existing state, banishing every citizen above the age of ten, and educating the remaining children according to the principles that have been laid out.

Book 8: The degeneration of the ideal state

In Book 5, Socrates had begun to enumerate the four vicious forms of the state before being interrupted by Polemarchus and Adeimantus. He now returns to the task. They are, from bad to worse: timocracy, oligarchy, democracy, and tyranny. States are not made of oak and rock, but of men, and come to resemble the men of which they are made. Aristocracies are made of just men; timocracies of honour-loving men; oligarchies of misers and money-makers; democracies of men who are overcome by unnecessary desires; and tyrannies of men who are overcome by unlawful desires.

Being human, the ideal state is bound, in time, to degenerate. Socrates provides a detailed account of the degeneration of the ideal state from aristocracy to tyranny via timocracy, oligarchy, and democracy.

Democracy in particular arises from the revolt of the poor in an oligarchy. The state is 'full of freedom and frankness' and every citizen is able to live as he pleases. 'These and other kindred characteristics are proper to democracy, which is a charming form of government, full of variety and disorder, and dispensing a sort of equality to equals and unequals alike.' However, the people in a democracy are overcome by so many unnecessary desires that they are forever spending and never producing, and are 'void of all accomplishments and fair pursuits and true words'. As a result, the state comes to be ruled by people who are not fit to rule.

As the ideal state degenerates from aristocracy and timocracy, it begins to harbour drones, that is, people such as beggars and criminals who do not belong to any class and so, do not have any role. These 'pests of the hive' may be fairly innocuous, or armed with terrible stings. In a democracy, they may even come to power, turning the democracy into a tyranny.

Book 9: Tyrants

Socrates gives a detailed account of the origins, mindset, and *modus operandi* of the tyrant, thereby demonstrating that this most unjust of men is also the most slavish and unhappy. The soul of the tyrant is full of disorder and regret, and incapable of doing what it truly desires.

The life of the political tyrant is even more wretched than that of the private tyrant, first, because the political tyrant is in a better position to feed his disordered desires, and second, because he is everywhere surrounded and watched by his enemies, of whom he is, in effect, the prisoner.

There are three classes of men, the lovers of wisdom, the lovers of honour, and the lovers of gain, and three corresponding kinds of pleasure. Every man claims that the life that has the most of what he loves is the best of lives, but only the lover of wisdom is to be believed, since only he has experienced every kind of pleasure. Moreover, only the pleasure of philosophy is pure and positive, whereas other forms of pleasure merely involve relief from pain. Socrates calculates that the king is precisely 729 times happier than the tyrant.

Justice is inherently desirable. Ideally, we are impelled by human nature and divine reason to be just. But if not, the laws are there to guide us, and impose from without what cannot be imposed from within.

Book 10: The Myth of Er

Socrates discusses poetry (the arts of imitation), which ought to be banned for three reasons. First, poetry can easily be wrought without knowledge of the truth, as when a painter represents a cobbler though he knows nothing about cobbling. Second, poetry indulges the histrionics of the inferior, irrational part of the soul. And third, poetry can lead even the best of us to empathize with the intemperate emotions of baser people, and carry those emotions into our lives. Socrates, who loves his Homer, regrets having to ban poetry from the ideal state.

Socrates discusses the 'greatest prizes and rewards which await virtue'. He begins by offering a proof for the immortality of the soul. Anything that is destroyed is destroyed by something that is bad for it. What is bad for the soul is vice and injustice. However, vice and injustice do not dissolve or destroy the souls of evil men. Therefore, the soul cannot be destroyed, and the greatest rewards of virtue lie beyond this life.

To show how this might be, Socrates concludes the discussion with an eschatological myth, the famous Myth of Er, which I detail and discuss in the *Meaning of Myth*.

Commentary

The first book of the *Republic* presents several attempts to
define justice.

Cephalus' concept of justice, 'to speak the truth and pay one's
debts', echoes the traditional, Hesiodic concept of justice.
Socrates undermines this definition with the counterexample
of not returning his weapon to a madman.

Polemarchus' definition of justice, to help one's friends and
harm one's enemies, is also based on the notion of justice as the
repayment of a debt. Socrates defeats it on the basis that it
seems counterintuitive for justice to involve doing harm, and
that most people are not friends with the most virtuous people.

In Classical Athens, sophists like Thrasymachus undermined
these received notions of justice and their roots in religious
belief. Thrasymachus, an embodiment of sophistic relativism,
does not define justice so much as reject it: the tyrant is the
happiest of men, and it is only from fear that people pay lip
service to justice. Socrates is made to defend the very value of
justice, notably by arguing that man is a social animal, before
he can return to his original task of defining it.

Book 2 picks up with Glaucon and Adeimantus, who wonder
whether justice is like health or knowledge: desirable in itself
as well as for what it brings. To press Socrates into proving that
it is, they adopt the other side of the argument, raising social
contract theory and the ring of Gyges. Plato's brothers are more
receptive and constructive than Thrasymachus, and typical of
the more sophisticated interlocutors, such as Phaedrus and
Theaetetus, of Plato's later dialogues.

In response to the brothers, Socrates does something original
and radical, which is to define justice structurally rather than

behaviourally, first in the city, where it is easier to locate, and then in the soul. In so doing he is making two important, and debatable, assumptions: that justice can be defined structurally, and that justice in the individual is analogous to justice in the state. He ends up concluding that justice, in imitating the Forms, is desirable in itself as well as for what it brings.

The *Republic* is often regarded as a work of political philosophy when it is more properly a work of ethics—although the divide between ethics and politics was not so marked in antiquity, when ethics was more about human flourishing than right action *per se*. It is for the sake of an ethical concept, justice, that Socrates conjures up the ideal state, and it is not justice in the state so much as justice in the individual that he is after.

To wit, Socrates does not think that the ideal state is realistic or possible. Even a pale imitation of the ideal state could not exist 'until all philosophers are kings...' and would be prone to degeneration. Were the ideal state possible, it would have no place for the very person advocating it, the gadfly (or drone) who shunned politics to take to the streets. The constitution in Plato's last work, the *Laws*, is far more pragmatic and realistic than the blueprint for the ideal state.

At the same time, if it is solely to search for justice, Socrates says much more than he needs to about the ideal state, whose spirit lives on in the *Laws*. It may be that many of the passages about the ideal state are ironic, intended not as a blueprint, but to invite thought on political matters while fleshing out the issues, trade-offs, and connexions involved. Irony is, after all, what we have to come to expect from Socrates.

All the same, what can be read into Plato's own politics? Plato may not have cared for Athenian democracy, but the tyranny of his own aristocratic relatives had proven much worse. Reflecting his lived experience, the degeneration of the ideal state ends in democracy followed by tyranny. Long before the advent of psychoanalysis, he paints penetrating psychological portraits of the oligarch and tyrant, even tracing the greed of the oligarch back to childhood loss.

The ideal state has many parallels with Ancient Sparta, which had a small, specialized, and very successful class of warriors at its apex. When Socrates tells Adeimantus that an army of however many rich men would be no match for an army of however few trained warriors, Plato is almost certainly thinking of Sparta. But the Spartiates owned property, and, of course, were far from being philosophers.

The ideal state has been attacked, notably by Karl Popper (d. 1994), for being totalitarian— although there are also elements, especially among the guardians, of communism. This unusual, unique set-up aims to keep each class in check and functioning as it should. The banning of poetry as a form of uncritical imagination is even more radical than it sounds, since Homer was the Bible of the time, and poetry the basis of education. But the most surprising totalitarian aspect is not the censorship or even the eugenics, but the mythmaking, coming as it does from a philosopher who places truth on a pedestal. If justice in the state amounts to doing what we do best, or are told we do best, then this justice, the principle of specialization, trumps the truth. The principle of specialization not only creates harmony but helps to preserve it by ensuring that unsuitable people such as drones (unspecialized people) do not come to power.

When Adeimantus objects that people would be unhappy without the ability to enjoy luxuries, Socrates counters that the ideal state aims at the greatest happiness of all, and that, in any case, the guardians may well be happier for their deprivations. That he may be right is deeply thought provoking, especially in our materialistic age. Still today, monks and nuns make the positive choice to renounce the world and obey the rules.

Between the lines, the *Republic* also offers a 'philosophy of philosophy': a defence of philosophy, the philosopher, and the philosophical life. One argument that Socrates gives for the life of philosophy is that lovers of gain (like bankers) and lovers of honour (like politicians) may one day become lovers of wisdom, but never the other way round.

Only philosophers can have knowledge. Because they are absorbed in the Forms, their appetites are subdued, ensuring that they are virtuous with a virtue that stems from philosophy rather than mere civicism—although even civic virtue, in being harmonious, imitates the Forms. The true philosopher has no ulterior motive to rule (or indeed to write) other than seeking to replicate the harmony of the Forms.

Only by imitating or partaking in the Forms, that is, by being just and virtuous, can we be happy—even if, through bad luck, we may not be. Hence Themistocles' reply to the Seriphian: 'Had you been a native of my country or I of yours, neither of us would have been famous.' One purpose of the Myth of Er is to persuade us that, even though the virtuous might be unhappy in this life, they will fare better over several lives. Even if we cannot see it, in the long run we get exactly what we deserve.

When Plato first appeals to the Forms at the end of Book 5, he assumes that the reader is familiar with the concept. The universe is divided into that which is completely, that which is in no way, and that which both is and is not. That which is completely is the object of knowledge, that which is in no way is the object of ignorance, and that which both is and is not is the object of opinion. Only the Forms are completely, and only philosophers can grasp them. Thus, only philosophers can have knowledge. The influence of Parmenides (that which is completely, that which is in no way) and Heraclitus (that which both is and is not) in the metaphysics of the Forms is easily felt.

But now Plato introduces the elusive Form of the Good. As the Form of the Good is impossible to describe, and difficult to imagine, Socrates tries to convey its essence through three connected metaphors: the sun, line, and cave. The Good seems to be the source of all existence and knowledge, and yet to lie beyond them.

In the *Timaeus* (37c-e), Plato suggests that the Good is unity, or the One, while the universe exists in number, and, thus, in time and movement. The passage in question is the source of the famous misquotation, 'Time is the moving image of eternity.'

> When the father creator saw the creature which he had made moving and living, the created image of the eternal gods, he rejoiced, and in his joy determined to make the copy still more like the original; and as this was eternal, he sought to make the universe eternal, so far as it might be. Now the nature of the ideal being was everlasting, but to bestow this attribute in its fullness upon a creature was impossible. Wherefore he resolved to have a moving image of eternity, and when he set in order the heaven, he made this image eternal but moving according to number, while eternity itself rests in unity; and this image we call time.

Looking beyond the West, it seems to me that the Form of the Good is very similar to the Hindu concept of Brahman.

More generally, Ancient Greek philosophy is a lot closer to Indian philosophy than modern Western philosophy—which raises some interesting questions.

Just as Plato elaborates on the Forms, so he elaborates on the soul, which now has three parts. The tripartite soul mirrors the three classes of the ideal state: the rational, truth-loving part mirrors the guardians; the spirited, honour-loving part mirrors the auxiliaries; and the appetitive, pleasure-loving part mirrors the producers.

The tripartite soul seems to contradict the precept in the *Phaedo* that the soul is uncompounded, and therefore indissoluble and immortal. In the *Timaeus*, Plato is even more specific, locating the rational part, or *logos*, in the head, the *thymos* in the chest, and the *eros* in the gut.

The tripartite soul is prefigured in the *Phaedrus*: in the chariot allegory, the unruly horse corresponds to the *eros*, the tame horse to the *thymos*, and the charioteer to the *logos*.

Freud's structural and topographical models of the mind may 'on some level' have been influenced by the tripartite soul, with the id corresponding to the *eros*, the ego to the *thymos*, and the superego to the *logos*. The same might be said of Kierkegaard's three spheres of existence, with the aesthetic life corresponding to the *eros*, the ethical life to the *thymos*, and the religious life to the *logos*.

Another important theme in the *Republic* is education. Plato focuses on the education of the guardians because it is they who govern the *polis*. For the same reason, the guardians, and only the guardians, are barred from property and family, which may undermine or divide their loyalty to the state.

Plato's curriculum emphasizes the study of mathematics, which raises the mind from the visible realm of sensible particulars to the intelligible realm of the Forms. Also raising the mind is dialectic, although dialectic should not be taught to anyone under the age of thirty. Even if they pretend otherwise, young people (and most old people) are more interested in themselves than in the truth, so that dialectic for them becomes all about confirming their prejudices or winning the argument.

Under the rubric of education, Plato also discusses the love between man and boy, which is to be encouraged but not to be consummated. As per the *Phaedrus* and *Symposium*, love is the force that raises the mind from the sensible to the intelligible realm, and there are correspondences between the ladder of love and the divided line, which are both to be ascended. Love, like the Forms, is temperate and harmonious, but lust issues from the appetitive part of the soul.

There are also correspondences between the divided line and the journey out of the cave: the shadows in the cave correspond to imagination, the statues to perception, the real objects to reason, and the sun to understanding.

The purpose of education is to drag the prisoner as far out of the cave as possible; not merely to instil knowledge into his soul, but to turn his whole soul towards the light of the sun.

Knowledge without understanding is, at best, information; knowledge illuminated by understanding is wisdom.

18

THEAETETUS

*T*he *Theaetetus* is the founding treatise of epistemology, or theory of knowledge, and asks the question, 'What is knowledge [*epistēmē*]?'

The *Theaetetus* is a 'dialogue within a dialogue'. The short frame dialogue is set in Megara, about thirty years after the death of Socrates. Terpsion, who had been a follower of Socrates, runs into Euclid in front of the latter's house. Euclid tells Terpsion that he has just met with the injured and dying Theaetetus, who was being carried up to Athens from the army at Corinth.

Euclid recalls that Theaetetus, when very young, had conversed with an elderly Socrates, who had been impressed by the boy's character and intellect. Socrates related their conversation to Euclid, who wrote it down in the form of a direct dialogue. As Terpsion is keen to hear the dialogue, Euclid asks one of his slaves to read it out to them.

The dramatic date of this 'dialogue within a dialogue' is 399, since, at its end, Socrates says that he must be off to the porch

of the King Archon to 'meet Meletus and his indictment'. In
fact, if such internal references are reliable, the *Theaetetus* must
have taken place on the exact same day as the *Euthyphro*.

The *Theaetetus* probably stands as Plato's tribute to his friend
Theaetetus of Athens (417-369 BCE), who, like Plato, was a
student of Socrates' friend Theodorus of Cyrene. Among his
many achievements, Theaetetus demonstrated that there are
no more than five regular convex polyhedrals: tetrahedron,
cube, octahedron, dodecahedron, and icosahedron. In the
Timaeus, Plato associates each one with a classical element, so
that they are more commonly known as the Platonic solids.
Today, Theaetetus is also remembered by a lunar crater.

Going by his stated birth year of 417, Theaetetus would have
been a mere sixteen years old when he conversed with Socrates.

The Theaetetus

Socrates asks Theodorus about the Athenian youths. Is any one
of them showing signs of turning out well? Theodorus heaps
praise on Theaetetus, whom he describes as snub-nosed and
globe-eyed and outwardly similar to Socrates. Theodorus
beckons Theaetetus and Socrates offers to examine him.

Socrates says that to learn is to become wiser about that which
one is learning. What makes men wise is wisdom, which is the
same as knowledge, since the things that men know are the
things that they are wise about. But what exactly is knowledge?

Theaetetus replies that subjects such as geometry and music
are knowledge, as are crafts such as cobbling and carpentry.
Socrates points out that he asked what knowledge is, not what
one might have knowledge of: listing areas of knowledge is
neither necessary nor sufficient for a definition of knowledge.

Theaetetus contrasts his ease in defining mathematical terms with his difficulty in defining knowledge. He has long pondered the problem of knowledge and suffers from his lack of an adequate solution. Socrates tells him, 'These are the pangs of labour, my dear Theaetetus; you have something within you which you are bringing forth.'

Socrates goes on to compare himself to a midwife who works with men rather than women, and the soul rather than the body. Just as the midwife is beyond bearing age, so he too is barren—not of children, but of wisdom. All he can do is bring forth the wisdom of others and thoroughly examine it.

So, once again, can Theaetetus tell him: what is knowledge? Theaetetus replies that one who knows something is one who perceives what he knows: in short, knowledge is perception. Socrates claims that this was in fact the opinion of Protagoras, who held that 'man is the measure of all things'. But if one man feels cold in the wind, and another feels warm, must this mean that the wind is both warm and cold?

Protagoras must have put out his saying as a riddle for common people, while teaching a secret doctrine to his students, namely, that, since everything is in a state of becoming, nothing can truly be called warm or cold, or great or small, or heavy or light. Heraclitus, Empedocles, and everyone but the Eleatics agree with Protagoras that all things are in flux, and that flux and motion are the source of being and becoming. There are many ways in which this can be demonstrated. For instance, physical exertion is good for the body and study is good for the soul, whereas rest and idleness lead to wasting and forgetting.

Applying this doctrine to the senses, a given colour comes into being through the interaction of the eye and the object of perception, so that the colour is neither in the object nor in the eye but in something that has come into being in between

them, and which is private to the percipient. This explains why
colour does not appear the same from person to person, or
from person to animal, or even to the same person from
moment to moment. Yet, nothing can truly become different
unless it changes. For example, six dice may be more by half
than four, and fewer by half than twelve, but in either case
there are still six dice.

> Yes, Socrates, and I am amazed when I think of [these kinds of
> contradiction]; by the Gods I am! And I want to know what on
> earth they mean; and there are times when my head quite
> swims with the contemplation of them.

> I see, my dear Theaetetus, that Theodorus had a true insight
> into your nature when he said that you were a philosopher,
> for wonder is the feeling of a philosopher, and philosophy
> begins in wonder.

If, says Socrates, everything is just as it appears, how might one
account for dreams, madness, and illusions of the senses, which
give rise to false perceptions? Who is to say that we are not
asleep and our thoughts but a dream? Whenever one says that
a thing is or becomes, perhaps one ought to stipulate that it is
or becomes *in relation to something else*, rather than absolutely.

With this caveating, Theaetetus feels confident enough to
conclude that knowledge is perception, that we have knowledge
of what we perceive, and that what we perceive is true to us.

Socrates responds:

> Then this is the child which you and I have with difficulty
> brought into the world. And now that he is born, we must run
> the hearth with him, and see whether he is worth rearing, or
> is only a wind-egg and a sham.

Theodorus asks Socrates whether Theaetetus is correct. Socrates says that he is not 'a bag full of theories' and knows only enough to bring out the theories of others. However, he does offer a series of objections to the idea that knowledge is perception. For instance, if knowledge is perception, why should a pig or a 'dog-faced baboon' not also be the measure of all things? And why should Protagoras be any more correct than the majority who would contradict him? We are often said to know things (from memory) even though we are not currently perceiving them. Adverbs such as 'sharp' and 'dull' are often used to describe perceptions but not to describe knowledge, suggesting, yet again, that perception does not amount to knowledge.

Socrates regrets that Protagoras is no longer alive to defend his doctrine. Posing as Protagoras, he argues that one must attend to the meaning of terms as they are commonly employed. For instance, people who know things from memory can be said to 'perceive' those things. More pertinently, since there are no such things as false beliefs, one cannot be said to have true or false beliefs, but only good or bad beliefs. While all beliefs are true, not all beliefs are useful—the goal of education being to replace true but harmful beliefs with true and beneficial ones.

Socrates switches back to argue against his 'Protagoras'. If all beliefs are true, the ordinary belief that 'not all beliefs are true' must also be true—which is a paradox. Moreover, in arguing that truth is relative but the beneficial is absolute, 'Protagoras' has let slip that his theory is not general in its application.

Socrates embarks on a long digression in which he sets the orator apart from the philosopher, whom he portrays as an absent-minded stargazer. His purpose, it seems, is to contrast a life of relative expediency, which is mundane and miserable, with a life of absolute justice, which is divine and blissful.

> I mean to say, that those who have been trained in philosophy and liberal pursuits are as unlike those who from their youth upwards have been knocking in the courts and such places, as a freeman is in breeding unlike a slave.

Socrates picks up where he left off. The doctrine that 'man is the measure of all things' cannot be extended to judgements about the future, since things do not simply happen as one anticipates. In any case, if the Heraclitean doctrine does indeed pertain, everything is in a constant state of flux, so that nothing can be said of anything. Finally, the universal notions that we apply to the objects of perception, such as being and not-being, sameness and difference, and odd and even, are not themselves perceived by the sense organs, but built into the mind.

> Indeed, Socrates, I cannot answer; my only notion is, that these [universal notions], unlike objects of sense, have no separate organ, but that the mind, by a power of her own, contemplates the universals in all things.

> You are a beauty, Theaetetus, and not ugly, as Theodorus was saying; for he who utters the beautiful is himself beautiful and good. And besides being beautiful, you have done me a kindness in releasing me from a very long discussion, if you are clear that the soul views some things by herself and others through the bodily organs. For that was my opinion, and I wanted you to agree with me.

On this basis, Socrates suggests that knowledge consists not in sense perception, but in *reasoning* about sense perception.

⁓

Taking his cue from Socrates, Theaetetus offers that knowledge is belief, and more specifically *true* belief, since not all beliefs are knowledge.

If knowledge is true belief, how, asks Socrates, can there be such a thing as false belief? All things are either known or unknown, so that one cannot suppose to know what one does not, or not know what one does. Perhaps one could have a false belief in thinking of something that is not. However, if one who perceives something necessarily perceives something that is, it stands to reason that one who thinks of something necessarily thinks of something that is—so that one cannot think about something that is not. Or perhaps one could have a false belief by mistaking one thing for another. However, not even the mad try to persuade themselves that an ox is a horse, that two are one, or that the noble is base.

To address this problem of false belief, Socrates supposes that his memory is like a block of wax impressed with those things which he remembers and therefore knows.

- If he knows both Theaetetus and Theodorus and perceives neither, he cannot possibly form a false belief that the one is the other.
- If he knows either Theaetetus or Theodorus and perceives neither, he cannot possibly form a false belief that the one whom he knows is the one whom he does not.
- If he knows neither Theaetetus nor Theodorus and perceives neither, he cannot possibly form any false belief about them at all.

The only way that he can form a false belief about Theaetetus and Theodorus is by mismatching a perception of the one or the other to an impression on the block of wax. In other words, a false belief cannot result from a mismatch between two objects of perception, nor between two objects of thought, but only between one object of each type.

Unfortunately, this account excludes and even precludes certain false beliefs such as false beliefs about arithmetic which do not involve objects of perception.

To account for such false beliefs, Socrates compares the memory to an aviary with all kinds of birds, each one a separate piece of knowledge.

Once a bird has been entered into the aviary, retrieving it is a simple matter of catching it in the hand.

A false belief arises when the wrong bird is caught. For instance, if one thinks that 5 and 7 make 11, this is because one mistakenly caught 11 instead of 12, a pigeon instead of a ring-neck dove.

Unfortunately, this solution to the problem about confusing two things involves a regress, in which we are simply confusing another corresponding two things, birds for beliefs. Theaetetus helpfully suggests that the aviary may contain ignorance-birds as well as knowledge-birds. Even so, says Socrates, it would still be a matter of confusing birds.

Following these several attempts at explaining the possibility of false belief, Socrates offers a direct argument against the thesis that knowledge is true belief. Since an orator can bring one into a state of true belief (or correct opinion) without this being a state of knowledge, knowledge and true belief cannot be one and the same thing.

~

Theaetetus remembers having once heard that knowledge is true belief *with an account*.

Socrates tells of a dream that he had in which all was either a simple or a complex of simples. Whereas it is possible to provide an account of complexes in terms of their elements, no account can be given of the elements themselves. Thus, if knowledge is true belief with an account, knowledge can only be of complexes and not of simples, which, though they can be perceived, cannot be known.

Assuming that the dream theory is an accurate reflection of reality, a complex such as the first syllable of 'SOCRATES' is either no more than its elements, 'S' and 'O', or something over and above its elements. In the first instance, one cannot know the syllable without also knowing its elements, such that there can be no knowledge of complexes without prior knowledge of simples—which are, however, unknowable. In the second instance, one cannot know the syllable without also knowing something above and beyond its elements, such that its elements no longer suffice to define the syllable. In this case, the syllable is itself an element or 'single form', and therefore unknowable.

Although the dream suggested that there can be no knowledge of simples, ordinary experience suggests that it is more basic and important to learn elements such as letters and musical notes than complexes such as words and tunes.

Thus dismissing the dream, Socrates explores what might be meant by 'an account'. Perhaps an account consists simply in vocalizing one's thoughts, in which case anyone who vocalizes an accurate judgement could be counted to have knowledge. Or perhaps an account consists in a statement of the elements of the thing being accounted for, in which case anyone able to string out the letters in 'Theaetetus' in their correct order could be counted to have knowledge of 'Theaetetus'. Or, more likely, an account consists in marking out the thing being accounted for from all other things [by providing its *sêmeion* or *diaphora*, its sign or difference, or diagnostic feature], for instance, marking out the sun from all other things by saying that it is the brightest object in the sky.

However, if knowledge of the sun requires it to be marked out from all other things, so does mere true belief, if it is not to be true belief about something else. Thus, knowledge of the sun requires us not merely to form a true belief about the sun, but to *know* it, so that knowledge would amount to true belief + knowledge—which is circular!

Socrates concludes that knowledge is neither perception, nor true belief, nor justified true belief.

> And are you still in labour and travail, my dear friend, or have you brought all that you have to say about knowledge to the birth?
>
> I am sure, Socrates, that you have elicited from me a good deal more than ever was in me.
>
> And does not my art show that you have brought forth wind, and that the offspring of your brain are not worth bringing up?
>
> ...
>
> But if, Theaetetus, you should ever conceive afresh, you will be all the better for the present investigation, and if not, you will be soberer and humbler and gentler to other men, and will be too modest to fancy that you know what you do not.

Commentary

In this dense, difficult, and rather dry dialogue, Theaetetus offers four definitions of knowledge, all of which end up being rejected by Socrates. The first definition, in which he merely lists areas of knowledge, is not strictly a definition, although, unlike Meno, he is quick to understand what is being asked of him. The next three are proper definitions: knowledge as perception, knowledge as true belief, and knowledge as true belief with an account.

Socrates compares Theaetetus's perplexity to the pangs of labour, and himself to a midwife who brings forth the wisdom in others. This midwifery of the mind, called maieutics [*maia*, midwife], is often assimilated with the Socratic method, but whereas the Socratic method aims at aporia, the maieutic method aims more properly at hypothesis generation. Thus, the *Theaetetus*, even though it ends in aporia, is more of an experimental or exploratory dialogue than an aporetic one. It is no coincidence that Theaetetus is a model of humility and perplexity: because he begins in aporia, he is an ideal candidate for the more positive, collaborative maieutic method. We should all aim to be like Theaetetus.

Socrates' response to Theaetetus' bewilderment after the discussion of the Protagorean and Heraclitean doctrines includes one of the most quoted lines in all of Plato: '...for wonder is the feeling of a philosopher, and philosophy begins in wonder.' In the *Metaphysics*, Aristotle says that it is wonder that led the first philosophers to philosophy, since a man who is puzzled thinks of himself as ignorant and philosophizes to escape from his ignorance. Notice that this kind of puzzlement or perplexity is not the same as the wonder excited by grand vistas, circus tricks, and the like, which can be experienced even by young children and higher-order primates. The rarer and more rarefied wonder of the philosopher, also known as Socratic wonder, is not so much wonder in the sense of awe as wonder in the sense of broken knowledge. I discuss wonder, including Socratic wonder, at greater length in *Heaven and Hell*.

When Theaetetus offers that knowledge is perception, Socrates is quick to assimilate this thesis with Protagoras' *homo-mensura* ['man the measure'] doctrine, which he presents as a position of radical truth relativism. Having painted him into a corner, Socrates is charitable to 'Protagoras', introducing the radical reality relativism of Heraclitus as an ontological underpinning for the perceptual infallibility that the Protagorean doctrine appears to entail (even though this is almost certainly not the 'secret doctrine' of Protagoras). Later, Socrates goes so far as to put himself into Protagoras' sandals to defend his position from his imagined perspective, although this only ends up damning him further.

Even if the relativism of Protagoras and Heraclitus does apply to sense perception, there is more to knowledge than sense perception. Once this has been recognized, the thesis that knowledge is perception leads to all manner of absurdity. There is more to knowledge that what is in front of us, and it is in this cognitive space and cognitive distancing that knowledge resides. This understanding prompts Theaetetus to redefine knowledge as true belief, and, later, as true belief with an account [*meta logou alêthê doxan*, or justified true belief].

It is striking that these attempts to define knowledge do not explicitly make use of the Forms, not even in their discussion. In earlier dialogues such as the *Phaedo*, *Phaedrus*, and *Republic*, Socrates keenly and creatively expounds on the Forms, which he presents as the source of all knowledge. Could Plato by now have abandoned the Forms? After the *Republic*, Plato probably wrote the *Parmenides*, followed by the *Theaetetus*. In the

Parmenides, 'Parmenides' attacks the Theory of the Forms with five successive arguments which may have hit their mark. Whereas the *Phaedo*, *Phaedrus*, and *Republic* are brimming with bold and colourful schemes, the *Theaetetus* harks back to the early aporetic dialogues in which Socrates and his interlocutors attempt, and fail, to define a particular concept—marking a return, perhaps, to the Plato of before the Forms.

Alternatively, the *Theaetetus* may represent a bid to bolster, or salvage, the Theory of the Forms by showing how rival accounts of knowledge fall short. If Plato did have serious doubts about the Forms, writing the *Theaetetus* may have served to assuage them. Some of Socrates' arguments are hasty, not to say poor, so that Plato appears to be orchestrating an aporetic climax, or anticlimax, in which he and the reader are left crying out for the Forms. None of the three accounts of 'an account' are the favoured one given in the *Meno*, 'an account of the reason why'. There are several junctures at which the Forms seem to suggest themselves, even though Socrates holds back from discussing them. Whatever Plato might have been feeling about the Forms, the *Theaetetus* represents his attempt to do epistemology without recoursing to them.

The *Theaetetus* is explicitly connected to two later dialogues, the *Sophist* and the *Statesman*, which are both set on the morrow of the conversation in the *Theaetetus*. Theodorus and Theaetetus introduce Socrates to an Eleatic Stranger who, unusually, does most of the talking. In the *Sophist*, the Eleatic Stranger employs the method of collection and division to define and describe the sophist and distinguish him from the statesman and philosopher. In the *Statesman*, he does the same for the statesman. The continuity with the *Theaetetus* is not merely in the cast, timing, and setting, but also in the theme, since the sophist, statesman, and philosopher each embody a particular kind of knowledge.

PART IV

ARISTOTLE

If someone asked me what book I think everyone should read, I would reply without hesitation, Aristotle's *Nicomachean Ethics*. Its subject is quite simply, how best to live. This section outlines all of Aristotle's major works, but covers the *Nicomachean Ethics* in more depth than the rest. Aristotle spent almost twenty years in Plato's folds, before emerging as Plato's greatest critic: 'Plato is my friend' he said, 'but truth is a greater friend still.' Comparing and contrasting these two towering figures is a source of endless fascination.

LIFE, BIOLOGY, AND WORKS

*A*ristotle was born in 384 BCE in Stageira, on the Chalcidice peninsula of north-eastern Greece. In 348, Philip II of Macedon occupied and destroyed the city, but then had it rebuilt and repopulated in honour of Aristotle, who had been his childhood friend, and whom he had appointed to tutor his son, Alexander, the future King of the *Oikouménē*, or Known World.

The Stagirite's father, Nicomachus, served as physician to Philip's father, Amyntas III of Macedon, and descended, purportedly, from the god of medicine, Asclepius—as did his mother, Phæstis. With the healing arts running so thickly in his blood, Aristotle would have been expected to follow in his father's footsteps. Certainly, his medical background, and the empiricism of physicians such as Hippocrates (d. c. 370 BCE), informed his method and philosophy.

Aristotle had a sister, Arimneste, and a brother, Arimnestus. The symmetry of these names, which both mean 'Greatly remembered' or 'Everlasting memory', suggests that Aristotle may have been the youngest of the three siblings.

At the age of about thirteen, Aristotle lost both his parents, and became the ward of Proxenus of Atarneus (in Æolis, Asia Minor), who rounded whatever medical training he had received from his late father.

Arimneste married Proxenus, and from this union came a daughter, Hero, and a son, Nicanor. Hero in turn had a son, the historian Callisthenes of Olynthus, great nephew to Aristotle.

In 367, Proxenus sent the seventeen-year-old Aristotle to study at Plato's Academy, which had by then become a pre-eminent centre of learning. If Diogenes Laertius is to be believed, the grown-up Aristotle had small eyes and slender calves, dressed fashionably, and spoke with a lisp.

Aristotle remained at the Academy for nearly twenty years, only leaving after Plato's death in 347. The reasons for his departure are unclear: he may have felt slighted at being passed over for the scholarchship of the Academy in favour of Plato's nephew, Speussipus; or he may have fled, possibly even before Plato's death, for fear of the growing anti-Macedonian feeling. In 351, the orator Demosthenes had delivered his First Philippic denouncing Philip II's imperial ambitions, and in 348, the year before Plato's death, Philip had razed Athenian ally Olynthus to the ground.

Then in his thirty-seventh year, Aristotle travelled with fellow Platonist Xenocrates of Chalcedon to Assos (in the Troad, Asia Minor) to join the court of Hermias of Atarneus, who had studied at the Academy. Aristotle may or may not have gone to Assos as an ambassador of Philip, who wished to have Hermias for an ally. In either case, it seems that he exerted a moderating influence on Hermias, who softened his harsh tyrannical rule —enabling him, in short succession, to win over neighbouring peoples and expand his territory.

In 344, Hermias was captured by a mercenary in the service of Artaxerxes III of Persia and tortured for information about the invasion plans of his ally Philip. But Hermias held his silence, his dying words being that he had done nothing shameful or unworthy of philosophy. Aristotle honoured the memory of his perfect friend with a statue at Delphi and a still extant hymn to virtue. At around this time, he married Hermias' niece and adoptive daughter, Pythias, who helped him in his work and bore him a daughter, also Pythias.

After the death of Hermias, Aristotle and his student Tyrtamus crossed over to Lesbos to research the flora and fauna of the island and its remarkable lagoon, then known as the Pyrrha lagoon, now known as the Gulf of Kalloni. Tyrtamus went down in history as Theophrastus ['Divinely-speaking'], the nickname given to him by Aristotle. Supposedly, the more empirical Theophrastus concentrated on the flora while the more speculative Aristotle concentrated on the fauna, so that the one is remembered as the father of botany and the other as the father of zoology. In fact, Theophrastus also wrote on animals, and Aristotle on plants, but these works have been lost, as have almost all of Theophrastus' wide-ranging works.

It would reward us to tarry on Aristotle's relatively early biological works, which represent the first systematic study of biology and reveal a great deal about the man and his method. These works are usually ignored, though they make up a quarter of his extant corpus, and were revered by naturalists such as Georges Cuvier and Charles Darwin—who, in the year of his death, 1882, wrote to William Ogle that 'although Linnaeus and Cuvier have been my two gods ... they were mere schoolboys to old Aristotle.'

Aristotle accompanied his *History of Animals* (a somewhat misleading title, cf. 'natural history') with a now lost book of anatomical drawings. His other biological writings are the *Parts of Animals*, *Movement of Animals*, *Progression of Animals*, and *Generation of Animals*, as well as *On the Soul* and seven shorter works collectively known as the *Parva Naturalia*.

On the Soul may seem out of place, until one remembers that the very word 'animal' [*anima*] means 'having breath' or 'having soul'. The soul, says Aristotle, is the principle of life, and the knowledge of it contributes greatly to our understanding of nature and truth in general. *On the Soul* includes a detailed discussion of the senses and established our notion of the 'five senses', with Aristotle explicitly stating that 'there is no sixth sense in addition to the five enumerated'.

In his biological works, Aristotle outlines more than five hundred species, some in more detail than others. He describes the chambered stomachs of ruminants, the social organization of bees, and the embryological development of a chick. He notices that some sharks are viviparous, and that whales and dolphins differ from other fish in breathing air and suckling their young. He infers that brood size decreases with body mass, whereas gestation period, and overall lifespan, increases. In a playful by the way, he remarks that 'after drinking wine, the Indian parrot becomes more saucy than ever'.

For centuries, some of Aristotle's accounts seemed too fanciful to be true, for instance, that the young of a dogfish grow inside their mother's body, that the male of the river catfish guards the eggs for forty or fifty days after the female has left, or that male octopuses have a sperm-transferring tentacle that sometimes snaps off during mating. Each of these wonders of the world had to wait until the nineteenth century to be confirmed.

Unlike Plato, Aristotle privileged observation over speculation. Like our scientists, he began with a systematic gathering of data, from which he attempted to infer explanations and make predictions. He carried out dissections and even rudimentary experiments such as cutting out the heart of a turtle to discover that it could still move its limbs for a surprisingly long time.

However, he did not carry out anything like modern case-control studies, and relied uncritically on the lay testimony of beekeepers, fishermen, travellers, and the like. This lack of rigour led to some embarrassing errors, such as the claim that lions copulate back-to-back, while bears adopt the missionary position and hedgehogs stand on their hind legs to face each other. Or the claim that the female of several species has fewer teeth than the male. Among these species, he included humans, when he could simply have looked into Pythias' mouth (wife or daughter).

Aristotle was not simply doing biology for the sake of biology, but for the sake of philosophy. Like Plato, he was searching for universals, but this time from the ground up. 'We should' he said, 'venture on the study of every kind of animal without distaste; for each and all will reveal to us something natural and something beautiful.'

An animal gives birth to the same animal because of its form [*eidos*] or ordering pattern—an idea that resonates with modern genetics. The male supplies the form, which is also the soul, in his semen, while the female provides the material in her menses. When the semen meets the menses, they congeal into an egg or embryo 'like fig juice which curdles milk'. If the semen fails to 'master the menses', a female is born. The soul is not superadded or even supervenient, but corresponds to the animal's ordering pattern and dynamic processes. Aristotle's interest in biology informs his theory of the form, which in turn informs his entire physics and metaphysics (Chapter 23).

All beings, from minerals to plants and animals, have a form, the potential of which determines their position on the eleven-rung *scala naturae*, or great chain of being. The Church adapted the concept of a great chain of being, which later helped to justify slavery, colonization, and evangelization. Plants have a vegetative soul, capable of growth and reproduction. Animals, as well as a vegetative soul, have a sensitive soul, capable of sensation and movement, and hence of desire and imagination. Humans, uniquely, also have a rational soul, capable of thought and reflection. Contra Plato, the soul inheres in the organism, and dies with it—except for the rational soul, which, being a part of God, is immortal. Thought cannot die, since, unlike all else, it is not the function of a particular organ—the brain and the lungs being, in Aristotle's view, mere radiators for the heart, which is the site of the internal fire and the seat of intelligence, motion, and sensation.

Although he held that all beings have a form, and that the form is injected by the male (a male being defined as 'an animal that breeds inside another'), Aristotle also believed that many lower animals spontaneously generate: that eels grow out of mud, and insect maggots from putrefying flesh, even though Homer had said otherwise—when, in *Iliad* XIX, Achilles fears that flies will 'breed worms' in the corpse of Patroclus. To be fair to Aristotle, he had observed that eels have no gonads, and could hardly have guessed that they only develop them in the course of their epic migration to the Sargasso Sea. The earliest challenge to spontaneous generation came as late as 1668, when Francesco Redi covered jars of rotting flesh with gauze and found that only the controls, that is, the uncovered jars, grew maggots.

Figure 14. The Great Chain of Being.
From Retorica Christiana, *by Didacus Valades (1579).*

Aristotle was not a Darwinist nor even a Creationist, but an
eternalist who believed that the plants and animals before him
had always existed and would always exist. One argument that
he gives for eternalism is that, if motion had a beginning, this
beginning must itself have resulted from a movement, which is
a paradox. Although he privileged observation over theory, his
eternalism, albeit logically held, blinded him to the significance
of the petrified forest of Lesbos, which would have confronted
him with fossilized trees from millions of years ago.

Such are the main lines of Aristotle's biology and associated philosophy. Many of his inferences have not stood the test of time. Salacious animals do not age more quickly than continent ones. Hair is not grown at the expense of semen, even if women and eunuchs don't grow bald. And it is not because they lack fatness that bloodless animals are shorter lived than sanguineous ones.

But was the beginning of science not bound to look like this? And is it not remarkable that we can still read its record?

Aristotle spent no more than two years on Lesbos. In 343, King Philip commissioned him to tutor his son Alexander, who was then around thirteen years old, promising in return to rebuild his native Stageira and repatriate its former citizens. In the Temple of the Nymphs at Mieza, near the Macedonian capital of Pela, Aristotle taught not only Alexander but also his close friend or lover Hephæstion, and two other future rulers, Ptolemy and Cassander.

It is said that Aristotle prepared for Alexander an annotated copy of the *Iliad*, which inspired the prince to model his life on that of the demy-divine Achilles. Even if the story is invented, Aristotle's influence over Alexander is indicated by the crowd of zoologists and botanists that accompanied him on his Eastern conquests, and by the official chronicler of these conquests, who was none other than Aristotle's great nephew, Callisthenes of Olynthus.

According to both Plutarch and Aulus Gellius, upon hearing that Aristotle had published some of his teachings, Alexander wrote to him from Asia:

Alexander to Aristotle, greeting. You have not done well to publish your books of oral doctrine; for what is there now that we excel others in, if those things which we have been particularly instructed in be laid open to all? For my part, I assure you, I had rather excel others in the knowledge of what is excellent, than in the extent of my power and dominion. Farewell.

Later, as pharaoh in Egypt, Ptolemy built the Great Library of Alexandria, turning the city, which had been founded by Alexander, into a major centre of learning. Alexander, and Ptolemy after him, did much to disseminate Greek culture, so that three centuries later Greek seemed like the natural choice of language for the New Testament.

In around 339, Speussipus suffered a stroke and died, and Xenocrates became the third scholarch of the Academy, with Aristotle passed over for a second time. Among those who frequented the lectures of Xenocrates at the Academy were Zeno of Citium, founder of the Stoic school, and Epicurus of Samos, founder of the Epicurean school.

In 334, Aristotle, now returned to Athens, established his own school in a public exercise and training ground dedicated to the god Apollo Lyceus ['Apollo the Wolf-god'], whence its name, the Lyceum. A temple had once stood on the expansive site, which in Aristotle's time had different areas dedicated to different purposes. Both Socrates and Plato had spoken or taught there, to the extent that the Lyceum is the setting of Plato's *Euthydemus*, which features Socrates and Cleinias, the grandson of Alcibiades, in conversation with Euthydemus and Dionysodorus, a pair of moronic brothers and sophists.

Aristotle taught in the morning, and in the afternoon would sometimes give a public lecture. He often did his thinking and teaching while walking along the Lyceum's shaded paths, or *peripatoi*, so that his students, who doubled up as his colleagues and researchers, came to be known as the peripatetics.

Over the next twelve years, Aristotle wrote many of his works and collected the West's first great library, including copies of the constitutions of 158 cities. He also developed the world's first botanical garden and zoological park from the plant and animal specimens that Alexander kept returning from the East.

After the death of his wife Pythias, he became involved with Herpyllis of Stageira, who bore him a son whom he named Nicomachus after his father. To this son, he dedicated his major work of ethics, the *Nicomachean Ethics* (Chapter 20). According to the Suda, he also had an *eromenos*, the historian Palæphatus of Abydus.

Aristotle's school lived or limped on until 86 BCE, when Athens was sacked by Sulla, the only man in history to have occupied both Athens and Rome. According to Plutarch, Sulla felled the ancient planes of the Academy and Lyceum to build siege engines. In antiquity, the Lyceum had stood to the east of the city wall. In 1996, its remains were uncovered in a park behind the Hellenic Parliament, while clearing space for the new Museum of Modern Art.

In the East, Callisthenes had become increasingly critical of Alexander's adoption of Persian customs, especially those, such as proskynesis (falling down before the king and kissing the ground or his feet), which fed into his mounting megalomania.

When a former pupil implicated Callisthenes in a regicidal plot, Alexander left Aristotle's great nephew to perish in prison. According to Diogenes Laertius, Callisthenes was 'confined in an iron cage and carried about until he became infested with vermin through lack of proper attention; and finally he was thrown to a lion and so met his end.' The death of his great nephew soured Aristotle's relationship with Alexander, and prompted Theophrastus to write a treatise on grief, the now lost *Callisthenes*.

Even so, Aristotle's long-time association with Alexander had led the Athenians to perceive him as Macedonian. After Alexander's death in Babylon in 323, anti-Macedonian feeling in Athens flared up, and Demophilius and Eurymedon the Hierophant charged Aristotle with impiety, possibly for praying to his late friend Hermias rather than anything in the *Physics* or *Metaphysics*. Aristotle fled to the solitude, or loneliness, of his country house at Chalcis in Eubœa, an island off the Attic coast and the homeland of his mother's family. Referencing the trial and execution of Socrates, he explained, 'I will not allow the Athenians to sin twice against philosophy.'

In the event, Aristotle died within the year, in 322, aged sixty-two, possibly from an abdominal condition. Theophrastus, who was not Macedonian but Lesbian, had remained in Athens as scholarch of the peripatetic school. In his will, Aristotle named him as his successor and bequeathed him his works and library. On the family side, he left a furnished house, three female slaves, and a talent of silver to his wife or concubine Herpyllis. And he appointed his nephew Nicanor as guardian to the still young Nicomachus. Nicomachus became a pupil of Theophrastus and, according to Aristippus, his *eromenos*. He died in battle while still young.

Cicero, himself one of the greatest stylists of antiquity, lauded Plato's mellifluous dialogues, but then added that, if Plato's prose was silver, that of Aristotle was 'a flowing river of gold'.

This may come as a surprise to modern readers of Aristotle, whose prose often seems poor.

Since it is difficult to doubt Cicero, it can only be assumed that he had before him works that have since been lost, such as the dialogues that Aristotle is known to have written early in his career, probably while still at the Academy. These 'exoteric' dialogues were intended for publication, to be read and enjoyed by non-specialists.

The few fragments that remain suggest that the exoteric dialogues resembled the works of Plato, both in style and substance.

For instance, in his invitation to philosophy, the *Protrepticus* [*protrépō*, 'to urge upon'], Aristotle portrays the soul's yoking to the body as a punishment for some original sin, comparing it to the Etruscan practice of chaining captives face to face with the dead. This reprising of the *Phaedo* is far removed from his later account of the soul in *On the Soul*. The *Protrepticus* inspired and informed Cicero's also lost *Hortensius*, which became even more famous for being in Latin.

Other lost Aristotelian works have such alluring titles as *Concerning Love, Of Wealth, Of Friendship, On the Beautiful, On Pleasure, On Kingship, On Medicine, On Drunkenness*... Theophrastus even wrote one *On Honey*.

My dearest fantasy is for these works, or at least some of them, to be recovered. No doubt they are lying buried somewhere, if only we knew where.

The second part of the *Poetics*, which addressed laughter and comedy, has been lost in all but name, and is the rose, or one of the roses, in Umberto Eco's *Name of the Rose* (1980). The novel's last line, which is a variation of a verse in Bernard of Cluny's *Contemptu mundi,* reads, *Stat rosa pristina nomine, nomina nuda tenemus*: 'The rose of old remains only in its name; we possess naked names.'

In his *Lives*, Diogenes Laertius catalogues over 150 works by Aristotle. Only about 29 have come down to us, none of which seem to have been intended for publication. This so-called *Corpus Aristotelicum*, which still amounts to around a million words, consists of esoteric treatises intended for inner circle use. These probably originated as lecture notes or student texts, which were then reworked and rearranged over the years. Although their prose is unadorned, this does not usually detract from their philosophical content, and some scholars even come to admire them, or parts of them, for their compressed clarity.

According to Plutarch and Strabo, Theophrastus bequeathed Aristotle's esoteric writings to his student Neleus, who removed them to his native Scepsis. Neleus' heirs hid them from the bibliophilic Pergamon kings in a cellar, to be discovered some two hundred years later by the famous book collector Apellicon of Teos. Apellicon repatriated the dilapidated manuscripts to Athens, wherefrom Sulla, who occupied Athens in 86 BCE, removed them to Rome. In Rome, they were recopied, and then edited and published by Andronicus of Rhodes, the eleventh and last scholarch of the Lyceum. Although the tale seems breathless, it is mostly accepted that the current arrangement of the *Corpus Aristotelicum* owes to Andronicus.

Aristotle referred to the branches of learning as 'sciences', and divided them into three groups: practical sciences, productive sciences, and theoretical sciences. Practical sciences are concerned with right action and beautiful behaviour both at the level of the individual, as in ethics, and at the level of the community or society, as in politics. Productive sciences are concerned with products or outcomes as broadly conceived, and include, among many others, agriculture, architecture, medicine, music, and rhetoric. Theoretical sciences are concerned with knowledge for the sake of knowledge and comprise both natural sciences and non-empirical forms of knowledge such as mathematics and metaphysics.

Logic, that is, the branch of learning that is concerned with the principles of intellectual inquiry, does not fit into this tripartite division of the sciences, but underpins them all, and stands alone and apart under the heading of *Organon* or 'Tool'.

The works in the *Corpus Aristotelicum* can be classified under those four headings. Not all the works are considered genuine, and the following list includes only those that are. The works are referred to by their English titles, but scholars often use their Latin titles or standard abbreviations, which are also given. Any part of the text can be referenced by a Bekker number, named after August Immanuel Bekker, editor of the Prussian Academy of Sciences edition in Greek of the complete works of Aristotle. Bekker numbers are based on the page numbers of the Bekker edition and take the format of up to four digits, followed by a letter for column 'a' or 'b', and then the line number. For instance, the first line of *On the Soul* is given by 402a1, which corresponds to the first line of the first column on page 402 of the Bekker edition. The equivalent numbering system for the *Corpus Platonicum* is the Stephanus pagination (Chapter 13).

Practical Sciences

- Nicomachean Ethics [*Ethica Nicomachea*, EN]
- Eudemian Ethics [*Ethica Eudemia*, EE]
- Politics [*Politica*, Pol.]

Productive Sciences

- Rhetoric [*Ars rhetorica*, Rhet.]
- Poetics [*Ars poetica*, Poet.]

Theoretical Sciences

- Physics [*Physica*, Phys.]
- Metaphysics [*Metaphysica*, Met.]
- On the Heavens [*De cælo*, DC]
- Generation and Corruption [*De generatione et corruptione*, Gen. et Corr.]
- Meteorology [*Meteorologica*, Meteor.]
- History of Animals [*Historia animalium*, HA]
- Parts of Animals [*De partibus animalium*, PA]
- Movement of Animals [*De motu animalium*, MA]
- Progression of Animals [*De incessu animalium*, LA]
- Generation of Animals [*De generatione animalium*, GA]
- On the Soul [*De Anima*, DA]
- Brief Natural Treatises [*Parva naturalia*, PN]:

Sense and Sensibilia
On Memory
On Sleep
On Dreams
On Divination in Sleep

On Length and Shortness of Life
On Youth, Old Age, Life and Death, and Respiration

Organon

- Categories [*Categorie*, Cat.]
- On Interpretation [*De interpretatione*, DI]
- Prior Analytics [*Analytica priora*, APr]
- Posterior Analytics [*Analytica posteriora*, APo]
- Topics [*Topica*, Top.]
- Sophistical Refutations [*De sophisticis elenchis*, SE]

20

PRACTICAL SCIENCES
ETHICS AND POLITICS

*W*hen people refer to Aristotle's *Ethics*, they usually mean the ten-book *Nicomachean Ethics*, which is arguably the best treatise on ethics ever written.

The *Nicomachean Ethics* seems like a later and more developed reprisal of Aristotle's other ethical treatise, the eight-book *Eudemian Ethics*, named for Aristotle's student, Eudemus of Rhodes. In fact, Books 5, 6, and 7 of the *Nicomachean Ethics* are identical to Books 4, 5, and 6 of the *Eudemian Ethics*—suggesting that the *Nicomachean Ethics* may have been compiled or pieced together from various ethical writings.

Aristotle's *Ethics*, which seeks to determine the nature of human happiness, is closely connected to his *Politics*, which, in eight more books, seeks to determine the form of government that might maximise this happiness.

What follows are outlines of the *Ethics* and the *Politics*, which I'll discuss in the round at the end of the chapter.

Nicomachean Ethics

A thing is best understood by looking at its end, purpose, or goal [*telos*]. For example, the purpose of a knife is to cut, and it is by seeing this that one best understands what a knife is; the goal of medicine is good health, and it is by seeing this that one best understands what medicine is (or ought to be).

Now, if one does this for some time, it becomes clear that some goals are subordinate to other goals, which are themselves subordinate to yet other goals. For example, a medical student's goal may be to qualify as a doctor, but this goal is subordinate to his goal to heal the sick, which is itself subordinate to his goal to make a living by doing something useful. This could go on and on, but unless the medical student has a goal that is an end-in-itself, nothing that he does is inherently worth doing.

What is this goal that is an end-in-itself? People agree that the chief good is *eudaimonia* [happiness, success, flourishing] but disagree as to its nature. The many identify happiness with sensual pleasure, but a life of sensual pleasure is no better than that of a beast. Finer people identify it with honour, but honour is merely a mark of virtue [*arete*, also, 'excellence'], and beholden to the vagaries of opinion. Neither can it be virtue itself, or else it would be compatible with a lifetime of sleep or inactivity, or with the greatest sufferings and misfortunes.

According to Plato, there is such a thing as the Form of the Good in which all good things share. Aristotle raises eight objections to the Theory of the Forms but claims that this is not the proper place to investigate it. He revisits the subject in the more theoretical *Metaphysics*. This passage contains the oft quoted line, 'Plato is my friend, but truth is a greater friend still,' or words to that effect.

A goal that is an end-in-itself is worthier than one that is merely a means to an end, but worthiest of all is the goal that is only ever an end-in-itself.

> Now such a thing happiness, above all else, is held to be; for this we choose always for itself and never for the sake of something else, but honour, pleasure, reason, and every virtue we choose indeed for themselves (for if nothing results from them we should still choose each of them), but we choose them also for the sake of happiness, judging that by means of them we shall by happy. Happiness, on the other hand, no one chooses for the sake of these, nor, in general, for anything other than itself.

All well and good, but what is happiness?

It is by understanding the distinctive function of a thing that one can understand its essence. For example, one cannot understand what it is to be a gardener unless one understands that the distinctive function of a gardener is something like, 'to tend to a garden with a certain degree of skill.' Whereas humans need nourishment like plants and have sentience like animals, their distinctive function is their unique capacity to reason. Thus, our supreme good, or happiness, is to lead a life that enables us to use and develop our reason, and that is in accordance with reason.

Unlike amusement or pleasure, which can be enjoyed also by pigs, happiness is not a state but an activity [*energeia*]. It is not the merely strong and beautiful who are crowned at the Olympic Games, but those who perform well. Similarly, it is not the merely wise and virtuous who win the good and noble things in life, but those who act well. The life of those who act well is in any case more pleasant, since virtuous actions are by nature pleasant, and all the more so to the lover of virtue.

Now, for most men their pleasures are in conflict with one
another because these are not by nature pleasant, but the
lovers of what is noble find pleasant the things that are by
nature pleasant; and virtuous actions are such, so that these
are pleasant for such men as well as in their own nature.
Their life, therefore, has no further need of pleasure as a sort
of adventitious charm, but has its pleasure in itself.

True, our good or bad fortune can play a part in determining
our happiness. For instance, our happiness might be affected
by our material circumstances, our place in society, even our
physical appearance. Yet, by living life to the full according to
our essential nature as rational beings, we are bound to become
happy regardless of our good or bad fortune. Thus, happiness is
more a question of behaviour and habit—of excellence and
virtue—than of luck. A person who cultivates reason and lives
rationally can bear his misfortunes with equanimity, and thus
can never be said to be truly unhappy.

The soul has a rational and an irrational part. The irrational
part has a vegetative element concerned with nutrition and
growth, and an appetitive, impulsive element that more or less
obeys the rational part. Similarly, there are two kinds of virtue,
one that pertains to intellect [*dianoia*] and another that pertains
to character [*ethos*, the root of 'ethics'].

Book 2: The golden mean

Intellectual virtues are developed by instruction, while moral
virtues are developed by habit. Unlike sight and hearing, which
are given to us, moral virtues are not in our nature. But neither
are they contrary to our nature, which is adapted to receive
them. Just as a sculptor becomes a sculptor by sculpting, so the
virtuous become virtuous by exercising virtue.

One cannot define virtue with any precision, as the goodness of a feeling or action is highly person- and context-dependent. What can be said is that virtue, like strength, is undermined by a lack or excess of training. For instance, he who flees from everything becomes a coward, while he who runs headlong into every danger becomes rash. Courage, in contrast, is indicated and produced by the mean.

Moral excellence is related to pleasure and pain. It is in the pursuit of pleasure and avoidance of pain that bad deeds are committed, and good deeds omitted. Hence, it is by pleasure and pain that bad people are bad. There are three objects of choice, the noble, the advantageous, and the pleasant, and three objects of avoidance which are their contraries, the base, the injurious, and the painful. The good tend to go right about these, whereas the bad tend to go wrong. This is especially true of pleasure, which is common to the animals, and also contained in the advantageous and the noble. The good feel pleasure at the most beautiful [*kalos*] actions, but the bad or not-good are often confused about what is most pleasant. It is harder to fight with pleasure than with anger, but virtue, like art, is concerned with what is harder, and the good is better when it is harder.

A person may perform an apparently virtuous action by chance or under duress. An action is only virtuous if it is recognized as being virtuous and performed for that sake by a person with a set, unvarying character. In sum, an action is only virtuous if it is such as a virtuous person would perform.

Three things are found in the soul: passions, faculties, and dispositions [*hexeis*]. As the virtues are neither feelings nor faculties, they must be dispositions: dispositions to aim at the intermediate, or mean, between deficiency and excess.

Hitting this mark is a form of success and worthy of praise. While it is possible to fail in many ways, it is possible to succeed in one way only, which is why the one is easy and the other is difficult. By the same token, men may be bad in many ways, but good in one way only.

So far so good, except that not every passion or action admits of a mean, for instance, not envy or murder. It is never a question of murdering the right person, at the right time, in the right way, for murder is neither a deficiency nor an excess but always and intrinsically vicious.

The principal virtues along with their corresponding vices are listed in Table 1.

In some cases, one vice can be closer to the virtue than the contrary vice, for instance, rashness is closer to courage than cowardice, and prodigality closer to liberality than meanness. This is partly because the contrary vice, whether cowardice or meanness, is the more common. Hence, people oppose not rashness but cowardice to courage, and not prodigality but meanness to liberality.

It is no easy task to be good. To increase the likelihood of hitting the mark, we should (1) avoid the vice that is furthest from the virtue or mean; (2) consider our vices and drag ourselves towards their contrary extremes; and (3) be wary of pleasure and pain.

> For in everything it is no easy task to find the middle ...
> anyone can get angry—that is easy—or give or spend money;
> but to do this to the right person, to the right extent, at the
> right time, with the right motive, and in the right way, that is
> not for everyone, nor is it easy; wherefore goodness is both
> rare and laudable and noble.

Table 1: The principal virtues and vices			
Sphere of feeling or action	Excess (vice)	Mean (virtue)	Deficiency (vice)
Fear and confidence	Rashness	Courage	Cowardice
Pleasures and pains	Self-indulgence	Temperance	Insensibility (rare)
Getting and spending (minor)	Prodigality	Liberality	Meanness
Getting and spending (major)	Tastelessness	Magnificence	Niggardliness
Honour and dishonour (major)	Vanity	Proper pride	Pusillanimity
Honour and dishonour (minor)	Ambition	Proper ambition	Lack of ambition
Anger	Irascibility	Good temper	Lack of spirit
Self-expression	Boastfulness	Truthfulness	Mock modesty
Conversation	Buffoonery	Wittiness	Boorishness
Disposition to others	Obsequiousness	Friendliness	Cantankerousness
Shame	Bashfulness	Modesty	Shamelessness
Indignation	Envy	Proper indignation	Spite

Sometimes, we may somewhat miss the mark, for instance, get angry too soon or not enough, yet still be praiseworthy. It is only when we deviate more markedly from the mean that we become blameworthy.

Book 3: Praise and blame

Actions are either voluntary, in which case they can be praised or blamed, or involuntary, in which case they can be pitied or ignored. An action is involuntary if it occurs under compulsion or out of blameless ignorance of particulars. In other words, an action is involuntary if it is impelled from without. An action that is impelled from within, but under threat or duress, is in a grey area, but more akin to a voluntary action.

An action that occurs out of ignorance of universals is not to be counted as involuntary, since ignorance of universals is precisely what makes a person bad. Divulging a secret because we did not know it to be a secret is not the same as divulging it because we do not know the difference between right and wrong. In the first instance we repent our action, in the second we do not.

Even children and animals are capable of voluntary actions, so that it is choices rather than actions that reveal character. Choices, which relate to means, are not the same as wishes, which relate to ends. Neither are choices the same as opinions, which may be true or false but not strictly good or bad. Our character is determined not by our opinions but by our choices, and the people who have the best opinions are not necessarily those who make the best choices.

In deliberating choices, the good wish for the good, whereas the not-good may wish only for the apparent good, which is vice. It may seem that the not-good are acting involuntarily, but this is not so, for it is from their successive choices that they became as they are. It is as with those who became ill through incontinence: although they may now be incurable, it was open to them at the beginning not to become ill.

Turning from the general to the particular, courage is a mean with respect to things that inspire fear and confidence. Courage is not the same as fearlessness, since there are some evils such as disgrace or envy that even a courageous person ought to fear. A deficiency of fearfulness is rashness; an excess of fearfulness is cowardice. Those who may appear courageous even though they are not include those who act out of self-interest, those who act out of habit, those who act out of passion, those who act because they are likely to prevail, and those who act without knowledge of the danger.

Temperance is a mean with respect to bodily pleasures.
Because these pleasures attach to us qua animals, to delight in
them and love them above all others is brutish. A deficiency of
temperance is self-indulgence; an excess of temperance—
which is rare—is insensibility. Temperate people desire as they
should the pleasant (although not extravagant) things that
make for health and fitness. Self-indulgence is more voluntary
than cowardice in that it concerns a pleasure to be pursued
rather than a pain to be avoided.

Book 4: Virtues and vices

Liberality is a mean with respect to the taking and, especially,
the giving of things that can be bought and sold. A deficiency of
liberality is meanness, an excess is prodigality. As liberals are
useful, they are loved. They give with pleasure and without
pain, to the right people, in the right amount, at the right time,
in the right way. Liberality resides in the giver, so that the
person who gives less may well be the more liberal. Meanness
is more common than prodigality, and worse, for it involves
wickedness as well as foolishness, and is harder to overcome.

Liberality on a public scale is called magnificence, and the
magnificent person is like an artist who spends large sums
fittingly. A deficiency of magnificence is niggardliness; an
excess of magnificence is tastelessness.

A person is proud if he both is and thinks himself to be worthy
of great things. If he both is and thinks himself to be worthy of
small things, he is not proud but temperate. On the other hand,
if he thinks himself worthy of more than he is worthy of, he is
vain; and if he thinks himself worthy of less than he is worthy
of, he is pusillanimous. Although the proud person is an
extreme in respect of the greatness of his claims, he is, like the
temperate person, a mean in respect of their truthfulness.

The proud person is avid of his just deserts and particularly of honour, 'the prize of virtue and the greatest of external goods.' He is mildly pleased to accept great honours conferred by good people, but utterly despises trivial honours proffered by casual people on trifling grounds. As one who deserves more is better, the proud person is good, and as he is good, he is also rare.

True, the proud person is liable to disdain, but as he reasons rightly, he does so justly. Although he may be haughty towards the high and mighty, he is always unassuming towards more middling sorts, for it is a difficult and lofty thing to be superior to the former, but easy to be so to the latter, and a lofty bearing over the former is no mark of ill-breeding, but among humble people is as vulgar as a display of strength against the weak.

> Again, it is characteristic of the proud man not to aim at the things commonly held in honour, or the things in which others excel; to be sluggish and to hold back except where great honour or a great work is at stake, and to be a man of few deeds, but of great and notable ones. He must also be open in his hate and in his love … and must speak and act openly; for he is free of speech because he is contemptuous, and he is given to telling the truth, except when speaking in irony to the vulgar.

The mean for smaller honours is called proper ambition. Its excess is ambition; its deficiency is lack of ambition.

Good temper is a mean with respect to anger. It is closer to its deficiency, lack of spirit, than to its excess, irascibility, which is the commoner of the two vices. A good-tempered person may sometimes get angry, but only as he ought.

Aristotle also discusses the virtues of friendliness, truthfulness, and wittiness, along with their corresponding vices.

Book 5: Justice

Whereas virtue pertains to our moral condition, justice pertains to our relations with others. The best people are those who exercise their virtue towards others. Besides this kind of universal justice, there is a particular justice pertaining to greed for goods such as money or honour. Particular justice can be divided into distributive justice and rectificatory justice. Distributive justice pertains to the distribution of goods such as money or honour, which are to be distributed according to virtue and participation in the *polis*. Rectificatory justice pertains to the rectification by a judge of unjust transactions, regardless of personal merit. Rectificatory justice can be further divided into rectification of voluntary transactions such as sales and loans, and rectification of involuntary transactions such as theft and assault.

There is another type of justice, reciprocal justice ('an eye for an eye'). However, reciprocal justice does not bind people together and is not fit for the *polis*.

Political justice, which relies on the rule of law (a combination of natural law and legal convention), ought to be distinguished from domestic justice, which relies instead on respect. Although the political justice of citizens and the domestic justice of a father or master are akin, there can be no injustice in the unqualified sense towards one's own property [women, children, and slaves].

To act justly is not easy. The ability to distinguish just from unjust comes not so much from familiarity with the law as from a virtuous disposition. If laws are inadequate, equity may be required to ensure justice. For this reason, equity is better than legal justice, although not better than absolute justice.

Book 6: Intellectual virtues

As has been mentioned, there are two kinds of virtue, one that pertains to character [*ethos*], which has already been treated, and one that pertains to intellect [*dianoia*].

The soul comprises an irrational and a rational part, and the rational part can be further divided into a contemplative part concerned with invariable truths and a deliberate part concerned with practical matters, that is, with right choice.

The types of disposition by which the soul can arrive at truth are five in number: (1) scientific knowledge [*episteme*], which arrives at necessary and eternal truths through induction and deduction; (2) art or technical skills [*techne*], which is a rational capacity to make; (3) practical wisdom [*phronesis*], which is a rational capacity to secure the good life; (4) intuition [*nous*], which apprehends the first principles or unarticulated truths from which scientific knowledge is derived; and (5) philosophic wisdom [*sophia*], which is scientific knowledge combined with intuition of the things that are highest by nature.

Philosophic wisdom is the highest intellectual virtue; however, practical wisdom is the one most closely associated with the deliberation and choice required for just action.

Although it is by the moral virtues that we may do what is just, it is by the intellectual virtues that we may know what this is.

But the intellectual virtues are also ends-in-themselves. As such, they are intrinsically, as well as instrumentally, productive of happiness.

Book 7: Incontinence and pleasure

Three kinds of moral state are to be avoided: vice, incontinence [*akrasia*], and brutishness. Their respective contraries are virtue, continence, and a heroic and divine kind of virtue. Both the hero and the brute are rare, although brutishness is more common among barbarians [non-Greeks].

Incontinence differs from vice in that the person knows what is right. Incontinence is near to self-indulgence, the difference being that the latter is a positive choice whereas the former implies a lack of self-control. As self-indulgence is a positive choice, it is more disgraceful than incontinence, and also less corrigible since the self-indulgent person is less likely to repent.

Continence differs from temperance in that it implies bad appetites, or a lack of good ones. Continence is better than endurance since it consists in conquering whereas endurance consists merely in resisting. If the opposite of continence is incontinence, the opposite of endurance is softness.

Of the kinds of incontinence, impulsive incontinence is more curable than wilful incontinence. Similarly, those who are incontinent by habit are more curable than those who are incontinent by nature or design.

There are some philosophers who believe that no pleasure is good, others who believe that only some pleasures are good, and yet others who believe that all pleasures are good although not the highest good. While some pleasures can be harmful, the higher pleasures enjoyed by the temperate are not harmful in any sense. If it can be agreed that pain is bad and to be avoided, it can also be agreed that pleasure is good and to be pursued. Indeed, it is hard to conceive of an ideal of happiness that is devoid of pleasure.

All animals avoid pain and pursue pleasure: that some of their pleasures are bad need not imply that all pleasures are bad. Things that act as restoratives and that are only incidentally pleasurable ought to be distinguished from things that are inherently pleasurable. These higher pleasures do not admit of pain, and, therefore, neither of excess. It is to be deplored that most people prefer incidental pleasures to higher ones.

Books 8 & 9: Friendship

> After what we have said, a discussion of friendship would naturally follow, since it is a virtue or implies virtue, and is besides most necessary with a view to living. For without friends no one would choose to live, though he had all other goods; even [the rich and powerful] are thought to need friends most of all; for what is the use of prosperity without the opportunity of beneficence, which is exercised chiefly and in its most laudable form towards friends?

Other than this, friendship safeguards prosperity, alleviates poverty and adversity, assists the elderly and infirm, guides the young, and stimulates to noble actions those in the prime of life. Friendship deepens thought and reinforces action. Parents feel it for their offspring, and offspring for their parents, even among the animals. It so binds the state that lawgivers value it more highly than justice. Friends have no need for justice, but the just need friendship as well, and the truest form of justice is a kind of friendliness.

Some say that friendship is likeness, others say the opposite. But is there only one type of friendship? For two people to be friends it is necessary that they bear goodwill to each other and wish good things for each other, without this escaping their notice. A person may bear goodwill to another for one of three reasons: that he is good (that is, rational and virtuous), that he is pleasant, or that he is useful. That being said, relationships based on advantage alone or pleasure alone have a smaller claim to the name of friendship that those based partly or wholly on virtue.

> Perfect friendship is the friendship of men who are good, and alike in virtue; for these wish well alike to each other qua good, and they are good themselves. Now those who wish well to their friends for their sake are most truly friends; for they do this by reason of their nature and not incidentally; therefore their friendship lasts as long as they are good—and goodness is an enduring thing.

Perfect friendship produces a high degree of mutual benefit, including such rare and precious goods as companionship, dependability, and trust. More importantly, to be in such a friendship and seek out the good of one's friend is to exercise reason and virtue, which is the distinctive function of human beings, and amounts to happiness.

Unfortunately, the number of people with whom one can sustain a perfect friendship is very small, first, because reason and virtue are rare, and second, because perfect friends need to spend a lot of exclusive quality time together. Thus, even if entirely surrounded by virtuous people, one could only have at most a small handful of perfect friends.

Acts of friendship are undertaken both for the good of one's friend and for the good of oneself, and there is no reason to suppose that the one precludes the other. In any case, having a perfect friend is like having another self, since perfect friends make the same choices as each other and each one's happiness adds to that of the other.

Like loves like, and this is especially true in the case of virtue, for the virtuous hold fast to one another, and neither go wrong nor let their friends go wrong. The wicked, on the other hand, are not even consistent with themselves, and become friends only for a short time to delight in one another's wickedness. People who are vastly unequal in virtue or anything else cannot be friends, and men of no account do not expect to be embraced by the best or wisest men.

Reproaches are more likely in friendships of utility. Also more unstable are friendships of superior and inferior, in which each person expects to extract the more out of the other. Ideally, the superior person should receive greater honour, and the inferior person greater gain. Even then, it is usual for the benefactor to love the beneficiary more than the beneficiary loves him back, because giving is more pleasurable than receiving, and because the benefactor has in some sense shaped the beneficiary, much like an artist shapes a work of art.

Most people, being avid of flattery, prefer to be loved, but friendship depends more on loving than on being loved. The love of others is motivated by self-love, and there is no conflict in this: what is best for us is also best for all, and *vice versa*. The virtuous, even if self-sufficient, will seek out friends, and seek to benefit them, for friendship is one of life's greatest goods, and the exercise of virtue is called happiness.

Friendship is closely related to justice. Just as friendship binds individuals, so justice binds communities. There are three kinds of constitution: monarchy, aristocracy, and timocracy [rule by property owners], monarchy being the best kind and timocracy the worst. Their respective perversions, in which privileges are not extended according to merit and the ruling faction privileges its own interest over the common interest, are tyranny, oligarchy, and democracy. Of the perversions, tyranny is the worst and democracy the least bad, so that the perversion of the best is the worst, and that of the worst, the best. Monarchy is analogous to the relation between father and son; aristocracy to that between man and wife; and timocracy to that between brothers. These relations are supported by friendship and justice, without which the state is liable to degenerate.

Book 10: Pleasure and happiness

Aristotle revisits pleasure, since 'to enjoy the things we ought ... has the greatest bearing on the virtue of character'.

Eudoxus [a scholar and student of Plato] thought that, since all things seek pleasure and avoid pain, pleasure must be the greatest good. Pleasure, he argued, is sought for its own sake and not the sake of something else. And when it is alloyed with something else, it makes that thing more worthy of choice.

However, these arguments merely show that pleasure is a good, rather than the greatest good. No one would choose to live with the intellect of a child, however pleasing that may be, or take pleasure from the most heinous crimes. Clearly, then, pleasure is not the highest good.

Pleasure is a concomitant of activity, and it is because we are incapable of continuous activity that we are incapable of continuous pleasure. Upon being presented with a pleasure, the mind is stimulated, but then relaxes so that the pleasure is dulled. If we desire pleasure, it is because we aim at activity, which is life. Activity and pleasure are so inextricably linked that it is impossible to tell whether we choose life for the sake of pleasure or pleasure for the sake of life.

Just like activities, pleasures can be good or bad, to be pursued or to be avoided. Every animal has its proper functions and proper pleasures, and the pleasures of man are far more varied than those of any other. Just as the perception of the healthy is more accurate than that of the ill, so the judgement of the virtuous is more accurate than that of the not-good.

Having spoken of virtue, friendship, and pleasure, it remains to outline the nature of happiness, which is the end of living. Happiness is not a disposition but an activity, or else it might belong to someone who slept through his whole life, or to someone suffering the greatest misfortunes.

Some activities are chosen for the sake of something else, while others are chosen for their own sake. It is among the latter that happiness is to be found, for happiness is not in want of anything. Activities that are chosen for their own sake are those from which nothing more is sought than the activity itself, and it is of this kind that virtuous actions are thought to be.

It would be strange if happiness lay in amusement rather than activity, for then man would toil and trouble all his life only to amuse himself. In truth, he amuses himself only so that he may exert himself. Amusement is a sort of relaxation, necessary only because of the impossibility of continuous activity.

Any chance person, even a slave, can enjoy the bodily pleasures no less than the best man; but no one assigns to a slave a share in happiness—unless he assigns to him also a share in human life. For happiness does not lie in sensual pleasure, but, as we have said, in virtuous activity.

Of all the virtues, it is philosophic contemplation that leads to the greatest pleasure, for philosophic contemplation is the best thing in man, and the most continuous. The pleasures of philosophy are marvellous both for their purity and their enduringness. Man, more than anything, is reason, and the life of reason is the most self-sufficient, the most pleasant, the happiest, the best, and the most godlike of all.

Indeed, the activity of God, which surpasses all others in blessedness, must surely be contemplative. All life aims at God and eternity: plants and animals participate in the eternal through reproduction, but man can come nearer through contemplation. Contemplation and happiness are the fruit of leisure [*schole*], for we are busy that we may have leisure, and make war that we may live in peace.

The person who is to be happy does not need many things or great things, and the life of contemplation and virtue can be practised, indeed, more easily practised, with but moderate means. The happy person is bound to seem strange, since the many only perceive, and judge by, external possessions.

A person is made good by one of three things: nature, reason, or habit. Nature is not in our control, and few people are inclined to listen for very long to the voice of reason. After nature and reason, all that remains is habit, and most of what passes for virtue is no more than force of habit.

> Now if arguments were in themselves enough to make men good, they would justly, as Theognis says, have won very great rewards, and such rewards should have been provided; but as things are, while they seem to have the power to encourage and stimulate the generous-minded among our youth, and to make a character which is gently born, and a true lover of what is noble, ready to be possessed by virtue, they are not able to encourage the many to nobility and goodness.

Good habits come down from good laws, with justice in the state eventually translating into justice in the individual. And so I turn my pen to the *Politics* ['Affairs of the *polis*'].

Politics

The state [*polis*], being the greatest of all communities, aims at the greatest good. The family arises from need, then the village, and then the state, which meets every need. The state is a creation of nature, for man is by nature a political animal [*zoon politikon*]. Man is the most political of all animals, since he alone has the faculty of speech and the knowledge of good and evil. Since the isolated individual is not sufficient for himself, the state is prior to the individual, and, like his hand and mind, enables him. For man, when perfected, is the best of animals, but when separated from law and justice, the worst of all. He who is unable to live in society, or who has no need because he is sufficient for himself, is either a beast or a god.

The state consists of households, which consist of the relations of master and slave, husband and wife, and father and children. The rule of a household, which is under one head, resembles a monarchy. Some men are born for subjection, and it is better for such men to be ruled by a master. However, it is unjust to enslave those who are not natural slaves. In a household, the head stands to his wife as a statesman to his people, and to his children as a king to his subjects. Unlike slaves, women and children are possessed of the deliberative faculty, although it is immature in children and weak in women. The same must be supposed of the virtues. For instance, the courage of a man is in commanding, that of a woman in obeying.

The art of household management includes wealth-getting, although this should stop at natural acquisition: unnatural acquisition, that is, money for its own sake, is as unlimited as it is unnecessary. All wealth-getting is illiberal and irksome, but the most detestable sort is usury, for money is intended to be used in exchange, not to increase at interest.

Book 2: Constitutions

Aristotle proposes to examine a number of theoretical and actual constitutions, beginning with Plato's *Republic*, which he criticizes for its communism of wives, children, and property. It is not uniformity but plurality that secures self-sufficiency, and people do not care for the common interest as much as they do for their own. Plato's guardian class would be deprived of happiness, which cannot be said to exist in the whole unless it exists also in the parts.

> We should not disregard the experience of the ages; in the multitude of years these things, if they were good, would certainly not have been unknown; for almost everything has been found out...

Aristotle also criticizes Plato's *Laws*, and examines two further theoretical constitutions, those of Phaleas of Chalcedon and Hippodamus of Miletus. By equalizing land possessions, Phaleas may eliminate necessity and so petty crime, but the greatest crimes are not committed out of necessity. 'Men do not become tyrants in order that they may not suffer cold; and hence great honour is bestowed, not on him who kills a thief, but on him who kills a tyrant...' It is not land possessions but desires that need to be equalized, and this can only be achieved through education.

Aristotle raises further objections to the constitutions of Phaleas and Hippodamus, in the course of which he says that laws should only be changed with great caution, when the benefit of making the change is both clear and considerable. 'For the law has no power to command obedience except that of habit, which can only be given by time, so that a readiness to change from old to new laws enfeebles the power of the law.'

He now turns to a number of actual constitutions, namely, those of Sparta, Crete, and Carthage. The fundamental problem with the Spartan constitution is that it has regard for only one part of virtue, namely, the virtue of the solider. As a result, the Spartans never engage in any employment higher than war and know nothing of the arts of peace.

The Carthaginian constitution is so superior that the Carthaginians have never suffered a rebellion or been ruled by a tyrant. Although the Carthaginian government tends to oligarchy, it avoids the evils of oligarchy by sending its citizens to be enriched in its colonies.

Book 3: Forms of government

A citizen is not a citizen by virtue of living in a certain place or having certain rights, or else metics and slaves would also be citizens, but by virtue of taking part in the administration of the state. In practice, this usually means that a citizen is one born of citizen parents.

At the same time, the state does not amount to its citizenry, or indeed to its territory, but to its constitution, so that a change in the constitution, or form, amounts to a change in the state.

The virtue of a citizen varies from one constitution to another, so that it is possible for a person to be a good citizen without being a good person. It also varies from citizen to citizen, according to their function in the state.

A government may be just and aim at the common interest, or unjust and aim only at the interest of the rulers. Whether just or unjust, a government may be in the hands of one, a few, or the many (Table 2).

Table 2: Aristotle's six forms of government		
Rule of	**Just (in the common interest)**	**Unjust (in the interest of the rulers)**
One	Kingship or royalty	Tyranny
A few	Aristocracy	Oligarchy
The many	Constitutional government (rulers excel in military virtue only)	Democracy (rule is in the interest of the poor only)

If the end of the state is wealth, the state should be apportioned according to property, as in an oligarchy. If it is life or security, it should be apportioned equally, as in a democracy. However, the end of the state is neither wealth nor life, but the good life. Those who contribute most to the good life ought to be given a greater share in the state, regardless of birth or wealth.

Rule by one man or a few deprives the rest from the honour of public office. Moreover, compared to the many, the one and the few are more liable to accidents of passion. Rule by the law may be preferable to rule by one or a few, but laws are only as good as those who framed them. Constitutional government can overcome many of these difficulties. Laws, when good, should reign supreme, with institutions only intervening when, and insofar as, they are deficient. As a collective, the many often come to better decisions, and are a better judge of whether they are being well governed. While the many should not serve singly in the great offices of state, they should share in certain deliberative and judicial functions.

All arts and sciences have a good for an end. The end of politics is justice, which is the greatest good. Everyone agrees that justice is some sort of equality, although not everyone agrees as to what. If wealth and freedom are necessary qualifications for holding office, so too are justice and valour. All states that rely on only one of these attributes are perversions. As a collective, the many are often richer and better than the few. But once in a blue moon, there arises a person so exceptional as to outshine the political capacity of all the rest. This god among men ought to be made king.

Customary laws have more weight, and relate to weightier matters, than written laws. A single man may be a safer ruler than the written law, but not a safer ruler than the customary law. Where the law is silent or deficient, it is better for many men to decide, so long as they are of equal merit.

The earliest governments were kingships. But when many meritorious persons arose, they wished for a commonwealth and set up a constitution. The ruling class soon deteriorated and enriched itself out of the public treasury. Riches became the path to honour, and oligarchies sprang up. These passed into tyrannies, and tyrannies into democracies.

Book 4: Democracy, oligarchy, and polity

The two principal forms of government are democracy and oligarchy. To determine the types of democracy and oligarchy, it is necessary to number the parts of the state: farmers, artisans and artists, merchants, serfs or labourers, warriors, wealthy patrons, and the deliberative, executive, and judicial branches of government. The parts of the state may overlap, but not so the poor and the rich. If the poor, which are usually the many, are in power, this is democracy. If it is the rich, it is oligarchy. There are five forms of democracy and five forms of oligarchy. Polity or constitutional government is a fusion of democracy and oligarchy, although generally inclines towards democracy. Of tyrannies there are three forms, the commonest being the arbitrary use of power by an individual who governs for his own advantage.

In most cases, the best constitution is polity. If the happy life is the life of virtue, and if virtue is a mean, then the life which is in a mean, and a mean attainable by everyone, must be best. Because the rich find it hard to obey, and the poor find it hard to command, a city of the rich and poor is a city of masters and slaves, with the masters being full of spite and the slaves full of envy. Good fellowship springs from friendship, so that a city ought, in as far as possible, to be composed of similars, that is, of the middle classes. Compared to states with a large middle class, states of the rich and poor tend to strict oligarchy or rampant democracy, and, ultimately, to tyranny. Unfortunately, few states have a large middle class, so that the middle form of government is rare.

Every state is made up of quantity and quality. A democracy is preferable if the quantity of the poor exceeds the quality of the rich. Otherwise, an oligarchy is preferable. The form of the democracy or oligarchy depends on the precise composition of the state. But in all cases, the middle classes must be included in government. The rich and the poor mistrust one another, and the middle classes are able to mediate and arbitrate between them. To ensure their contribution, the poor should be paid to participate, and the rich fined for not participating. But the minimum qualification for participation should be drawn at those who carry arms.

Constitutions have three elements, the judicial, executive, and deliberative. The role of the deliberative, and supreme, element is to enact laws, set foreign policy, inflict severe punishments such as death and exile, and elect magistrates. The executive element governs in the name of the deliberative. The judicial element resolves disputes and punishes offences, both in the public and the private spheres. In a polity, offices may be appointed by all or only some citizens, and from all or only some citizens, depending on the office.

Book 5: Kingship and tyranny

Democracy and oligarchy are the two principal forms of
government because numbers and wealth are common,
whereas good birth and virtue are rare. Both are based on a
mistake, and cannot endure, although democracy is the more
stable of the two. An aristocracy is a kind of oligarchy, albeit
with a different qualification. Aristotle discusses the causes of
revolution in democracies, oligarchies, and aristocracies, and
how their constitutions might best be preserved.

Although democracy and oligarchy are departures from the
most perfect form of government, they may be good enough so
long as they do not degenerate into their extreme forms, which
approximate to tyranny.

About monarchies, a kingship is of the nature of an aristocracy,
whereas a tyranny is a compound of oligarchy and democracy
in their extreme forms. A king is usually a virtuous man taken
from the notables by the notables for the notables; a tyrant is
usually a demagogue taken from the people by the people for
the people. A king protects the rich against injustice and the
poor against oppression, but a tyrant has no regard for any
interest other than his own. A king is guarded by citizens, a
tyrant by mercenaries.

Tyrannies may be destroyed from within by the hatred of the
people, or from without by some opposite and more powerful
form of government. Kingly rule, though rarer, is longer lasting,
and generally destroyed from within if royals quarrel or if the
king turns tyrant. A kingship is best preserved by limiting the
powers of the king. A tyranny, if it must be preserved, is best
preserved by harsh repression, or by the tyrant masquerading
as a king.

Book 6: Political stability

Justice in a democracy is that to which the majority agree; in an oligarchy, that to which the wealthy agree. In both principles there is some injustice.

The best material for democracy is an agricultural population, as farmers and herdsmen are too poor, too busy, and too rural to attend the assembly. Instead, they are content simply to elect qualified officials and hold them to account. The people are satisfied because they are governed with competence and accountability, and the notables are satisfied because they are not governed by their inferiors.

To create a state is one thing, but to preserve it is another. The legislator should not be tempted by pure democracy or pure oligarchy, which are both highly unstable. In a democracy, both the rich and the poor should be looked after. In an oligarchy, there should be one standard of qualification for holding high office, and another, much more modest, standard for filling minor offices.

Books 7 & 8: The ideal state

Before determining the best form of state, it is necessary to determine the best form of life. Happiness, whether consisting in pleasure or virtue or both, is more often found in those who are most highly cultivated in mind and character. Unlike external goods, virtue cannot be acquired by chance, and there can be no such thing as too much virtue. The best state is that in which everyone can behave best and live happiest.

Which is to be preferred, the life of the statesman or that of the philosopher? If happiness is virtuous activity, the active life is preferable to the inactive. At the same time, virtuous activity is the product of contemplation, so that the life of the statesman ought to go hand in hand with that of the philosopher.

A state should not be judged on its size, but on its collective virtue, and a very populous state is rarely well governed. If offices are to be distributed according to merit, citizens need to know one another's character. Although the population and the territory should be large enough for self-sufficiency, neither should exceed that which can be taken in by the eye. The state's territory should be well situated and readily defensible. Access to the sea may lead to an undesirable influx of foreigners, which is however outweighed by the benefits of increased trade and a naval force.

Peoples from the North are full of spirit but lack intelligence and political organization. Peoples from the East are intelligent and inventive but lack spirit and live in a state of subjection and slavery. The Greeks, being intermediate in character, are both intelligent and spirited. If only the Greeks could come together, they would rule the world.

For a state to be self-sufficient, it must provide six indispensable things: food, crafts, arms, property, worship, and government. To make time for leisure and the cultivation of virtue, citizens should not engage in farming or artisanry but only in the four other functions. The young should bear arms, those in middle age should govern, and the elderly should tend to the temples.

The state should aim at something more than mere survival or self-sufficiency:

> Men must be able to engage in business and go to war, but leisure and peace are better; they must do what is necessary and indeed what is useful, but what is honourable is better ...
> If it be disgraceful in men not to be able to use the goods of life, it is peculiarly disgraceful not to be able to use them in

time of leisure—to show excellent qualities in action and war, and when they have peace and leisure to be no better than slaves.

Although reason is the end of man, habit should be taught first, for the irrational is prior to the rational. Men and women should marry in the prime of life: women at about 18 years old, men at about 37. Men should not beget children much after the prime of their intelligence, which is at around 50 years old. Education should take place in two periods, from the age of 7 to puberty, and thereon to the age of 21.

The education of the citizens should match the character of the constitution. As the state has but one end, education should be the same for all, and should be public. Children should not be taught vulgar things, that is to say, things that deform the body or lead to paid employment. All paid employment absorbs and degrades the mind.

Aristotle lays out the curriculum. Like Plato, he believes that there is a close connection between music, ethics, and politics, and concludes the *Politics* with a discussion of music:

> Since then music is a pleasure, and virtue consists in rejoicing and loving and hating aright, there is clearly nothing which we are so much concerned to acquire and to cultivate as the power of forming right judgments, and of taking delight in good dispositions and noble actions. Rhythm and melody supply imitations of anger and gentleness, and also of courage and temperance, and of all the qualities contrary to these, and of the other qualities of character, which hardly fall short of the actual affections...

Commentary

Like Socrates and Plato, Aristotle emphasizes reason, virtue, and education, with an end to the good. But contra Plato, he rejects the Form of the Good, and the *Nicomachean Ethics* can be read as an attempt to do moral philosophy without appealing to the Forms.

In general, Aristotle is less inventive but more systematic than Plato. He is also more of a small-c conservative, for example, when he argues that laws should only be changed with great caution, or when he criticizes the *Republic* for disregarding 'the experience of the ages'.

The purpose of Book 2 of the *Politics* is to review rival political theories. Aristotle approaches political science like he approached biology, by collecting and parsing all the data, in this case, the 158 constitutions in his library. That his criticism of the *Republic*, a theoretical constitution, falls so squarely on the communism of the guardians suggests that he looked upon Plato's ideal state as a genuine proposition rather than a thought experiment. By focusing on city-state constitutions in an age of empire, he may have been passing commentary on his student Alexander, or simply digging his head in the sand: when Thebes rebelled in 335, Alexander summarily razed it to the ground.

Aristotle's interest in biology informs both his ethics and his politics. Man is a rational animal, and he is also a political animal, and it is only by participating in the life of the *polis* that he can make full use of his reason and be the kind of animal that he is. He who is unable to live in society 'is either a beast or a god'. The state is a kind of species, for it has a form, which resides in its constitution.

That happiness is the supreme good is obvious enough, although it is all too easy especially in modern life to miss the wood for the trees, or not know of what the wood is made.

Happiness is not a private, subjective feeling, but comes from self-actualizing through the *polis*, from our contributions to society and our relations with others, both of which involve the exercise of reason and virtue.

Although *eudaimonia* ['good spirit'] is usually translated into English as 'happiness', it also has connotations of longer-term success and flourishing. As King Priam of Troy found out, eudaimonia requires a complete life, as well as complete virtue. Aristotle reinforces this point by quoting from Æsop's *Young Man and the Swallow*: 'One swallow does not make a summer, nor does one day; and so too one day, or a short time, does not make a man blessed and happy.' A life is not led for today or for tomorrow, but over a lifetime, and even after death.

But even if our happiness is not completely in our hands, we can overcome, or at least outshine, our bad fortune through the continued practice of reason and virtue, as Priam did when he retrieved the corpse of Hector from Achilles. This notion that happiness is more a question of excellence, or character [*ethos*], than of luck became a central tenet of Stoic philosophy.

Virtue is not knowledge or wisdom, as per Socrates and Plato, but a disposition [*hexis*] to happiness. If virtue is a disposition to happiness, happiness itself is the exercise of virtue. It is not merely the strong and beautiful who are crowned at the Olympic Games, but those who perform well—for which it helps to be 'strong and beautiful'.

Since virtue seems important, and reason seems important, what is the relationship between reason and virtue?

Virtue is not primarily acquired by reason, but by habit. Giving
a bad person reasons to be good, if you've ever tried, is like
whistling at the wind. But with a degree of virtue in place, it
becomes possible, through reason, to refine it. Thus, the
already good person will readily, even hungrily, engage with the
Nicomachean Ethics, whereas the not-good person will think it a
bore. 'A book is like a mirror' said GC Lichtenberg, 'if an ape
looks into it an apostle is hardly likely to look out.'

Reason also serves to implement virtue, to determine ends and
the means of attaining them. The intellectual virtue that
reasons about virtue is philosophic wisdom, or *sophia*. The
intellectual virtue that implements virtue is practical wisdom,
or *phronesis*. Phronesis also pertains to political means and
ends, and Aristotle identifies Pericles as a paradigm of foresight
and *phronesis*. Had he not perished in the plague, Pericles
would almost certainly have saved Athens from the disaster of
the Sicilian Expedition (Chapter 6).

Aristotle assumes free will: we are responsible for our choices,
if not for the consequences of our actions. As with the Stoic
archer, our concern should be to shoot accurately, not to hit the
mark. If we are the kind of person who reflexively makes bad
choices, this is our own fault since it was once open to us not to
become that kind of person. Aristotle fails to consider factors
such as early trauma and poor parenting or schooling that may
make it harder to become a good person.

At the same time, Aristotle agrees with Socrates that no one
ever knowingly does evil: the bad, who are the ignorant, do not
wish for evil but for the 'apparent good', which happens to be
evil. Ignorance, for Aristotle if perhaps not for Socrates, comes
by degrees. In particular, the incontinent person knows what is
good, but not well enough to resist temptation.

Aristotle's idea of placing the virtues on a spectrum of their extremes, which are vices, is ingenuous, and even flushes out vices, such as 'lack of ambition' and 'lack of spirit', that are not named in language.

Aristotle, who is ever pragmatic and never dogmatic, concedes that not every passion or action admits of a mean, not, for instance, envy or murder. The Stoics made a much longer list, and considered that passions such as anger and fear, which Aristotle had in a mean, are always inappropriate.

Aristotle lacks an underlying philosophy of what makes a virtue a virtue and takes his list of virtues for a given. He waxes lyrical about pride, also called magnanimity or 'greatness of soul' [*megalopsuchia*], but in the Christian tradition pride of any sort is one of the seven deadly sins. More than that, it is the original and most unforgivable sin, since it is from pride that the angel Lucifer fell from Heaven. At the opposite end of the scale, the three great theological virtues of faith, hope, and charity are not even mentioned by Aristotle, while humility for him is a vice, pusillanimity.

Two of Aristotle's virtues, pride and magnificence, can only inhere in aristocrats such as himself, and the *Nicomachean Ethics* is open in many places to charges of elitism. Aristotle condones slavery and misogyny, defining women and slaves as property to remove them from the full scope of the law. In times of peace, better-off citizens need not do any work other than running the household and taking part in government. But the people who make their leisure, and so their happiness, possible are natural slaves born for subjection. While better-off citizens are ends in themselves, slaves, serfs, and women are mere means to that end. We work to live, not live to work—unless, that is, we are a slave.

Aristotle's objection to usury, which in the mind of many Ancient Greeks epitomized 'money for the sake of money', bolstered the Church's ban on moneylending, which, later, created a fertile ground for anti-Semitic feeling.

Aristotle also looks down on non-Greeks, or 'barbarians', although, unexpectedly, holds the Carthaginian constitution in higher regard than the Greek ones that he surveys.

To be rational and virtuous may seem difficult and unpleasant but, once ingrained, is in fact easier and more pleasant than the alternative. Whereas Plato dismisses pleasure as an incidental process of restoration, Aristotle sees it as a product or by-product of activity and an important part, and driver, of the good life. Activity and pleasure are so intimately related that it is unclear whether we choose life for the sake of pleasure or pleasure for the sake of life. In Book 10 of the *Nicomachean Ethics*, Aristotle says: 'Pleasure completes the activity not as the corresponding permanent state does, by its immanence, but as an end which supervenes as the bloom of youth does on those in the flower of their age.'

However, not all pleasures are equal, and higher pleasures are to be preferred. Because higher pleasures are inherently rather than incidentally pleasurable, they do not admit of pain, and neither, therefore, of excess. In renewing the distinction between higher and lower pleasures, John Stuart Mill (d. 1873) essentially provided an Aristotelian correction to Jeremy Bentham's crude utilitarianism.

When offered a hypothetical choice between a life of limitless pleasure as a brain in a vat, or a genuine human life along with all it struggles and suffering, most people opt for the latter, suggesting that Aristotle is correct in identifying pleasure as a good but not the highest good.

Figure 15: Woodcut of Aristotle ridden by Phyllis (detail), by Hans Baldung (1515). According to a mediaeval 'Power of Women' story, when Alexander the Great found Phyllis (by some accounts, Alexander's wife) riding Aristotle like a horse around the garden, he exclaimed, 'Master can this be!' Quick on his feet, Aristotle replied, 'If lust can so overcome wisdom, just think what it could do to a young man like you.'

That pleasure is discussed twice, once in Book 7 and again in Book 10, seems to confirm that the *Nicomachean Ethics* is a compilation—helping, perhaps, to account for some of its inconsistencies.

That friendship takes up two of its ten books may seem odd to contemporary readers. But man is a political animal, and it is friendship more than anything that brings people together, and provides opportunities for exercising reason and virtue.

Friendship, which binds individuals, is so near to justice, which binds the state, that the discussion of friendship is immediately followed by a discussion of constitutions. If you were scratching your head, the classification of constitutions in the *Ethics* differs somewhat from the one in the *Politics*, which seems, in turn, to have been informed by the one in Plato's *Statesman*.

As laid out in the *Politics*, good forms of government aim at the interests of all, whereas their corrupt forms aim only at the interests of the ruling faction. Although a corrupt form of government is all that may be realistically possible, it should at least attempt to approximate to a good form, notably by becoming more moderate and having regard for those who are excluded from power.

If bad people come to power, there is a risk that government will be overthrown. To prevent this from happening, Aristotle makes the law sovereign, that is, unalterable. That the law reigns supreme in most countries owes in no small part to the influence of Aristotle's *Politics*.

Returning to the subject of friendship, Aristotle tells us that people may be bad in many ways, but good in one way only. An implication, which Socrates drew, is that all good people are alike to one another. No surprise, then, that having a perfect friend is like having another self. Perfect friends, who are by definition good, naturally make the same choices. To quote Phaedrus in the *Phaedrus*, 'Ask the same for me, for friends should have all things in common.'

Despite the praise that he lavishes upon friendship, Aristotle is quite clear that the best and happiest life is not the one spent in friendship but the one spent in contemplation. There is a contradiction here. If the best life is one of contemplation, then friendship is either superfluous or inimical to the best life. It may be, as he tentatively suggests, that friendship is needed because it leads to contemplation, or that contemplation is only possible some of the time and friendship is needed the rest of the time, or even that a life of friendship is just as good as a life of contemplation. This fudging is as close as he comes to acknowledging the tension between the individual and the state—which, in fairness, was much weaker then than it is now.

Insightful and illuminating is the distinction drawn between leisure for the sake of amusement and relaxation, necessary because of the impossibility of continuous activity, and leisure for the sake of contemplation and virtuous activity. Economic imperatives have led us to associate leisure exclusively with amusement and relaxation, so that many people who retire, and no longer need to flop on a beach or in front of a screen, find themselves at a loss—essentially, because they have never been schooled in leisure. *Schole*, the Greek word for 'leisure', is the root of our word 'school', and the divide between primary and secondary school [French, *lycée*, after the Lyceum] also owes to Aristotle.

Like the hermit, the virtuous man of contemplation is content, if he must, to live on the margins of society, not as a beast but as a god. Contemplation enables us to participate in God, who is himself engaged in contemplation. This notion of a single and abstract God, found in both Plato and Aristotle, is a radical departure from the polytheistic Greek pantheon, and marks the beginning of monotheism in the West.

The contents of the *Nicomachean Ethics*, and its companion the *Politics*, are impressive enough. What is even more impressive is how they fit together, enabling the reader to connect the dots. As a moral philosophy, virtue ethics is surprisingly modern, even futuristic, with people poised to have much more leisure as robots take over from workers. So much has changed since the time of Aristotle, and yet so little.

21

ORGANON
LOGIC AND DIALECTIC

*A*ristotle's logic, or 'analytics' as he called it, is the earliest systematic study of human reasoning. At the end of *Sophistical Refutations*, he himself says that, in most cases, discoveries lean on the achievements of others, but in this case, 'Nothing existed at all... we had absolutely nothing else of an earlier date to mention, but were kept at work for a long time in experimental researches.'

More than two thousand years later, no less than Immanuel Kant deemed Aristotle's logic to be complete and unsurpassed. In fact, Chrysippus (d. c. 206 BCE), the third scholarch of the Stoic school, had developed a more sophisticated system of propositional logic. In the third century CE, Diogenes Laertius wrote that Chrysippus was so renowned for dialectic that 'most people thought, if the gods took to dialectic, they would adopt no other system than that of Chrysippus'. However, Stoic logic came to be lost, along with the more than seven hundred works of Chrysippus, while Aristotle's deductive or syllogistic logic came to dominate.

Because logic seemed capable of uncovering the hidden truths
of nature, the Aristotelian system was heavily taken up and
elaborated upon in the monasteries and madrasas—so that it
can be a challenge to disentangle the work of the monks and
mullahs from that of the Master. But however much the God
men tried, Aristotle's system was only superseded in the late
nineteenth century with the advent of predicate logic.

Several of Aristotle's logical works came to be grouped together
under the heading of *Organon* [Apparatus, Instrument, Tool,
Organ]. Whereas the Stoics thought of logic as an integral part
of philosophy, later Peripatetics thought of it more as a tool of
philosophy, hence 'organon'. The six books of the *Organon* are:
*Categories, On Interpretation, Prior Analytics, Posterior Analytics,
Topics,* and *Sophistical Refutations,* which may once have been an
appendix to the *Topics.* Some of Aristotle's logic is contained in
the *Metaphysics,* and more informal forms of argument are
covered in the *Rhetoric.* In Islamic scholarship, the *Rhetoric* and
Poetics came to be appended to the *Organon,* and it is true that
the works lie on a spectrum: whereas the *Organon* is about
uncovering the truth, the *Rhetoric* and *Poetics* are about
instilling it in less philosophical types.

In the *Categories,* Aristotle divides the 'things that are said' [*ta
legomena*] into ten distinct kinds that can form the subject or
predicate of a proposition: substance, quantity, quality, relation,
place, time, position, state, action, or passion—with substance
seeming to differ somewhat from the other nine (about which
more in Chapter 23). These *prædicamenta,* as they came to be
called in Latin, are not all that pertinent to Aristotle's logical

system, except that they reveal or betray a close connexion in his mind between language and reality, which in the *Categories* seem all but indistinguishable.

The second book, *On Interpretation*, is concerned with the formation of propositions. Because words in isolation do not assert anything, they cannot be either true or false. For them to assert something, they must be combined to form a statement or proposition. Typically, a proposition contains a subject, a predicate, and a connecting verb. Not every complete sentence is a proposition that asserts or denies something about the world. Questions, prayers, and commands cannot be either true or false, and fall more in the ambit of rhetoric or poetry.

Propositions have both a quality (affirmative or negative) and a quantity (universal or particular). On this basis, there are four types of propositions: universal affirmative (A, 'All men...'), universal negative (E, 'No men...'), particular affirmative (I, 'Some men...'), and particular negative (O, 'Some men are not...'). All statements can be recast into one or other of these four proposition types, A, E, I, or O.

Ancient thinkers represented the four proposition types and the relations between them in a 'square of opposition' (Figure 16). For instance, if A is true ('All S are P'), I ('Some S are P') must also be true, but E ('No S are P') and O ('Some S are not P') must be false. Other so-called immediate inferences can be obtained by conversion, obversion, or contraposition.

- Conversion: If 'No S are P', it must also be true that 'No P are S'.
- Obversion: If 'Some S are P', it must also be true that 'Some S are not non-P'.
- Contraposition: If 'All S are P', it must also be true that 'All non-P are non-S'.

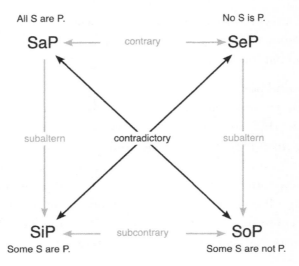

Figure 16. The square of opposition.

These inferences, and Aristotelian logic in general, rely on three 'laws of thought' formulated by Aristotle but also contained in Plato: the law of identity (each thing is identical with itself), the law of non-contradiction (no proposition can be both true and false at the same time), and the law of excluded middle (every proposition must be either true or false). Much later, GW Leibniz (d. 1716) formulated two additional principles: the principle of sufficient reason (everything must have a cause) and the identity of indiscernibles (there cannot be separate entities that have all their properties in common).

Although Aristotelian logic is primarily assertorial, it is able to deal with modalities, that is, with possibility or necessity, and *On Interpretation* is especially remembered for Aristotle's example of a hypothetical sea-battle in discussing the problem of future contingents. In essence, if a proposition about the future is said to be true, it may seem that things cannot turn out otherwise. Aristotle rejects this implication, breaking the bond between language and reality to salvage our notion of freedom.

A sea-fight must either take place tomorrow or not, but it is not necessary that it should take place tomorrow, neither is it necessary that it should not take place, yet it is necessary that it either should or should not take place tomorrow.

To go beyond immediate inferences, one needs to form arguments or make syllogisms, which is the subject of the *Prior Analytics*. A syllogism is a deduction which consists of two premises and a conclusion that necessarily follows from the premises.

For example:

> All mammals are warm-blooded.
> All marsupials are mammals.
> Therefore, all marsupials are warm-blooded.

Notice that the two premises have a term in common, which is called the middle term. The predicate of the conclusion is called the major term, while its subject is called the minor term. The premise that contains the major term is called the major premise. The premise that contains the minor term is called the minor premise. The major premise, which contains the broader truth, is conventionally placed above or prior to the minor premise. In the above example, 'mammals' is the middle term, 'warm-blooded' is the major term, and 'marsupials' is the minor term.

Syllogisms can be classified according to figure and mood. Syllogisms fall into one of four figures, as determined by the position of the middle term. Syllogisms in the first figure (with the middle term on the left of the major premise and on the right of the minor premise) are closest to natural reasoning.

Mood, which is a mediaeval development, is determined by the arrangement of the propositions, for instance, AAA, as in our example with marsupials.

Tabulating mood against figure yields 256 possible syllogistic forms. Of the 24 valid ones, only 15 are unconditionally valid, with the remaining 9 only valid if a particular term exists.

The four unconditionally valid forms in the first figure are AAA, EAE, AII, and EIO, also known as BArbArA, CElArEnt, DArII, and FErIO.

These four first-figure syllogisms are 'perfect syllogisms' in that they are transparently true. This means that they can be used to demonstrate the validity of the other, imperfect syllogisms through conversion or 'reduction' according to the relations in the square of opposition.

Aristotle intended his dialectic and rhetoric for argument and debate. His logic he intended for science, which he did not conceive as hypothesis testing as we do today but as a search for essential definitions of species. Paradigmatically, for a given species, one would identify its larger natural group [*genus*] and the unique features that mark it out from this group [*differentia*] —although, it has to be said, his own biology is usually a lot more informal, and pragmatic, than that.

This means that Aristotelian logic is not intended for entities such as gorgons, sirens, and unicorns that do not exist in nature. Nor is it intended for singular terms such as 'Socrates', even if examples with 'Socrates' are rife in the literature (and scanned as something like 'All instances of Socrates').

It also means that, unlike modern symbolic logic, Aristotelian logic is not agnostic to the meaning of the terms involved. Logic is one thing, causality is another. Valid relations that appear necessary, and that are, therefore, more deeply embedded in the fabric of the universe, are more significant than those that are merely contingent (subject to chance or circumstances).

Although Aristotelian logic is primarily deductive, it reserves an important place for induction.

Induction begins with the sense perception of individual cases, which are entered into memory. From this accumulated store, it becomes possible to draw generalizations, that is, to derive universal propositions that can then be inputted into deductive syllogisms. This process of inductive reasoning can itself be cast into a sort of syllogism.

If induction serves to build on the perceptible, deduction serves rather to reveal the imperceptible. Thus, for Aristotle, and contra Plato, sense perception is the beginning of knowledge. There is a parallel in the ethical realm, in which repeated actions (habits) give rise to virtues, which can then be leaned upon to illuminate more complex or unusual moral problems.

The place of induction in Aristotelian logic helps to explain the issue with singulars such as 'Socrates' or 'a dog', which are more the material of induction than of deduction, that is, more the material of sense perception than of reason and abstraction.

If the less rigorous and secure rhetorical equivalent of the deductive syllogism is the enthymeme, the less rigorous and secure rhetorical equivalents of the inductive syllogism are argument from analogy and argument from example.

Although knowledge derives from perception and induction, this derivation is supported by intuition [*nous*], which supplies the first principles [*archai*] of human knowledge, such as the laws of thought and the concepts of 'some' and 'all'. The first principles must be irreducible, without which 'there would be an infinite regress [with] still no demonstration'. At the end of the *Posterior Analytics*, Aristotle affirms that intuition is even more reliable than scientific knowledge—as indeed it must be if it is to provide a solid foundation for scientific knowledge.

The *Topics* is essentially a textbook of dialectic. To argue successfully, it is necessary to go back to premises that are founded on commonly held opinions [*endoxa*] which even our opponent can or must endorse, and from these premises derive a conclusion that contradicts our opponent's position. *Topoi* are the 'places' from which such arguments can be constructed.

On Sophistical Refutations is a guide to logical fallacies that can be concealed to deceive.

Aristotle identifies 13 logical fallacies which he divides into two groups: those that are in the language (formal fallacies) and those that are not (informal fallacies).

Formal fallacies include equivocation and amphibology, which both introduce ambiguity, semantical ambiguity in the case of equivocation, syntactical ambiguity in the case of amphibology.

Informal fallacies include irrelevant conclusion, begging the question, and affirming the consequent.

I'll close with Aristotle's discussion of affirming the consequent:

The refutation which depends upon the consequent arises because people suppose that the relation of consequence is convertible. For whenever, suppose A is, B necessarily is, they then suppose also that if B is, A necessarily is. This is also the source of the deceptions that attend opinions based on sense perception. For people often suppose bile to be honey because honey is attended by a yellow colour: also, since after rain the ground is wet in consequence, we suppose that if the ground is wet, it has been raining; whereas that does not necessarily follow. In rhetoric proofs from signs are based on consequences. For when rhetoricians wish to show that a man is an adulterer, they take hold of some consequence of an adulterous life, viz. that the man is smartly dressed, or that he is observed to wander at night. There are, however, many people of whom these things are true, while the charge in question is untrue. It happens like this also in real reasoning; e.g. Melissus' argument, that the universe is eternal, assumes that the universe has not come to be (for from what is not nothing could possibly come to be) and that what has come to be has done so from a first beginning. If, therefore, the universe has not come to be, it has no first beginning, and is therefore eternal. But this does not necessarily follow: for even if what has come to be always has a first beginning, it does not also follow that what has a first beginning has come to be; any more than it follows that if a man in a fever be hot, a man who is hot must be in a fever.

22

PRODUCTIVE SCIENCES
RHETORIC AND POETICS

*A*ristotle's *Rhetoric* is, if perhaps not the first, then at least the most important treatise on rhetoric, and is remembered also for its insightful psychology of the emotions. It exerted an important influence on Roman orators such as Cicero and Quintilian.

The *Rhetoric* has come to consist of three books. The first treats of the divisions of rhetoric and the means of persuasion, the second of the emotions of the hearers and the character of the orator, and the third of style and delivery.

The *Poetics* [*poētēs*, maker, author] seems even more mangled than the *Rhetoric*. Its theme is not poetry as we now think of it, but the broader imitative arts. The first book treats especially of tragedy and epic poetry. Because the second book addressed comedy, it was less likely to be recopied, and came to be lost. What remains of the *Poetics* is the oldest extant work of dramatic and literary theory, and may have done even better under the title of, *What Makes a Story Work* or, *How to Write a Good Story*.

Fittingly or not, Aristotle approaches rhetoric and poetry in the same scientific manner that he approached biology, gathering, analysing, and categorizing a ream of data before abstracting from it. But one wonders whether the endless listicles owe more to his student notetakers than to the master himself. He was, after all, the author of at least two books on style—the contents of which may or may not have been decanted or distilled into Book 3 of the *Rhetoric*.

For all his scientism, Aristotle often cites the *Œdipus Rex* of Sophocles as a paradigm of the tragic form, even though many extant Greek tragedies, not least those by Euripides, vary markedly in their construction. Although Aristotle is not nearly so prescriptive, the *Poetics* inspired the three 'classical unities' or 'Aristotelian unities' of action, place, and time, according to which a tragedy should consist of a single action that unfolds in a single place over the course of a single day. These compressive rules held sway from the sixteenth century for three centuries and were strictly observed especially by French playwrights such as Pierre Corneille and Jean Racine.

Plato famously disapproved of the 'irrational' imitative arts, which he banned from the ideal state. However, in the *Phaedrus* he does say that the truth is more persuasive when allied with rhetoric, and that dialectic and rhetoric ought to go hand in hand. It is no doubt in this spirit of a necessary evil that the *Rhetoric* ought to be approached. But although Aristotle never comes close to advocating the mock logic of the sophists, one is left wondering to what extent it is acceptable to deceive and manipulate in the service of the truth.

Truth needs not only to make itself heard, but also to defend itself, and it is notable that Socrates used only dispassionate dialectic at his trial, going so far as to tell the jurors that emotional appeals would not have been worthy of him or them.

Rhetoric

Rhetoric, which is the study of modes of persuasion, is the counterpart [*antistrophos*] of dialectic. Rhetoric is useful in that some people cannot be persuaded by knowledge alone. That said, people have a natural instinct for truth, and that which is true and good tends to be easier to prove and easier to believe.

Of course, even artful rhetoric might not persuade, just like artful medicine might not cure. But just as a man should be able defend himself with his limbs, so he should be able to defend himself with his reason, for reason is more proper to man.

Rhetoric may be defined as the ability, in any given case, to grasp the available means of persuasion. The three technical means of persuasion are the character of the speaker [*ethos*], the emotional state of the audience [*pathos*], and the argument itself [*logos*]. To master them, the orator needs to have studied human nature, the emotions, and logical argument. He should be able to take up both sides of an argument, not for the sake of vice, but to better confute his opponents.

If the proof of a proposition is founded on the truth of some other propositions, this is syllogism in dialectic and enthymeme in rhetoric. Speeches that rely on enthymeme, though no more persuasive than those that rely on example, excite the louder applause.

Rhetoric has three divisions: political, legal, and ceremonial (Table 3). Political oratory, which recommends or urges, concerns the future; legal oratory, which accuses or defends, concerns the past; and ceremonial oratory, which praises or censures, concerns the present. When speaking, the orator should not lose sight of the division and its ends.

Table 3: The Three Divisions of Rhetoric			
Division	**Content**	**Time**	**End**
Political (deliberative)	Exhortation/ Dehortation	Future	Expediency/ Inexpediency
Legal (forensic)	Accusation/ Defence	Past	Justice/ Injustice
Ceremonial (epideictic)	Praise/Censure	Present	Honour/ Dishonour

Because the end of oratory, and all else, is happiness, Aristotle discusses happiness and goodness along the same lines as in the *Ethics*. For political oratory, he discusses the various forms of government and their respective ends. For ceremonial oratory, he discusses the nature of virtue and vice. For legal oratory, he discusses the psychology of wrongdoers.

The doer of an action must either intend or not intend it. If he intends it, it must be either from deliberate purpose or from passion, and it is deliberate purpose that constitutes criminal guilt. Even then, it should be possible to distinguish criminal acts that owe to moral badness from those that owe to errors of judgement or great misfortunes. This is called equity.

> Equity bids us be merciful to the weakness of human nature; to think less about the laws than about the man who framed them, and less about what he said than about what he meant; not to consider the actions of the accused so much as his intentions, nor this or that detail so much as the whole story; to ask not what a man is now but what he has always or usually been.

The five non-technical means of persuasion—laws, witnesses, contracts, tortures, and oaths—pertain most of all to legal oratory. Aristotle discusses each one in turn.

If the written law is unfavourable, the orator can appeal to natural law, as Antigone did when she buried her brother. Or he might argue that the relevant law contradicts itself or another law, or is open to interpretation, or is antiquated.

In the absence of a witness of fact, the orator can call upon a witness of character, but best of all is an ancient witness such as Solon, Homer, or a proverb.

Book 2: Emotion and character

Having treated of the arguments [*logos*], Aristotle turns to the emotions of the hearers [*pathos*] and the character of the orator [*ethos*], which are also means of persuasion. *Pathos* is especially important in legal oratory, and *ethos* in political oratory.

The things that inspire confidence in the orator are three: good sense, good moral character, and goodwill. How to seem good and sensible can be deduced from the analysis of goodness in Book 1. The analysis of goodwill and friendliness is yet to come, to be contained in the discussion of the emotions.

Aristotle goes on to discuss the emotions, starting with anger, which he defines as an impulse, accompanied by pain, to a conspicuous revenge for a conspicuous slight. I discuss his treatment of anger in my book on the emotions. The orator, he says, ought to portray his opponent as deserving of anger.

Aristotle's discussion of friendliness and enmity coheres with the discussion of friendship in the *Nicomachean Ethics*. In contrasting anger to hatred, he makes the point that, whereas anger pertains to individuals, hatred can also pertain to entire groups, for instance, the entire class of thieves rather than a single thief. Anger aims at pain, hatred at harm. Time can quell anger, but not hatred.

From the discussion of friendliness and enmity, the orator can prove people to be friends or enemies, or refute their claims to friendship or enmity, or attribute their actions to either anger or hatred.

Fear is pain or disturbance from a mental image of some future evil. Anything that inspires pity can also inspire fear. But there can be no fear unless there is also at least the illusion of some small chance of escape.

The opposite of fear is confidence. Among others, a person feels confident if he believes that he has often been successful, or often escaped danger. Anger breeds confidence because a person who feels wronged also believes that the gods must be on his side.

Aristotle also treats of shame, kindness, pity, indignation, envy, and emulation, before turning to the types of human character.

The young have strong but volatile passions, while the elderly are small-minded, cynical, and distrustful. The character of those who are in the prime of life is a vigorous mean between these two extremes. The prime of life is defined as 30 to 35 years old for the body, and around 49 years old for the mind. In a memorable line, Aristotle says that the young 'are fond of fun and therefore witty, wit being nothing but well-bred insolence.'

Aristotle next considers the gifts of fortune by which human character is affected, namely, good birth, wealth, and power. He remarks that to be wellborn is not to be noble, and that most of the wellborn are nonetheless wretches:

> In the generations of men as in the fruits of the earth, there is a varying yield; now and again, where the stock is good, exceptional men are produced for a while, before decadence sets in.

In degenerating, a clever stock will tend towards insanity, as did the descendants of Alcibiades, whereas a steady stock will tend towards torpor, as did the descendants of Pericles and Socrates. As in the *Ethics*, Aristotle fails to consider the effects of the opposites of good birth, wealth, and power.

Having done with *pathos* and *ethos*, Aristotle returns to *logos*. Argument by example has the nature of induction, which is the foundation of reasoning. An example can be a past fact or an invented fact such as a fable. If an orator can argue by enthymeme, he should only use examples as supplemental evidence, in effect turning his examples into witnesses.

If a maxim is a general statement about matters of practical conduct, an enthymeme is a deduction concerning these matters. Thus, the premises or conclusions of enthymemes are of the nature of maxims. The greatest advantage of the maxim is that it lends character to a speech. Another great advantage of the maxim is that people love to hear expressed in general terms that which they already believe in some particular connexion. For instance, one who has bad children is ready to agree with anyone who tells him, 'Nothing is more foolish than to be the parent of children.' Maxims that declare something to be universally true when it is patently not are useful for stirring people up. For instance, an orator who is calling for war in the absence of favourable signs might say, 'One omen of all is best, that we fight for our fatherland.' Some proverbs are also maxims and contradicting them can heighten people's opinion of the character of the orator. For instance, the orator might say, 'We ought not to follow the saying that bids us treat our friends as future enemies: much better to treat our enemies as future friends.' If one is to pose as a moral authority, one has to be credible, and it is unbecoming for young men to utter maxims.

Aristotle ends by running through various types of enthymeme, such as returning an accusation to a morally inferior accuser, for example, 'Would you take a bribe to betray the fleet? No? Well, if you would not, why would I?'

The most effective enthymemes are those that are short and clear, and whose conclusion, while not being entirely obvious, can be gleefully anticipated.

Book 3: Style and delivery

In Book 3, Aristotle turns to addressing style and delivery: 'It is not enough to know what we ought to say; we must also say it as we ought...'

Oratory should be clear and simple. The orator should use everyday speech but lend it a subtly unfamiliar air. The fitting use of metaphor brings clarity, charm, and distinction. Delivery essentially involves the appropriate expression of emotions by modulating volume, pitch, and rhythm.

Bad taste in language may take one of four forms: strange words such as 'spoliative' and 'witless'; awkward compound words such as 'flame-flushed' and 'sombre-hued'; grandiose epithets such as 'monarchs of states' (laws) and 'world-concourse of the Isthmian games' (Isthmian games); and strained or maladroit metaphors such as 'events that are green and full of sap' and 'foul was the deed you sowed and evil the harvest you reaped'.

Correctness of language is the foundation of good style and has five elements: the avoidance of ambiguity; the use of specific names instead of vague and general ones; the proper use and arrangement of connecting words or clauses; the observance of gender (male, female, and inanimate); and the observance of number (unity, fewness, and plurality).

Here are six ways to make language seem more impressive. (1) A thing can be described rather than named, or, for concision, named rather than described. (2) A thing can be represented with epithets and metaphors. (3) The plural can be used for the singular, for example, 'Unto havens Achæan.' (4) One article can be tied with each word, or, for concision, two or more words can be bracketed under one article. (5) Plenty of connecting words can be used or, for concision, not many. (6) A thing can be described with attributes that it does not possess, for instance, 'a lyreless melody.'

Language is apt if it is suited to its subject and expresses emotion and character. Apt language leads people to believe in the truth and accuracy of what they are hearing. The form of a piece of prose should be neither metrical nor destitute of rhythm. In prose, metre is distracting, and, by seeming contrived, undermines trust. At the same time, prose that lacks rhythm is vague and unsatisfying. Prose should not be free-running but divided by periods. Divided or structured prose is easier to follow and remember and gives people the sense of having grasped something.

A speech is lively if it enables its audience to get hold of fresh ideas quickly and easily. Ideas are best conveyed through metaphor and simile. Simile is almost identical to metaphor, but longer and less direct. Arguments should not be too obvious or too lengthy, the most effective arguments being those that the mind only just fails to keep up with. The most appealing or satisfying arguments are antithetical in form, for instance, 'judging that the peace common to all the rest was a war upon their own private interests.' Events should be described in progress so that people may picture them, for instance, 'and the point of the spear in its fury drove full through the breastbone.' This phrase is lively because it mixes activity, metaphor, and surprise.

Each kind of rhetoric has its own fitting style. The style of written prose is different to that of spoken oratory, and the style of political speaking is different to that of legal speaking. Written prose is more finished, but spoken oratory better admits of dramatic delivery.

With regard to arrangement, a speech has a minimum of two parts: stating a case, and then proving it. To the Statement and Argument may be added an Introduction and Epilogue. The discussion of introductions includes strategies for allaying or exciting prejudice. For instance, to allay prejudice, Iphicrates admitted to having harmed Nausicrates, but not to having wronged him.

The appropriate amount, content, and style of any narration (relating of past events) varies according to the kind of rhetoric. Narration ought to depict character. Emotion should be described rather than merely stated, for example, Æschines described Cratylus as 'hissing with fury and shaking his fists'. 'Such details carry conviction: the audience takes the truth of what they know as so much evidence for the truth of what they do not.' If a detail seems incredible, it needs to be accounted for, as when Antigone explained that she cared more for her brother than for her husband and children because, unlike her husband and children, her brother could not be replaced.

Although arguments should bear upon the question in dispute, any falsehoods about irrelevant matters should be highlighted, as they will look like proof that other statements are also false.

Argument by enthymeme is highly suitable for legal oratory, and argument by example for political oratory. Refutative enthymemes are better received than demonstrative ones because their logic is more striking. Enthymemes should be used judiciously and sparingly: successive enthymemes risk spoiling one another's effect.

In most instances, the first speaker should begin with his own arguments before attacking his opponent's likely arguments. On the other hand, the second speaker should begin by attacking the first speaker's points.

When burnishing one's own character or demolishing that of an opponent, it helps to put one's words into the mouth of some third person.

Interrogation should only be used at opportune moments, such as when the opponent is contradicting himself or that which everyone believes, or when it is impossible for him to give anything but an evasive answer.

Jesting can be used to kill the opponent's earnestness, and earnestness to kill his jesting. However, irony befits a gentleman better than buffoonery: the ironical man jokes to amuse himself, the buffoon to amuse the gallery.

The aims of the epilogue are four: summarize the argument; magnify or minimize the leading facts; excite an appropriate state of emotion; and bring the hearer on side. For wrapping up, the disconnected style is effective: 'I have done. You have heard me. The facts are before you. I call for your judgement.'

Poetics

Poetry is defined as imitation or mimesis, not merely as verse form. Thus, poetry might also take the form of prose, and not all verse is poetry. However, all kinds of poetry use language, rhythm, and harmony.

Even for abstract forms of poetry such as dancing and flute-playing, the objects of imitation are men. In epic poetry and tragedy, men are represented as better than in real life; in comedy, as worse.

Man, by far, is the most imitative of animals and learns and derives pleasure from imitation: even a dead body can seem delightful if skilfully imitated. Moreover, humans have an instinct for rhythm and harmony, which find their highest expression in poetry.

Serious poets imitate good and noble actions in hymns and epic poetry; more trivial sorts imitate the actions of meaner persons in lampoons and satires. These opposing tendencies lie at the origins of tragedy and comedy. Comedy, then, imitates inferior characters. They are not bad in the full sense, but merely ridiculous. Tragedy imitates superior characters, as does epic poetry.

Tragedy is a serious and substantial imitation, in the form of action as opposed to narrative, and in language embellished by rhythm and harmony. It arouses emotions of pity and fear, leading to the purification or purgation [*katharsis*] of these emotions. As well as song and diction, it requires a stage and some actors.

An actor is distinguished by thought and character, since it is these that give rise to actions, and actions that determine success or failure. Thus, every tragedy has six parts: actions or plot [*mythos*], character, thought, diction, song, and spectacle. Of these six, *mythos* is the most important, for life consists in action, and the end of life is not a quality but a mode of action.

Plot must have a beginning, a middle, and an end. Since beauty depends on magnitude as well as order, each of these parts must be of a certain magnitude. Plot should be long enough for the main character to transition from fortune to misfortune or vice versa, but not so long as to lose the audience. Unity of action does not imply unity of the main character. For instance, the *Odyssey* does not include every adventure that Odysseus ever embarked upon, but only those that form part of a single, if broad, narrative. If a thing's presence or absence makes no difference, that thing is not an organic part of the whole and ought to be omitted.

The poet works in the realm not of the actual, but of the possible and hypothetical. He differs from the historian not in that he writes verse but in that he writes fiction.

> Poetry, therefore, is a more philosophical and a higher thing than history: for poetry tends to express the universal, history the particular ... It clearly follows that the poet or 'maker' should be the maker of plots rather than of verse; since he is a poet because he imitates, and what he imitates are actions. And even if he chances to take a historical subject, he is none the less a poet; for there is no reason why some events that have actually happened should not conform to the law of the probable and possible, and in virtue of that quality in them he is their poet or maker.

Actions should succeed one another with necessity, or at least probability, to provide insight into general principles of conduct. At the same time, tragedy is most effective at arousing feelings of fear and pity if actions, though credible, come as something of a surprise. Even a coincidence can be made more striking by lending it an air of design, as when the statue of Mitys at Argos fell upon Mitys' murderer and killed him.

In a simple plot, transition occurs without reversal of fortune [*peripeteia*] and without discovery or recognition [*anagnorisis*], whereas in a complex plot, it occurs with one or both of these elements. The best kind of *anagnorisis* coincides with *peripeteia*, as when the Œdipus of Sophocles finds out who he is. A third plot element besides *peripeteia* and *anagnorisis* is the scene of suffering, which involves a destructive or painful action such as murder or mutilation.

The parts that are common to all tragedies are prologue, episode, exode, and choric song (parode and stasimon). Some tragedies also have songs of actors from the stage and a *commos*, that is, a lamentation sung by both actors and chorus. The proper ordering of these parts is: prologue, parode, episode, stasimon, exode.

The plot of a perfect tragedy is complex and imitates actions that inspire pity and fear. The *peripeteia* should not involve a good man passing from prosperity to adversity, since this inspires shock more than pity and fear. Nor should it involve a bad man passing from adversity to prosperity, since there is no tragedy in that. Nor again should it involve the downfall of an utter rogue, which although satisfying, does not inspire pity and fear—for pity is inspired by unmerited misfortune, and fear by the misfortune of one who is our similar. Instead, it should involve a man who is neither particularly good nor bad, and whose misfortune is brought about by some great error or frailty [*hamartia*]. Although not virtuous, the man should be illustrious, like Œdipus, Thyestes, and their ilk.

The plot, however complex, should have a single focus. The change of fortune should be from prosperity to adversity and result not from common vice but from some great error or frailty. The hero should never be worse than the average man and is often significantly better. Tragedies used to be inspired by legends, but nowadays the best are founded on the fortunes of a few houses, those of Alcmæon, Meleager, Œdipus, Orestes, Telephus, Thyestes, and others who have done or suffered something terrible. Pity and fear should be inspired by the plot itself, not by mere spectacle. Actions that most inspire pity and fear are those that take place between intimates, rather than between strangers or enemies. In the strongest scenarios, the protagonist is about to act out of ignorance, but then discovers the truth and refrains from acting.

Figure 17. Œdipus and the Sphinx (detail), by Ingres (1808).
Musée du Louvre, Paris.

The character of the tragic hero should be good, and proper to his station. It should be consistent, so that the plot's unravelling [*lusis*] arises out of the plot itself rather than improbable actions or divine intervention [*apò mēkhanês theós*].

There are six kinds of *anagnorisis*. The most common but least artistic is recognition by signs such as necklaces and bodily marks. Next is recognition so contrived that it stretches the unity of the plot. Third is recognition that relies upon memory, such as when a disguised character bursts into tears upon seeing a picture or hearing a tune. Fourth is recognition that relies on a false inference on the part of a disguised character. Fifth and second best is recognition by deductive reasoning. Sixth and best of all is recognition that arises from the actions themselves, as in the *Œdipus* of Sophocles.

In plot-making, the poet should go so far as to put himself into the sandals of his characters, enact their actions, and feel their emotions. To be able to do this, the poet must have a special gift, or else a strain of madness. He should outline the plot before filling its episodes. For instance, the outline of the *Odyssey* could fit into under three sentences. Every tragedy consists of complication [*desis*] and unravelling or denouement [*lusis*]. Reversal of fortune [*peripeteia*] is their turning point. As a tragedy could never contain the entire *Iliad*, the poet should confine himself to a single plot.

Style ought to be clear without being mean. Language can be elevated by the judicious use of strange words, compounded words, and metaphor.

> It is a great thing, indeed, to make a proper use of the poetic forms, as also of compounds and strange words. But the greatest thing by far is to be a master of metaphor. It is the one thing that cannot be learnt from others; and it is also a sign of genius, since a good metaphor implies an intuitive perception of the similarity in dissimilars.

Epic poetry is narrative in form and employs a single meter. A paradigm of the form is the *Iliad*, in which Homer focuses on a single portion of the Trojan War. Epic poetry requires the same parts as tragedy, including *peripeteia* and *anagnorisis* but excluding song and spectacle. However, it is constructed on a larger scale, and is narrated in elevated heroic meter rather than spoken in commonplace iambic meter. In both forms, the poet should avoid the fantastical, and speak of himself as little as possible.

A work of poetry may be criticized for lacking verisimilitude, for contradictions arising from the language used, or for an irrational plot or depraved character. However, the fantastical or incredible might be justified if it renders the poem more striking, in which case a probable impossibility is preferable to an improbable possibility.

Unlike tragedy, epic poetry needs not pander to its audience with ill-judged antics and histrionics. In general, these faults pertain more to the actors than to the poet, and good tragedy can produce its effect even if it is not staged.

For all that, tragedy is superior to epic poetry because more vivid and concentrated: more vivid because it also has music and spectacle, and more concentrated because it is shorter and more unified.

THEORETICAL SCIENCES
PHYSICS AND METAPHYSICS

*A*ristotle's *Physics* and especially *Metaphysics* are some of the most abstract and challenging texts in the Western canon, not least because they do not have a thrust or even much of a thesis.

In his autobiography, Avicenna (d. 1037) claims that, after having mastered the natural sciences, logic, and mathematics, he returned to metaphysics and read Aristotle's *Metaphysics* forty times without understanding it, until a bookseller persuaded him to part with four dirhams for a commentary by Al-Farabi (d. 950). He devoured the commentary and the next day 'distributed much in alms to the poor in gratitude to Almighty God'.

The *Physics* [*ta physika*, 'natural things'] is a study of nature, that is, of the natural objects that are subject to change, and of change itself, which, for Aristotle, is closely tied to motion. Highlights of the *Physics* include the famous four causes, the concept of God as a 'prime unmoved mover', and an answer to the problem of infinity. The *Physics* is also remembered for the claim that heavier objects fall faster than lighter ones, disproved some two thousand years later by Galileo Galilei (d. 1642). Certain themes in the *Physics* are revisited in other works, especially the *Metaphysics, On the Heavens, Generation and Corruption,* and *Meteorology.*

The *Metaphysics* [*meta ta physika,* 'after the physics'] is so named for coming after the *Physics* in the *Corpus Aristotelicum.* Aristotle himself did not refer to its subject matter, which he defined as 'being qua being', as 'metaphysics' but as 'first philosophy'.

The *Metaphysics* is in fact a compilation of various works, with all the problems of ordering and consistency that this entails. It comprises 14 books traditionally referred to by Greek letters (Alpha, Alpha the Lesser, Beta, Gamma...). Kappa, which repeats earlier tenets of the *Physics* and *Metaphysics,* may not even have been written by Aristotle.

Alpha to Epsilon might be looked upon as groundwork for the investigation of substance that follows in Zeta and Eta. For Aristotle, substance is the most fundamental kind, or category, of being, and his metaphysics has been called a 'metaphysics of substance'. In short, a substance is neither an individual or particular (John), nor a general or genus (animals), but a specific or species or form (man), which unlike a particular contains only essential rather than 'accidental' (incidental) properties, and unlike a general can be 'specifically' picked out or defined.

Theta treats of potentiality, which is identified with matter, and actuality, which is identified with form and hence with substance. Actuality is more fundamental than potentiality, not least because a potentiality is only a potentiality by virtue of its actuality. For Aristotle, the chicken really does come before the egg, for what would it mean to be a chicken's egg without a chicken, or chickens?

Another important book is Lambda for its discussion of the prime unmoved mover, who is pure substance and actuality, and thinks only upon himself—his thinking being a thinking upon thinking [*noesis noeseos noesis*]. Without a first cause, or uncaused cause, or unmoved mover, there would be an infinite series of causes, so that there would be, strictly speaking, no cause at all, and, therefore, no knowledge. At the same time, time and motion are eternal, as are the heavens, which rotate unremittingly out of desire for the prime mover. So, although the prime mover is the first cause in the chain of being, he did not intervene at a point in time to set things into motion.

In Mu and Nu, on the philosophy of mathematics, Aristotle asks whether numbers and the objects of mathematics exist. Since they do not exist in sensible objects nor separate from sensible objects, they must not exist, or exist only in some special sense. Mathematics is more precise than other sciences because it 'separates that which is not separate'. Thus, harmonics and optics treat their objects not qua voice or qua sight, but qua lines and numbers—which bring out their order and symmetry, and hence their beauty. Aristotle finishes by raising several objections to the Theory of the Forms in order to reject Platonic and Pythagorean notions of number as Form or causation. In particular, several of the better arguments for the Forms lead to a 'third man', that is, to an infinite regress of Forms to explain how a man and the Form of man can both be man—a problem first raised by Plato (using 'largeness' rather than 'man') in the *Parmenides*.

What follows is an outline of the *Physics* and the first book of the *Metaphysics*, after which the *Metaphysics* becomes very arcane. If you are confused, it is because you should be: even Aristotle's definition of 'substance' is not consistent between the *Categories, Physics*, and *Metaphysics*. Remember also that the puzzlement of metaphysics is the larger part of its value.

Physics

To understand the natural world, it is necessary to uncover the first principles and primary conditions of motion or change. This can be done by advancing from what is clearer to us to what is clearer to nature.

Aristotle raises several arguments against the Eleatic notion that being is one and motionless, and therefore changeless. He reviews the other pre-Socratics and notices that they all identify the first principles with contraries such as Odd and Even, and Love and Strife. 'And with good reason, for first principles must not be derived from one another nor from anything else, while everything has to be derived from them.'

Everything that comes into being is a product of contraries, so that there must be at least two first principles. It stands to reason that there are more than two, 'for Love does not gather Strife together and make things out of it, nor does Strife make anything out of Love, but both act on a third thing different from both.' This presupposes the existence of an underlying something, namely, that which becomes, or 'matter'.

Although matter is numerically one, in form it is more than one. Thus, form must also be a principle of nature. Matter passes into and out of form but persists and perdures throughout these changes. If matter passes into and out of form, a third principle of nature must be 'absence of form'.

In conclusion, the three principles of nature are matter, form, and privation. The conservation of matter through form and privation presents a solution to the Parmenidean problem.

Book 2: The four causes

Of the things that exist, some exist by nature, some from other causes. Things that exist by nature, called 'substances', are the animals, the plants, and the simple bodies (earth, fire, air, water), for each has within itself a principle of motion in respect of place, coming-to-be, growth, or alteration. Aristotle argues that nature resides in form rather than in matter, for 'man is born out of man'. The nature or form of a thing is also its end.

Based on the discussion so far, Aristotle identifies four different types of causes or explanations [*aitia*] for change:

- The material cause: the material from which something is made.
- The formal cause: the form that that thing takes.
- The efficient cause: the source of the change.
- The final cause: the intended purpose of the change.

For example, a table is a flat surface on four legs (formal cause) that is made by a carpenter (efficient cause) out of wood or stone (material cause) for the purpose of eating and writing (final cause).

Three of the four causes—the formal, efficient, and final— often coincide because in nature the formal cause is the same as the final cause, while the efficient cause, or primary source of motion, comes from within the object. As the end of an object implies its material cause, this too can be said to be contained within the definition of the object.

Aristotle rejects chance as a fifth cause. An event that occurs 'by chance' occurs out of the coincidence of separate events, each with a separate set of causes. As a chance event does not have any causes of its own, it is purely incidental. 'Hence, however true it may be that the heavens are due to spontaneity, it will still be true that intelligence and nature will be prior causes of this All...'

Contra Democritus and Empedocles, Aristotle contends that it is absurd to suppose that nature does not have a purpose, and compares it to a doctor doctoring himself: 'the best illustration is a doctor doctoring himself: nature is like that.'

Books 3 and 4: Motion, infinity, place, void, and time

Motion and change can be defined as the actuality of that which exists potentially. Like teaching and learning, they require the actuality of both agent and patient, the completion of the one being an 'action' and that of the other a 'passion'.

Since motion requires place and time, and both are (at least potentially) infinite, it is necessary to discuss the infinite [*apeiron*, boundless]. The infinite is an unending series of magnitudes arrived at by either addition or division. While the infinitely large and infinitely small can potentially exist, they are never realized or actualized in nature. Distinguishing between potential infinity and actual infinity resolves many of the paradoxes that arise from a straight affirmation or denial of the existence of infinity.

Every sensible body is in place [*topos*], which is independent of body. Place is the innermost motionless boundary of the containing body at which it is in contact with the contained body. The heaven, with Earth at its centre, contains concentric spheres within itself. While these concentric spheres can be said to be in heaven, heaven itself cannot be said to be contained in anything else. Hence, heaven is not in place.

Figure 18. The Ptolemaic model of the universe, from Cosmographia, *by
Peter Apian (1539). In* On the Heavens, *Aristotle argues that the
sublunary world is composed of the four classical elements, or 'simple
bodies'. Earth rests at the centre of the world, which is also the centre of the
heavens, water rests just above the earth, air just above water, and fire just
above air. Hence, from where we are, we see fire and air moving up and
earth and water moving down. The celestial regions and heavenly bodies
are made of a 'first [fifth] element', æther. Æther moves in a circle, rather
than up or down, and is weightless. As circular motion does not have a
contrary, æther is not subject to generation and corruption, but, like the
planets and the stars, is eternal and unchanging. Because earth falls to the
centre, there can only be one Earth, and one universe, and the Earth is at
the centre of the universe. Ptolemy's* Almagest *(c. 150), in which he lays out
his geocentric model of the universe, begins with an uncritical review of
Aristotle's cosmology. The geocentric model was only overturned after the
publication of* On the Revolutions of the Celestial Spheres, *by Nicholas
Copernicus (1543). In* On the Heavens, *Aristotle also speculates that the
Earth is spherical and of no great size, so that one should not be too
surprised if the ocean that lies beyond the pillars of Herakles is the same as
that of the Indians—which is what Columbus ended up believing.*

Void [kenon] is place with nothing in it. Given our definition of place, and that void, if it exists, must be deprived of body, it is plain that void does not exist. To postulate the existence of void is unnecessary and leads to contradictions that make motion either unnatural or impossible. For instance, because the speed of a falling object is proportional to its weight, and inversely proportional to the density of the medium through which it is falling, all objects in a void would fall at infinite speed.

Time [chronos] consists of a part that has been and is not, and another that is going to be is and is not yet. Something that is made up of things that do not exist does not itself exist. 'Now' is not a part of time, for time is not held to be made up of 'nows'. Time is often thought of in terms of motion and change, but motion is only in the moving thing. And while motion can be said to be faster or slower, and therefore defined by time, time cannot be said to be defined by time. However, without motion 'now' would be one and the same, and time could not be said to exist. Thus, time is neither motion nor independent of motion. It is, in fact, the numerical aspect of motion. To exist, time requires soul or mind to number its movement.

Books 5 and 6: Change and indivisibility

There are three kinds of change: generation, corruption (destruction), and variation. Generation and corruption, which are in a relation of contradiction, are not motions. Of the several categories discussed in *On Categories* (Chapter 21), change can only take place in respect of quality (alteration), quantity (increase or decrease), and location (locomotion). As change is not a substance, it does not admit of properties, and, therefore, does not admit of change. The opposite of change is not some other change, but rest in one of the contraries, for instance, health or disease.

Aristotle presents a series of arguments to demonstrate that anything that is continuous cannot be composed of indivisibles, for example, that a continuous line cannot be composed of indivisible points. Thus, everything that is continuous, including space, time, and motion, is infinitely divisible.

On this basis, he sets out to resolve Zeno's four paradoxes of motion which purport to demonstrate the impossibility of change and motion. For instance, when Zeno says that an object in locomotion must arrive at the half-way stage before it arrives at the goal, and that to arrive at this half-way stage it must first arrive at another half-way stage, and so on to infinity, he ignores that time can be divided just as infinitely as space. More fundamentally, Zeno assumes that the infinity of points that must be crossed is an actual infinity when it is only a potential infinity.

Books 7 and 8: God and eternity

A thing that is in motion is moved by something else that is in motion, which is itself moved by something else that is in motion, and so on. As this series cannot be infinite, there must be some prime unmoved mover.

If all motion requires an earlier cause, there cannot have been an initial uncaused cause. Moreover, time cannot exist without motion. Therefore, time and motion are eternal, as is the prime unmoved mover.

The prime unmoved mover is not subject to change because change is a type of motion. As well as being eternal and unchanging, the prime unmoved mover is without parts or magnitude. He, or it, is the cause of the rotary movement of the heavens which in turn causes all other movements in the sublunary world.

Metaphysics, Alpha

All men by nature desire to know. Thus, the senses are valued not only for their usefulness but also in and for themselves. Animals are sensing, and from sensation memory is produced in some of them. These animals are thereby more intelligent and able to learn than those that are without memory. Still, they have little of connected experience, whereas man lives also by art and reason.

Men of experience succeed better than those with only theory, for actions are concerned with the particular rather than the universal. Yet people suppose artists to be wiser than men of experience because artists know the 'why' or the cause and can therefore teach. None of the senses are regarded as wisdom because, although they give the most authoritative knowledge of particulars, they do not reveal the causes of anything. The wise man can learn things that are difficult and farthest from sense perception, reaching to the first principles that are most truly knowledge.

The science which knows to what end each thing is done is the most authoritative, and this end is the good of that thing as well as the supreme good in nature. That this is not a science of production is apparent already from the earliest philosophers, whose wonder brought them to philosophize. A person who is puzzled and who wonders thinks of himself as ignorant and philosophizes to escape from his ignorance and accede to knowledge and wisdom, not for the sake of something else but for its own sake.

Aristotle reviews the opinions of the 'first philosophers', including Thales, Anaximenes, Heraclitus, Empedocles, Anaxagoras, and Democritus. However true it may be that all generation and corruption proceeds from one or several elements, it behoves to ask: why do they occur and what is their cause? When Anaxagoras first suggested that reason is present throughout nature as the cause of order and movement, he must have seemed like a sober man. Empedocles conceived not only of an aggregative first principle which he called love or friendship, but also of a contrary segregative first principle which he called strife. These philosophers were grasping, if only imprecisely, at two of the four causes identified in the *Physics*, namely, the material and the efficient cause.

In most respects, Plato, who in his youth became familiar with Cratylus, followed these thinkers. For the Pythagoreans, things exist by 'imitation' of numbers, whereas for Plato they exist by 'participation' in Forms, but what 'participation' and 'imitation' involve they do not say.

Aristotle ends by criticizing Plato's Theory of the Forms, for which, he says, there is no persuasive proof.

THE GANG OF THREE

As we saw, it is the pre-Socratics who began the journey from *mythos* to *logos*. At the same time, and in tandem, the focus of attention shifted from the gods to man, from the temple and palace to the public square and court of law.

But by the time of Socrates, the pre-Socratics, as epitomized by the finger wagging Cratylus, had got lost in a blind alley of remote and sterile speculation, creating an opening for a new breed of intellectuals. Compared to the pre-Socratics, the sophists were far more concerned with rhetoric than with metaphysics, with cosmetics than with cosmology.

Cicero claimed that Socrates was the first 'to call philosophy down from the heavens', but the merit may lie instead with the sophists—assuming that it was indeed philosophy that they were doing. The first and foremost sophist, Protagoras, who was thirty years older than his fellow Abderite Democritus, famously, or infamously, declared that 'man is the measure of all things'.

The sophists were a product of the pre-Socratics, but also of the agora and court of law, and of the wealth and self-confidence arising from the double defeat of the mighty Persians. Like Socrates, they had skeptical tendencies, making light of the gods and even of the pre-Socratics. But unlike Socrates, they were more interested in expediency than in knowledge for its own sake, their primary purpose being to create effective public speakers and enrich themselves in the process, without due regard for the wider or longer-term consequences. Whatever philosophy they did do was largely self-serving justification for their *modus operandi*, while their protean knowledge was little more than good marketing. Although the pre-Socratics had freed them from the gods and traditional moral codes, they had not yet evolved a stirring ethics by which to live, and, as a result, risked derailing the entire enlightenment project that had begun with Thales. They were, in many ways, in a similar place to where we are now.

Socrates understood all this. Caught between the horns of the solipsistic sophists and the onanistic pre-Socratics, he resolved to re-found philosophy. To address the pre-Socratic problem, he abandoned metaphysical speculation for ethics, opting this time for a universal ethics rather than the moral relativism of the sophists. To address the sophist problem, he made a show of his and their ignorance, and closed the perceived gap between our individual good and the public good.

For putting human beings and human happiness at the centre of his philosophy, Socrates might be considered the father of humanism. In so doing, he essentially created the self-conscious individual, which immediately found expression in the plays of Euripides. However tragic, Euripidean characters such as Electra and Phædra are no longer mere playthings of the gods but rational, self-reflective agents who agonize over their ethical choices.

To make the right choices, we need to think rationally, and we need to know who we are, that is, we need to know our nature and our good, which is also everyone else's nature and good. We are all in this together, and it is only by looking after one another, by doctoring one another with reason, that we might make progress. Socrates, the philosopher of the street, never did philosophy alone but in collaboration with one and all, for he conceived of philosophy not as a solitary, academic activity but as a collective human enterprise. By insisting that this kind of mutual therapy could change things for the better, he upended the traditional Hesiodic account of human history as a stepwise decline from an imagined golden age and offered tremendous hope and optimism.

In emphasizing human flourishing, Socrates doubled up as a spiritual leader who turned philosophy into something of a rational religion, as is even more evident in the various schools, such as Cynicism and Stoicism, that derived from his teachings. Thus, the unaffiliated Cicero, writing more than three hundred years later: 'Unless the soul is cured, which cannot be done without philosophy, there will be no end to our miseries.' Even the 'soul' of which Cicero speaks, the soul as the seat of human consciousness, originated with Socrates. In the *Charmides*, Socrates advises that we should treat the soul before treating the body, since health and happiness ultimately depend on the state of the soul. The treatment that he advocates is 'beautiful words', that is, reasoned discourse. When Zopyrus imputed him with all sorts of vices—including being a womanizer, which had Alcibiades in stitches—he stepped in to save the physiognomer's face by saying that he did have all those vices at birth but had been able to overcome them by the use of reason.

By offering a combination of regulation and salvation, the humanist philosophy inaugurated by Socrates could fill the void left behind by the old and retreating religion. Like Jesus four hundred years later, Socrates rejected the law of retaliation and replaced it with an absolute morality that might have prevented Medea from slaughtering her children or the ekklesia from massacring the Melians. Early Christians such as Justin Martyr (d. 165) and Origen (d. 253), who faced persecution for challenging the old religion, hailed Socrates as a precursor and compared their plight to his. In his *Second Apology*, Justin claims that Socrates 'exhorted [men] to become acquainted with the God who was to them unknown, by means of the investigation of reason...' Other early Christians, however, dismissed Socrates as a pagan who swore 'by the dog of Egypt' and, in his dying breath, sacrificed a cock to Asclepius—with Tertullian going so far as to dismiss his *daimonion* as a demon.

Although Socrates replaced the *lex talionis* with an absolute morality, there is no conflict in Socratism between our own good and that of others, if we understand that it is for our own good that we follow after virtue. Our own good coincides so exactly with the greater good that Socrates is at all times a model of moral integrity, even though he is never so vulgar as to preach or moralize. Instead, he assumes that we are or can be rational, and affably reasons with us. He is a model not only of moral integrity but of intellectual integrity as well, and of how the two can be tied. If his life was an inspiration, his death, which tested his mettle, proved even more so, and launching Plato, who preserved his outlook for posterity, was the greater part of his legacy. His failing, if he did have a failing, was that he overestimated us, for reasoned discourse does not suit the majority, and Neoplatonism and Stoicism came to be swept away by Christianity, which, by speaking to high and low, repaired a schism in society.

～

In *Process and Reality* (1929), the philosopher Alfred North Whitehead opined that 'the safest general characterization of the European philosophical tradition is that it consists of a series of footnotes to Plato'. To lock in the progress made by Socrates, Plato re-founded and formalized philosophy, and in the process created all its main branches, including ethics, aesthetics, political philosophy, logic, philosophy of language, epistemology, metaphysics, and philosophy of religion. In particular, he made philosophy its own incorruptible aim and accorded it a status higher than religion.

Plato also influenced countless others, not least Aristotle, who in attacking him time and again only betrays his preoccupation with him. Aristotle's forms, although immanent rather than transcendent, resemble Plato's Forms (capital 'F') in being the highest realities. Like Plato's Forms, they are immaterial and changeless and accessible by reason, and serve to actualize the greatest good. For all its difference in style, the philosophy of Aristotle is not a departure from Plato, so much as a correction that Plato had already begun to make.

After Plato's death, the Academy morphed over the decades and centuries. Speussipus, Plato's heir and nephew, was succeeded by Xenocrates, who was succeeded by Polemo, who was succeeded by his *eromenos* Crates of Athens, who upon his death in ~264 BCE was interred in the same tomb as Polemo.

Crates was succeeded by Arcesilaus, who inaugurated the Middle or Second Academy, the long period during which the Academy embraced philosophical skepticism. In the words of Diogenes Laertius, Arcesilaus 'was the first to argue on both sides of a question, and the first to meddle with the system handed down by Plato'—although he himself, like every other shade of scholarch, claimed simply to be returning *ad fontes*, in this case, to the original skepticism of Socrates. As a skeptic,

Arcesilaus opposed Zeno of Citium's kataleptic account of knowledge, which became the main bone of contention between the Academy and the Stoa.

After Arcesilaus, Lacydes, Evander, and Hegesinus came Carneades, who, by moderating the Academy's skeptical stance, inaugurated what later came to be known as the New Academy.

In 155 BCE, the ekklesia sent an embassy of three heads of school, including Carneades, to Rome to contest the fine of five hundred talents imposed upon Athens for the sack of Oropus —when only six years earlier, the Roman Senate had ordered the expulsion of 'corrupting' Greek orators and philosophers.

In Rome, Carneades delivered an oration on justice in which he commended the virtue of Roman justice. But the next day, he, being a skeptic, turned his cloak and refuted all the arguments that he had made in his first oration, to show that justice, rather than amounting to virtue, is no more than a social compact for maintaining some semblance of order. This, and the volte-face, horrified Cato the Censor, who agitated in the Senate to dismiss Carneades and his embassy.

Fortunately, Diogenes of Babylon, the fifth scholarch of the Stoa, did much better at impressing the Senate, who, in the end, reduced the fine to one hundred talents. More importantly, many leading Romans fell under the spell of Greek culture and philosophy. In the words of Horace, 'Conquered Greece took captive her savage conqueror and brought her arts into rustic Latium.'

After Carneades came Clitomachus and then Philo of Larissa, the twelfth and last undisputed scholarch of the Academy. In 87 BCE, during the First Mithridatic War, Philo moved to Rome, where a young Cicero came to sit at his feet. The following year, Sulla sacked Athens and destroyed the Academy.

Philo died in around 84 BCE, to be succeeded by Antiochus of
Ascalon. Although Antiochus had studied under Philo, he
came to reject the Academic skepticism that had dominated for
now almost two hundred years. By seeking to fold Peripatetic
and Stoic doctrines into Platonism, he inaugurated the stage of
Platonic philosophy later known as Middle Platonism (not to be
confused with the earlier Middle, or Second, Academy). In 79,
Antiochus taught Cicero in Athens, but he never returned to
the ruins of the Academy, and seems to have divided his time
between Athens, Alexandria, and Syria.

Plutarch (d. 199 CE), author of the *Parallel Lives*, became a
leading exponent of Middle Platonism, and, as part of a wider
trend, began to blend Platonism with religion and mysticism.
Another prominent Middle Platonist, Philo of Alexandria (d. 50
CE) sought to harmonize Greek philosophy with Judaism. In
time, Middle Platonism morphed into 'Neoplatonism', a school
of religious and mystical philosophy attributed by nineteenth
century scholars to Plotinus (d. 270 CE) and his successors
Porphyry and Iamblichus.

Philo's example inspired early Christians such as Clement of
Alexandria, Origen, and Augustine, who looked upon Neoplatonism as the best available tool with which to defend the
teachings of Scripture and Church tradition—even though the
likes of Porphyry and Iamblichus had developed Neoplatonism
in conscious and at times vehement opposition to Christianity.
In the end, Christianity assimilated Platonism so completely
that Nietzsche derided it simply as 'Platonism for the masses'.

In around 410 CE, some leading Neoplatonists revived the
Academy in a large house in Athens. This Neoplatonic
Academy thrived for a time, notably under Proclus (d. 485),
before being shut down by Justinian in 529. As part of his
programme to enforce Christian orthodoxy, the Eastern Roman

emperor issued an edict declaring: 'Henceforth never again shall anyone lecture on philosophy or explain the laws in Athens.' The last scholarch, Damascius, fled Athens, and may have sought refuge in the court of King Chrosroes I of Persia.

After the fall of the Western Roman Empire, the knowledge of Greek was lost in the West. In around 321 CE, the philosopher Calcidius had published a Latin translation of the first part of the *Timaeus* (to 53c) with an extensive commentary, which for almost eight hundred years remained the only substantial section of the *Corpus Platonicum* available to the Latin West. Christian commentators, notably from the twelfth century Chartres School, assimilated its contents, which are obscure and mystical, with the creation story in Genesis. In around 1160, Henry Aristippus of Calabria made Latin translations of the *Meno* and *Phaedo*, but these remained in limited circulation.

Fortunately, the study of Plato continued in the Byzantine Empire and Islamic World. The second Abbasid caliph Al-Mansur (d. 775) moved his capital from Damascus to Baghdad, where he founded a great library called the House of Wisdom and ordered texts in Greek and Syriac to be translated into Arabic. Working in the House of Wisdom, Al-Kindi, the 'father of Arab philosophy' (d. 873), sought to harmonize Islam with Greek philosophy, and ended up being flogged for his efforts. Later Islamic philosophers such as Al-Farabi (d. c. 950), Avicenna (d. 1037), and Averroes (d. 1198) commented very extensively on the works of Plato and especially Aristotle—so that, in the *Divine Comedy* (1321), Dante placed Avicenna and Averroes 'who the great Comment made' in the company of Socrates, Plato, and Aristotle.

The eminent Byzantine Greek scholar George Gemistos Plethon, who privately rejected Christianity, so admired Plato that he took the name 'Plethon'. At the 1438-39 Council of Florence, he reintroduced Plato to the West as part of a failed attempt to repair the Great Schism between the Eastern and the Western Church and present a united front to the Ottoman Empire (Constantinople finally fell to the Ottomans in 1453).

While in Florence, Gemistos Plethon made an impression on the banker, politician, and patron of the arts Cosimo de' Medici, who had, among others, commissioned the *David* of Donatello, the first freestanding male nude since antiquity. He persuaded Cosimo to establish an institute and informal discussion group, now known as the Platonic Academy of Florence, which, under Cosimo's protégé Marsilio Ficino, went on to translate all of Plato's extant works into Latin. Ficino seems to have coined the term 'Platonic love' [*amor platonicus*], which first appears in a letter that he wrote to Alamanno Donati in 1476. In 1492, he published a series of Platonic love letters to *Giovanni amico mio perfettisimo* ['Giovanni my most perfect friend'], the poet Giovanni Cavalcanti.

Cosimo appointed Ficino as tutor to his grandson Lorenzo de' Medici (1449-1492)—who, within his own lifetime, came to be known as 'the Magnificent'. Lorenzo retrieved large numbers of classical works from the East and established a workshop to have them copied and disseminated. His circle of friends, which included the likes of Poliziano and Pico della Mirandola, supported the development of Renaissance humanism. His handsome brother Giuliano served as the model for Mars in Botticelli's *Mars and Venus*, and Lorenzo also sponsored the likes of Ghirlandaio, Pollaiuolo, Verrocchio, Leonardo, and Michelangelo, who, for three years, lived and dined with him.

Lorenzo's second son Giovanni rose to the papacy as Leo X (r. 1513-21). According to Alexandre Dumas *père*, Christianity under Leo 'assumed a pagan, Greco-Roman character... Crimes for the moment disappeared, to give place to vices; but to charming vices, vices in good taste, such as those indulged by Alcibiades and sung by Catullus.'

After Giuliano's murder in the Pazzi conspiracy, Lorenzo raised his illegitimate nephew, Giulio di Giuliano, as his own son. As the second Medici pope, Clement VII (r. 1523-34), Giulio approved Copernicus' heliocentric model of the universe a century before Galileo's heresy trial for similar ideas. He also commissioned works by Cellini, Raphael, and Michelangelo, including Michelangelo's *Last Judgement* in the Sistine Chapel.

The works of Aristotle followed a somewhat different arc, with somewhat different effects. After Sulla removed Aristotle's dilapidated manuscripts to Rome, they were recopied and arranged into their current ordering by Andronicus of Rhodes (fl. 60 BCE). Alexander of Aphrodisias, who from 195 occupied the Peripatetic Chair endowed by the philosopher-king Marcus Aurelius, commented so extensively on these works as to be styled 'the Explainer'. But by late antiquity they had virtually fallen out of circulation, held down by the rise of the Church and Neoplatonism, the decline and fall of the Western Roman Empire, and the loss of Greek as a lingua franca.

The last of the ancients to comment on Aristotle were Boethius (d. 524) and Simplicius (d. c. 560). For disregarding the advice of Socrates and trying to do the right thing in politics, Boethius was convicted of treason against the Gothic emperor Theodoric. While in prison awaiting execution, he wrote the still extant *Consolation of Philosophy*. For centuries, Boethius' translations of the *Categories* and *On Interpretation* were the only substantial parts of the *Corpus Aristotelicum* available in Latin Christendom.

In the Orient, the quasi entirety of the *Corpus Aristotelicum*, with the notable omission of the *Politics*, had been translated into Arabic by the efforts of the scholars in the House of Wisdom. This then became the subject of extensive commentary by the likes of Al-Farabi, Avicenna, and Averroes. In his autobiography *Deliverance from Error*, the theologian and philosopher Al-Ghazali (d. 1111) noted that none of the Muslim philosophers did more to transmit Aristotle than Al-Farabi and Avicenna, and Al-Farabi even acquired the epithet, 'Second Teacher' or 'Second Master', with Aristotle the first. The Moor Averroes (d. 1198), who wrote commentaries on almost all of Aristotle's still extant works, sought a return to a purer form of Aristotelianism which, he maintained, had been polluted by the Neoplatonist tendencies of Al-Farabi and Avicenna. In his *Guide for the Perplexed* (c. 1190), the Sephardic Jewish philosopher Maimonides—who took to bed with depression when his brother drowned en route to India—sought to reconcile the Aristotelianism of the Islamic philosophers with the Torah. At around the same time in Constantinople, the Byzantine princess and first female historian Anna Comnena (d. 1153) gathered a circle of scholars to write commentaries on Aristotle —prior to which the Byzantine output on Aristotle had largely been limited to the works on logic.

At the turn of the twelfth century, scholasticism in Europe began to coalesce into the first universities, in places like Oxford, Paris, Padua, and Coimbra. Scholars sought out new learning from Central Spain and Sicily, which had returned to Christian rule, respectively, in 1085 and 1091. In the East, Jerusalem was taken in 1099 at the outcome of the First Crusade, and Constantinople sacrilegiously sacked in 1204 at the outcome of the Fourth Crusade. In around 1150, James of Venice, who was in Constantinople, translated the *Posterior Analytics* from Greek, thereby making the complete *Organon* available in Latin (three further works by Boethius had since resurfaced). He also translated the *Physics*, *Metaphysics*, and *On the Soul*. To exploit the rich collections in Toledo, Gerard of Cremona (d. 1187) taught himself Arabic. He translated several theoretical works by Aristotle, including the *Physics* and *On the Heavens*. Michael Scot (d. 1232), who had studied at Oxford and Paris and knew Greek, Arabic, and Hebrew, translated the *History of Animals* from Arabic or Hebrew. He also translated other Aristotelian works and commentaries, especially those by Averroes. He is the only Scot to feature in Dante's *Inferno*, albeit in the Eighth Circle among the sorcerers. In around 1246, Oxford man Robert Grosseteste made the first Latin translation of the *Nicomachean Ethics*. Finally, to guard against inaccuracies, William of Mœrbeke (d. 1286) undertook a literal translation of the complete *Corpus Aristotelicum* directly from the Greek.

Albert Magnus (d. 1280) began to harmonize Aristotelian philosophy with Christian theology (rather than the other way round), a project picked up by his pupil Thomas Aquinas (d. 1274), who was shot through and through with Aristotle and referred to him simply as 'the Philosopher'. All this activity did not go unnoticed by the Church, and it was not until 1323 that Aquinas was canonized, and not until 1567 that he was proclaimed a Doctor of the Church. Particular problem areas included creation versus eternalism, a personal versus an impersonal God, and an immortal versus a mortal soul. The Condemnations at the University of Paris, aimed especially at the theoretical treatises of Aristotle, came in three sets, in 1210, 1270, and 1277. The Condemnation of 1210, which applied only to the faculty of arts, banned several authors including 'the books of Aristotle on natural philosophy or their commentaries

... under penalty of excommunication'. The Condemnation of 1270 banned the teaching of thirteen Aristotelian and Averroist doctrines, including 'that the world is eternal', 'that there was never a first human', and 'that the soul cannot suffer from bodily fire'. The Condemnation of 1277 banned as many as 219 propositions or 'errors', including about twenty Thomist ones. Ironically, the Paris Condemnations, which were only ever local and partial in their application, fostered an atmosphere of skepticism and inquiry which contained the beginnings of modern science. In the end, Aristotelian ideas assimilated by the Church achieved such prestige and prominence that they proved difficult to displace by pioneers such as Galileo, Descartes, and Newton. For so many centuries, in so many fields, Aristotle became the giant that needed to be slayed— with some help from Plato or, more exactly, Socrates.

Each in their own way, Socrates, Plato, and Aristotle clearly emphasized reason, which they ended up assimilating with us and with God. But it is unfortunate, if not coincidental, that, for centuries, except for a section of the *Timaeus*, the values-free *Categories* and *On Interpretation* were the only substantial parts of their legacy available in Latin Christendom. This narrow logic, out of which scholasticism and the universities emerged, was the lens through which all else came to be interpreted.

To this day, we in the West tend to think of intelligence in terms of analytical skills, and it is only in 1990 that Salovey and Mayer published the seminal paper on emotional intelligence. I discuss the limits of logic and reason, and the potentialities of non-rational forms of cognition such as emotion, imagination, and intuition in *Hypersanity: Thinking Beyond Thinking*.

The large tracts of the *Nicomachean Ethics* and *Rhetoric* devoted to the emotions seem, quite simply, to have been overlooked, as has much else in Plato and Aristotle, such as the role of love and the Dionysian, the emphasis on friendship and community, the importance of leisure and contemplation, and the purpose or end of it all. Although the *Corpus Aristotelicum*, even as it stands, is awesome, many more Aristotelian works have been lost than have been recovered, including such titles as *On the Passions*, *Of Friendship*, and *Concerning Love*.

Also overlooked is the place of *mythos* in among the *logos*. Socrates had a divine voice as a corrective, and Plato is arguably the greatest of all mythmakers. Even Aristotle, who sought to do without the mystical, had to turn to it in the final resort.

Having been diminished, *mythos* soon came back to the fore, mounting up through Neoplatonism and then Christianity, which, for centuries, met our need for *mythos*. With the retreat of religion, we have, to meet this need, turned increasingly to fiction, and now spend much of our leisure time in books, films, and video games. Perhaps we ought to be more open about our need for the mythical and mystical, while still holding on to all the advantages of *logos*.

I have long argued that the current crisis in meaning and mental health owes, in large part, to our one-sidedness and its manifestations. But if it is the Gang of Three who have led us here—and Plato did warn about the dangers of the written word—their rich works also contain the elements of their own correction, as when the rediscovery of Plato inflamed the Renaissance. Although their logic and their science have been superseded, their ethics are more relevant than ever. In the absence of religion to guide and galvanize us, we need a deep, satisfying reason to be good, and only virtue ethics seems able to provide it, for it is by being good that we may be happy.

Socrates, Plato, and Aristotle were epitomes of sanity. If they visited us today and sat in our clinics, they would be appalled by our short-termism and short-sightedness. Surely, they would say, the best way to feel better is to *be* better, and we have shown you how. Your salvation lies simply in being what you were meant to be: a human being in the fullest sense. If you only aim at that, everything else will fall into place.

(Blank page)

David, *by Michelangelo (c. 1504). Galleria dell'Accademia, Florence.
Photo: Neel Burton.*

Wealth does not bring about excellence, but excellence makes wealth and everything else good for men, both individually and collectively.

— PLATO, *APOLOGY*

WHAT DO YOU THINK?

If you found this book useful or enjoyable, be virtuous and happy by leaving a rating or short review on Amazon.

To hear about new books, subscribe to my very occasional newsletter and receive a free e-copy of my booklet on eudaimonia.

The next book in the Ancient Wisdom series is *Stoic Stories*.

STOIC STORIES:
STOICISM BY ITS BEST STORIES

Introduction

This is a book of Stoic stories: stories about Stoics, stories told by Stoics, and stories with a Stoic bent. Snuck between these heroic tales, and exemplified by them, are the main tenets of Stoic philosophy, served up in small, bite-size chunks.

Romans by the imperial period had stopped believing in the hoary myths of old. In his *Letters to Lucilius*, Seneca remarks that 'no one is such a child as to be afraid of Cerberus and the dark and the skeleton figures of ghouls'. In any case, ancient religion privileged ritual over doctrine and offered little in the way of guidance and consolation. For that, people, especially educated people, turned instead to philosophy, which held out the promise of a flourishing life removed from wrongdoing and suffering. In that much, Stoicism can be thought of as the first and original self-help. The movement by this stage had become eclectic and syncretic, borrowing freely from other schools, and, in practical terms at least, represents the best that ancient philosophy and antiquity have to offer. Ancient though they are, Stoic precepts and practices are timeless and universal insofar as they speak to our deepest human nature: for all our progress in science, technology, and education, we are still plagued and tormented—perhaps now more than ever—by anger, fear, greed, grief, death, and mis-living.

Stoicism was originally known by the name of its founder, Zeno of Citium, as 'Zenonism'. But Zeno, being a Zenonist, was not given to megalomania, and the name was soon dropped in favour of 'Stoicism'. The word 'Stoicism' derives from the *Stoa Poikile* or 'Painted Porch', a colonnade on the northern side of the agora in Athens where, overlooked by mythic and historic battle scenes, Zeno and his followers met to discuss and disseminate their ideas.

Unfortunately, all the works of the earlier, Greek Stoics have been lost, leaving us to piece together their main lines from surviving fragments and later reports, especially by Diogenes Laertius, Cicero, and Sextus Empiricus, as well as the Roman Stoics Seneca, Musonius, and Epictetus. These reports are however less than reliable: Diogenes Laertius is often fanciful, Cicero and Seneca are prone to flourishes, Sextus Empiricus strongly opposed the Stoics, and what passes for Musonius and Epictetus are in fact lecture notes by their students. Compared to their Greek forebears, the Roman Stoics emphasized ethics over physics and logic, and liberally interpreted or adapted Stoic teachings. Even so, a story does not have to be true to be enlightening, and even those stories in Diogenes that are made up are likely to be in the spirit of the truth.

At the heart of Stoicism is the idea that human beings ought to act in accord with their nature, which means two things. First, we are social animals, and designed to work together 'like hands, or feet, or eyelids'. 'Human nature' said Musonius, 'is very much like that of bees. A bee is not able to live alone; it perishes when isolated. Indeed, it is intent on performing the common task of members of its species—to work and act together with other bees.'

Second, while ants and bees, and maybe even wolves, may be more social than human beings, we are by a country mile the most rational of all animals, so that reason might be said to be our distinctive or defining function. Just as leopards ought to excel at running if they are to count as good leopards, so human beings ought to excel at reasoning if they are to count as good human beings. If we aim instead to excel at running or jumping or making money, we have not properly understood what it means to be a human being. Thus, of one who boasted of his diving, Aristippus asked, "Are you not ashamed to be proud of that which a dolphin can do?"

As human beings, we ought at every moment to be rational and social. Unfortunately, we are all too readily waylaid by unwise attachments and the destructive emotions to which they give rise. These attachments dangle the promise of pleasure or happiness but really offer only slavery—whereas, if only we could see it, nothing leads to pleasure and happiness as surely as reason and self-control.

Today, most people think of ancient Stoicism in terms of modern stoicism, that is, as the simple suppression or closeting of emotions. This misleading modern derivation originated in the sixteenth century and should not be confused with the much older philosophical movement. The Stoic is not without emotions, but, ideally, without painful or unhelpful emotions such as anger, envy, and greed. To be without emotion, were that even possible, would be to be reduced to the inanimate state of a tree or a rock, whereas the Stoic seeks, on the contrary, to exist and excel qua human being. Thus, the Stoics invited positive and prosocial emotions such as compassion, friendship, and gratitude, which pour out of Marcus Aurelius' *Meditations*. Already in Book I, Marcus praises his tutor Sextus of Charonea for being 'free from passion and yet full of love'.

Those familiar with Stoicism often came to it in a crisis, but soon discovered that it is about much more than firefighting or even longer-term resilience building. While I was writing this book, a buttoned-up surgeon put me on the spot by asking how stoicism, the modern disposition, differs from Stoicism, the ancient philosophical movement. I ventured in reply, "stoicism today is about maintaining a stiff upper lip, whereas ancient Stocism is about seeking to maintain the ultimate perspective on everything, which then raises many interesting questions." Unlike many modern interventions, Stoicism is not merely about feeling better, but about *being* better—which is, all considered, the surest way of feeling better, and not just better but better than ever before.

STOIC STORIES

STOICISM BY ITS BEST STORIES

NEEL BURTON

NOTES

In quoting from Plato and Aristotle I have generally favoured the Jowett translation for Plato and the Ross translation for Aristotle.

Preface

- Edward de Bono regularly used 'the Gang of Three' to describe Socrates, Plato, and Aristotle, for example, in an article in the *Guardian* published on 24 April 2007: *Edward de Bono: 'Iraq? They just need to think it through.'*

Introduction

- Plutarch, *Apophthegmata Laconica*, 62.1

Chapter 1

- Aristotle, *Metaphysics*, 984b17-18.

Chapter 2

- *Physiologoi*: Aristotle, *Metaphysics*, 986b.
- On Thales: Aristotle, *Metaphysics*, 983b.
- Russell, Bertrand (1945): *The History of Western Philosophy*.
- Plato, *Theaetetus*, 174a.
- 'In all the worlds': Hippolytus, DK 12A11.
- Aelian, *Various Histories,* III, 17.
- Nietzsche, *Philosophy in the Tragic Age of the Greeks*, 4. Published posthumously.
- Nietzsche, *On the Genealogy of Morality* (1887), III, 25.
- Simplicius, DK 13A5.
- Herodotus, VI, 22.
- Herodotus, V, 105.

Chapter 3

- "To observe the heavens": Iamblichus, *Protrepticus*, IX, 51.
- Russell, Bertrand (1945): *The History of Western Philosophy*.
- Aristotle, *Metaphysics*, I, 5-6.
- Pythagoras: Xenophanes, Fragment 7.
- Xenophanes, Fragment 8.
- Xenophanes, Fragments 23, 24, 25 & 26.
- Xenophanes, Fragment 27.
- Xenophanes, Fragment 38.
- Xenophanes, Fragments 1 and 4.
- Theophrastus on Heraclitus' book, in: Diogenes Laërtius, IX, 1.
- Heraclitus, Fragment 62.
- Reply ro Darius, in: Diogenes Laërtius, IX, 1.

- Heraclitus mentions Pythagoras and Xenophanes in Fragment 40.
- Heraclitus, Fragment 30.
- Heraclitus, Fragment 117.
- Bible, NT, John 1:1 (KJV).
- Heraclitus, Fragments 50, 51 & 60.
- Giuseppe Tomasi di Lampedusa, *Il Gattopardo* (1958). *Se vogliamo che tutto rimanga come è, bisogna che tutto cambi.*
- Aristotle, *Metaphysics* 987a32-b1.
- Aristotle, *Metaphysics* 1010a12-15.
- Aristotle, *Physics* 239b14-18.

Chapter 4

- 'A mute fish in the sea': Empedocles, Fragment 117.
- Diogenes Laertius, II, 3.
- Plutarch, *Parallel Lives, Life of Pericles*.
- Aristotle, *Metaphysics*, 985a.
- Archimedes, *Method of Mechanical Theorems*.
- Democritus, Fragment 49.
- Democritus, Fragment 125.

Chapter 5

- Cicero, *Tusculan Disputations*, V, 10-11.
- Aulus Gellius, *Attic Nights*, V, 10.
- Isocrates, *Antidosis*, 155.
- Xenophon, *Memorabilia*, II, 1.
- Philostratus, *Lives of the Sophists*, I, 11.
- *Suda, Hippias*.
- Plato, *Lesser Hippias*.

Chapter 6

- Stealing potherbs: Plutarch, *Life of Solon*, XVII.
- Draco's justification: Plutarch, *Life of Solon*, XVII.
- Aristotle on Peisistratos: *Constitution of Athens*.
- Hippias' dream: Herodotus, VI, 107.
- Queen Artemisia: Herodotus, VIII, 88.
- Ring of Gyges: Plato, *Republic*, II.
- Thucydides, *History*, I, 22.
- Xenophon, *Hellenica*, II, 2, 3.

Chapter 7

- Aelian, *Varia historia*, II, 13.
- Aristotle, *Metaphysics*, XIII, 6.

Chapter 8

- Herodotus, *Histories*, VIII, 79.
- Pausanias, *Description of Greece*, IX, 35, 7.
- Theophrastus, *Phys. Opin.* Fragment 4.
- *Suda*, Sigma 829.
- Theodoretus of Cyrus, *Cure for the Maladies of the Greeks,* 315.18.
- Xenophon, *Memorabilia*, I.

Chapter 9

- Aelian, *Historical Miscellany*, II, 13.
- Confucius, as quoted in Henry David Thoreau (1954), *Walden*, Ch 1.

- *Dhammapada: The Sayings of the Buddha.* Trans. John Richards (1993).
- Cicero, *On the Orator*, II, 270.
- The source for the anecdote with Prof Peacocke is TP Wiseman (ed.): *Classics in Progress* (2002), p. 282.

Chapter 10

- Plato, *Laws*, VII.
- Plato, *Republic*, IV, 429c.

Chapter 11

- "Not as a woman, but as a lion!": Plutarch, *Life of Alcibiades*.
- Aristotle, *History of Animals*, VI, 26.
- Plutarch, *Life of Pericles*.
- On women: Plato, *Republic*, V.
- Cicero, *Fate*, V, 10.
- Cicero, *Talks at Tusculum*, IV, 37, 80.
- Fools and dullards: Aristotle, *Rhetoric*, II, 15.

Chapter 12

- Ohayon MM (2000): Prevalence of hallucinations and their pathological associations in the general population. Psychiatry Research 97(2-3):153-64.

Chapter 13

- Pyrilampes' peacocks, in: Plutarch, *Life of Pericles*.
- Dicaearchus quoted in: Diogenes Laertius, III, 5.

- Plato crossed to Cyrene: Diogenes Laertius, III, 6.
- Plutarch, *De genio Socratis*, 579B.

Chapter 16

- Pliny the Elder, *Natural History*, 24.38.
- Democritus, DK 68B33.

Chapter 17

- Gibbons, F (2001): *The thinking person's favourite thinkers*. The Guardian, 7 September 2001. https://www.theguardian.com/uk/2001/sep/07/books.humanities
- Thu-Huong Ha (2016): *These are the books students at the top US colleges are required to read*. Quartz, 27 January 2016. https://qz.com/602956/these-are-the-books-students-at-the-top-us-colleges-are-required-to-read

Chapter 19

- 'After drinking wine, the Indian parrot becomes more saucy than ever', in: Aristotle, *History of Animals*, VIII.
- The fig juice analogy, in: Aristotle, *Generation of Animals*, II.
- 'We should venture on the study of every kind of animal without distaste; for each and all will reveal to us something natural and something beautiful', in: Aristotle, *Parts of Animals*, I, 645a.21.
- Plutarch, *Life of Alexander*, 7.7.
- 'A flowing river of gold', in: Cicero, *Academica Priora* 38.119.

Chapter 20

- GC Licthtenberg, Notebook E, 49.

Chapter 21

- Diogenes Laertius, VII, 7: Chrysippus.
- Laws of Thought: Aristotle, *Metaphysics*, IV, 4 & 7.
- The sea-battle in: Aristotle, *On Interpretation*, 9.
- The quotation involving an infinite regress in: Aristotle, *Metaphysics* 10006a6ff.
- Discussion of affirming the consequent in: *Sophistical Refutations*, I, 5.

Chapter 23

- Avicenna, *Love of Learning*, on historymuse.net.

The Gang of Three

- Cicero, *Tusculan Disputations*, V, 10-1.
- Cicero, *Tusculan Disputations,* III, 6.
- Justin Martyr, *Second Apology*, X: Christ compared to Socrates.
- Whitehead AN (1979), *Process and Reality*, p. 39. Free Press.
- Diogenes Laertius, IV, 6.
- Horace, *Epistles*, II, 1.
- Nietzsche F (1886), *Beyond Good and Evil*, Preface.
- Dante, *Inferno*, Canto IV.
- Alexandre Dumas *père* (1598): *Celebrated Crimes,* Vol I, part 2, *The Cenci*.